ROWAN

40 iconic hand-knit designs

40
years

sixth&springbooks

Concept Development
ROWAN YARNS & QUAIL PUBLISHING

Archive Curation
ROWAN YARNS

Graphic Layout & Restyled Photography
QUAIL STUDIO

Copy Editor
ROSEE WOODLAND

Pattern Queries
MAIL@KNITROWAN.COM

104 W 27th St, 3rd Floor
New York, NY 10001
www.sixthandspring.com

Library of Congress Cataloging-in-Publication Data
is available upon request

Manufactured in China
1 3 5 7 9 10 8 6 4 2

First Edition

FOREWORD

....

I first became aware of Rowan in the late 1980's when I had my first business designing and making ready to wear garments. Back then I was introduced to Rowan's beautiful yarns initially for machine knitting and then later for hand knitting. The day I first saw the iconic Rowan shade card shade card I was smitten. It was a designer's dream − not only beautiful yarns, but available in a huge range of fabulous colours. Because of this, Rowan has always held a very special place in my heart.

As a quintessential British brand, Rowan has been both creative and inspiring, influencing hand knit design over the last few decades with designs from the heady days of the 80's, 90's and 00's still as relevant today. From 2005 to 2013, I was lucky enough to be responsible for the glorious *Rowan Magazine* and hopefully contributed to Rowan's rich heritage. The designs featured within this book reflect the work of some very celebrated knitwear designers, designers I personally have been proud to have met and worked with.

I hope you will enjoy this book, and as it takes you on a journey through these four glorious decades of spectacular knitwear design, I hope you will fall in love with Rowan all over again.

MARIE WALLIN

CONTENTS

ROWAN

40
years

At Rowan we take great pride in celebrating and continuing Britain's rich textile legacy.

Our name was inspired by the glorious flowering shrubs lining the banks of Yorkshire's River Holme. And from humble beginnings 40 years ago, Rowan has blossomed to become a British brand loved by knitters and crocheters around the world.

This new collection reaffirms that status, carefully curated from the last four decades of visionary Rowan design. With exclusive images of 20 restyled projects, and classic shots of many more, *Rowan 40 Years - 40 Iconic Hand-Knit Designs* is a must for any Rowan fan.

Knitting with Rowan takes you on a journey through Britain. Our designers are inspired by the elegance of our historic buildings, and the raw beauty of our landscape in equal measure.

Marie Wallin's Orkney cardigan, photographed at Ballone Castle near Inverness, is a subtle concoction of heathery tones that draws on centuries of Fair Isle tradition. For knitters seeking a palette rich in contrast, the glorious Soumak wrap, originally shot at historic Haddon Hall, Derbyshire, will prove irresistible.

Immerse yourself in Scotland's knitting heritage with Sharon Miller's delicate Shetland lace shawls, and Jennie Atkinson's plaid jacket. Or channel vintage style in impeccable tailoring from Kim Hargreaves and Jean Moss.

Of course, we've always chosen our shoot locations to perfectly complement our spectacular collections, and Rowan knitters will recognise many favourites here.

Wonder at the extraordinary foliage at Westonbirt Arboretum, the backdrop for the Robinia kimono cardigan in Felted Tweed. Wander in the bleached dunes at Holkham Beach, Norfolk, the breathtaking scene for Lisa Richardson's innovative Wayfarer loop top.

There are 40 projects here to knit with love and wear for a lifetime, from the bold colours of Kaffe Fassett's painterly pieces to the sumptuous texture of Martin Storey's classic cables.

Look back at some of our most iconic designs and choose your very own Rowan masterpiece to cast on today.

F 1152

FROM CONCEPT
TO COVER

ROWAN

Every edition of Rowan Knitting & Crochet Magazine is a collector's item, inspiring the creativity of knitters for years, even decades, after its publication.

The cover image for each issue is taken from one of the designs in the magazine, and chosen for both its impact and the sheer beauty of the garment portrayed.

Over the decades there have been many iconic covers, from the bare−faced beauty of Magazine 4, featuring the Sampler Cardigan by Kim Hargreaves, to Martin Storey's powder white Foxtail sweater on the front of Magazine 49. Turn to page 40 to rediscover Kaffe Fassett's Lidiya dress, cover star of the Russian Doll collection in Magazine 48, an edition so popular it had to be reprinted several times to meet demand.

The pattern collections within an issue are known as design stories, and each design story is twelve months in the making. Long before the magazine hits the shelves the in−house design team are dreaming up concepts based both on key trends, and themes they want to explore. These themes can be inspired by anything − a painting, a film, a piece of art. What they do is give a focal point to the design story − something to build the collection around.

The process moves forward with the creation of a mood board filled with inspirational images that represent elements of the story concept. This is sent out to Rowan's key designers, who then submit swatches and sketches to outline their ideas. The very best are selected from these, and the patterns are written, knitted up and go through an editing process to ensure they are accurate.

While all this is happening, planning for the photography for each design story is already underway. Locations must be scouted, models cast and clothes and accessories sourced. The settings for each of the stories in the magazine are often inspired by the original moodboard. You can see this in the Highlander shoot for Magazine 42, where the initial concept for the collection was echoed in the windswept shoot location at Cawdor Estate, Inverness − find Jennie Atkinson's Striven plaid jacket from the Highlander story on page 50.

After the shoot has taken place the photographs of all the designs are narrowed down to a number of potential covers. All the key images are laid out in the design room and then everyone in the team has their say, marking their favourite cover with their initials. Sometimes there is a clear winner, sometimes there is more than one obvious contender.

When it's just too close to call, Rowan's brand manager David MacLeod and brand director Sharon Brant make the final decision. Usually it comes down to the strength of the image alone.

While every Rowan cover is beautiful, there are some that are particularly memorable. The 'picture window' cover design of this very book is based on that of Magazine 10, itself a key moment in Rowan history. Not only was the style of the cover a break from the usual format, it featured a young Kate Moss, modelling Kaffe Fassett's Kilim jacket. At the time Moss was still an up and coming model, popular, but unknown outside of Britain. Just as Moss has since risen to become a global style icon, Rowan has grown tremendously since that moment, and now reaches knitters and crocheters around the world with every issue.

Magazine 44, which celebrated Rowan's 30th anniversary, also used the picture window format. We have returned to it here as an unusual way to represent all of Rowan's gorgeous covers and celebrate the iconic design which has made, and continues to make Rowan Knitting & Crochet Magazine so special.

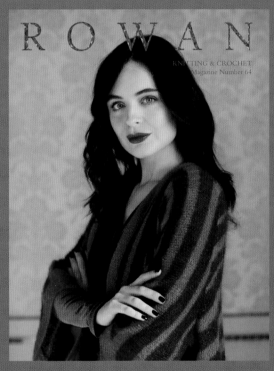

Rowan Magazine 64 Cover, 2018

ROWAN Magazine Front Covers (No. 01 - 16)

ROWAN
KNITTING Magazine Number 17
DESIGNERS
Kaffe Fassett
Kim Hargreaves
Louisa Harding
Susan Duckworth
Martin Storey
English Weather
FOURTY TWO
DESIGNS

THE INDIGO STORY
TRAVELLING LIGHT
THREE OF A KIND

ROWAN
KNITTING Magazine Number 18
DESIGNERS
Kaffe Fassett
Kim Hargreaves
Louisa Harding
Martin Storey
Sharon Peake
FORTY SIX
DESIGNS

ROWAN PEOPLE
OPULENT INTERIORS
A HELPING HAND

ROWAN
KNITTING Magazine Number 19
DESIGNERS
Kaffe Fassett
Kim Hargreaves
Louisa Harding
Martin Storey
Sharon Peake
OVER THIRTY
DESIGNS

ROWAN
KNITTING Magazine
Number 20
DESIGNERS
Kaffe Fassett
Kim Hargreaves
Louisa Harding
Sharon Peake
Debbie Jenkins
Justine Brown
OVER THIRTY
DESIGNS

ROWAN
KNITTING Magazine
Number 21
DESIGNERS
Kaffe Fassett
Kim Hargreaves
Louisa Harding
Sharon Peake
Martin Storey
OVER THIRTY
DESIGNS

ROWAN
KNITTING Magazine
Number 22
DESIGNERS
Kaffe Fassett
Kim Hargreaves
Louisa Harding
J & J Seaton
Sharon Peake
Martin Storey
Wendy Webster
OVER THIRTY
DESIGNS

ROWAN
KNITTING Magazine
Number 23
DESIGNERS
Kaffe Fassett
Louisa Harding
Martin Storey
Brandon Mably
Zoe Mellor
Debbie Abraham
OVER THIRTY
DESIGNS

ROWAN
KNITTING Magazine
Number 24
DESIGNERS
Kaffe Fassett
Kim Hargreaves
Louisa Harding
Martin Kidman
Sarah Dallas
Muir & Osborne
Erika Knight
Marie McLoughlin
OVER FORTY
DESIGNS

ROWAN
KNITTING Magazine
Number 25
DESIGNERS
Kaffe Fassett
Kim Hargreaves
Louisa Harding
Martin Storey
Sharon Peake
Zoe Mellor
Brandon Mably
Helen Dawson
OVER THIRTY
DESIGNS

ROWAN
KNITTING Magazine
Number 26
DESIGNERS
Kaffe Fassett
Kim Hargreaves
Louisa Harding
Jean Moss
Martin Storey
Sharon Peake
Brandon Mably
Elise Steedman
OVER THIRTY
DESIGNS

ROWAN
KNITTING Magazine
Number 27
DESIGNERS
Kaffe Fassett
Kim Hargreaves
Martin Storey
Zoe Mellor
Sarah Dallas
Brandon Mably
Fiona McTague
Carol Meldrum
THIRTY FIVE
DESIGNS

ROWAN
KNITTING Magazine
Number 28
DESIGNERS
Kaffe Fassett
Kim Hargreaves
Louisa Harding
Debbie Bliss
Sarah Dallas
Sharon Peake
Brandon Mably
OVER FORTY
DESIGNS

ROWAN
KNITTING Magazine
Number 29
DESIGNERS
Kaffe Fassett
Kim Hargreaves
Louisa Harding
Debbie Bliss
Susan Duckworth
Debbie Abrahams
Carol Meldrum
Julia Ryan Dinner
THIRTY FIVE
DESIGNS

ROWAN
KNITTING Magazine
Number 30
DESIGNERS
Kaffe Fassett
Kim Hargreaves
Louisa Harding
Debbie Bliss
Susan Duckworth
Sarah Dallas
Martin Storey
Livingstone Studio
Brandon Mably
OVER FORTY
DESIGNS

ROWAN
KNITTING Magazine
Number 31
DESIGNERS
Kaffe Fassett
Kim Hargreaves
Sarah Dallas
Martin Storey
Sharon Peake
Zoe Mellor
Amanda Griffiths
Brandon Mably
Carol Meldrum
OVER FORTY
DESIGNS

ROWAN
KNITTING Magazine
Number 32
DESIGNERS
Kim Hargreaves
Sarah Dallas
Sasha Kagan
Jean Moss
Sharon Peake
Muir & Osborne
Brandon Mably
Debbie Abrahams
Carol Meldrum
Leah Sutton
OVER FORTY
DESIGNS

ROWAN Magazine Front Covers (No. 17 - 32)

ROWAN Magazine Front Covers (No. 33 – 48)

ROWAN Magazine Front Covers (No. 49 – 64)

20 DESIGNS FROM THE ROWAN ARCHIVE

ROWAN

A Rowan pattern is one you can knit and wear for a lifetime. In our Archive collection you'll find iconic knits from the past 40 years encompassing elegant lace, richly interwoven cables and breathtaking colour work, as well as simple textured key pieces.

Discover groundbreaking designs dreamt up by some of the finest minds in the crafting world and wrap yourself in a piece of British knitting history, brought to life with your own two hands.

Designs featured:

Addison (Magazine 52)	Lidiya (Magazine 48)
Anice Shawl (Magazine 41)	Mist (Magazine 26)
Carlotta (Magazine 36)	Rapunzel (Magazine 34)
Evia (Magazine 31)	Restful (Magazine 47)
Fickle (Magazine 10)	Snowberry (Magazine 32)
Flora (Magazine 35)	Striven (Magazine 42)
Flourish (Magazine 29)	Tillie (Magazine 25)
Franziska (Magazine 56)	Valentina (Magazine 48)
Guiseley (Magazine 46)	Wentworth (Magazine 46)
Kintyre (Magazine 52)	Winter Flower (Magazine 28)

Please note that the following patterns have been collated from the Rowan archives and could be subject to slight formatting differences and discontinued yarns/shades.

ADDISON

Amanda Crawford
Magazine 52
Page 60

ANICE

Sharon Miller
Magazine 41
Page 62

CARLOTTA

Kim Hargreaves
Magazine 36
Page 64

FICKLE

Louisa Harding
Magazine 10
Page 70

F L O R A
Kim Hargreaves
Magazine 35
Page 74

FLOURISH

Kim Hargreaves
Magazine 29
Page 76

FRANZISKA
Galina Carroll
Magazine 56
Page 82

GUISELEY
Sarah Hatton
Magazine 46
Page 84

KINTYRE

Marie Wallin

Magazine 52

Page 86

LIDIYA
Kaffe Fassett
Magazine 48
Page 90

RAPUNZEL

Jean Moss
Magazine 34
Page 96

RESTFUL

Martin Storey
Magazine 47
Page 100

SNOWBERRY

Sasha Kagan
Magazine 32
Page 104

STRIVEN

Jennie Atkinson
Magazine 42
Page 108

TILLIE

Louisa Harding
Magazine 25
Page 110

VALENTINA

Martin Storey
Magazine 48
Page 114

WENTWORTH

Kaffe Fassett
Magazine 46
Page 118

WINTER FLOWER

Kim Hargreaves
Magazine 28
Page 120

ADDISON

Amanda Crawford

● ● ●

SIZE
S (M: L: XL: XXL)
To fit bust
81-86 (91-97: 102-107: 112-117:122-127)cm
32-34 (36-38: 40-42: 44-46: 48-50)in

YARN
Rowan Alpaca Cotton
9 (10: 11: 12: 13) x 50g balls
(photographed in Lichen 415)

NEEDLES
1 pair 4½mm (no 7) (US 7) needles
1 pair 5mm (no 6) (US 8) needles

TENSION
19 sts and 33 rows to 10cm (4in) measured over
pattern using 5mm (US 8) needles.

Pattern note: When working patt, work all
slipped sts with yarn at right side of work - this
is back of work (as sts are slipped on **WS** rows
only).

BACK
Using 4½mm (US 7) needles, cast on
99 [109: 119: 131: 145] sts.
Row 1 (RS): K1, *P1, K1, rep from * to end.
Row 2: P1, *K1, P1, rep from * to end.
These 2 rows form rib.
Work in rib until back measures 4cm, ending
with RS facing for next row.
Change to 5mm (US 8) needles.

Now work in patt as follows:
Row 1 (RS): Knit.
Row 2: K1, *sl 1 (see pattern note), K1, rep
from * to end.
Row 3: Knit.
Row 4: K2, *sl 1, K1, rep from * to last st, K1.
These 4 rows form patt.
Cont in patt until back measures
47 [48: 49: 50: 51]cm, ending with RS facing
for next row.
Shape raglan armholes
Keeping patt correct, cast off 3 sts at beg of next
2 rows. 93 [103: 113: 125: 139] sts.
Sizes S and M only
Next row (RS): K1, sl 1, K1, psso, K to last 3
sts, K2tog, K1.
Next row: P2, patt to last 2 sts, P2.
Next row: Knit.
Next row: P2, patt to last 2 sts, P2.
Rep last 4 rows 4 [0: -: -: -] times more.
83 [101: -: -: -] sts.
Sizes L, XL and XXL only
Next row (RS): K1, sl 1, K1, psso, K to last 3
sts, K2tog, K1.
Next row: P1, P2tog, patt to last 3 sts, P2tog
tbl, P1.
Rep last 2 rows – [-: 0: 4: 9] times more.
– [-: 109: 105: 99] sts.
All sizes
Next row (RS): K1, sl 1, K1, psso, K to last
3 sts, K2tog, K1.
Next row: P2, patt to last 2 sts, P2.
Rep last 2 rows 23 [32: 35: 33: 29] times more,
ending with RS facing for next row.
Cast off rem 35 [35: 37: 37: 39] sts.

FRONT
Work as given for back until 49 [49: 53: 53: 57] sts
rem in raglan armhole shaping.
Work 1 row, ending with RS facing for
next row.

Shape front neck
Next row (RS): K1, sl 1, K1, psso,
K8 [8: 10: 10: 12] and turn, leaving rem sts on
a holder. 10 [10: 12: 12: 14] sts.
Work each side of neck separately.
Keeping patt correct, dec 1 st at neck edge of
next 4 rows, then on foll 0 [0: 1: 1: 2] alt rows
and at same time dec 1 st at raglan armhole
edge of 2nd and foll 1 [1: 2: 2: 3] alt rows. 4 sts.
Next row (WS): Patt 2 sts, P2.
Next row: K1, sl 1, K2tog, psso.
Next row: P2.
Next row: K2tog and fasten off.
With RS facing, rejoin yarn to rem sts, cast off
centre 27 sts, patt to last 3 sts, K2tog, K1.
10 [10: 12: 12: 14] sts.
Complete to match first side, reversing shapings.

SLEEVES
Using 4½mm (US 7) needles, cast on
49 [51: 53: 53: 55] sts.
Work in rib as given for back for 4cm, ending
with RS facing for next row.
Change to 5mm (US 8) needles.
Now work in patt as given for back, shaping
sides by inc 1 st at each end of 7th [7th: 7th: 5th: 5th]
and every foll 8th [8th: 8th: 6th: 6th] row to
73 [73: 81: 67: 69] sts, then on every foll
10th [10th: 10th: 8th: 8th] row until there are
77 [79: 83: 87: 89] sts, taking inc sts into patt.
Cont straight until sleeve measures
44 [45: 46: 46: 46]cm, ending with RS facing
for next row.
Shape raglan
Keeping patt correct, cast off 3 sts at beg of next
2 rows. 71 [73: 77: 81: 83] sts.
Next row (RS): K1, sl 1, K1, psso, K to last
3 sts, K2tog, K1.
Next row: P2, patt to last 2 sts, P2.
Next row: Knit.
Next row: P2, patt to last 2 sts, P2.

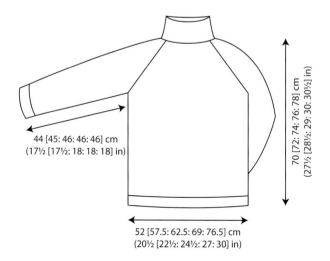

44 [45: 46: 46: 46] cm
(17½ [17½: 18: 18: 18] in)

70 [72: 74: 76: 78] cm
(27½ [28½: 29: 30: 30½] in)

52 [57.5: 62.5: 69: 76.5] cm
(20½ [22½: 24½: 27: 30] in)

Rep last 4 rows once more.
67 [69: 73: 77: 79] sts.
Next row (RS): K1, sl 1, K1, psso, K to last
3 sts, K2tog, K1.
Next row: P2, patt to last 2 sts, P2.
Rep last 2 rows 26 [27: 29: 31: 32] times more,
ending with RS facing for next row. 13 sts.
Keeping raglan decreases correct as now set, cont
as follows:
Left sleeve only
Dec 1 st at each end of next row, then cast off
3 sts at beg of foll row. 8 sts.
Dec 1 st at end (front neck edge) of next row
and at same edge of foll 3 rows, **and at same
time** dec 1 st at beg (back raglan edge) of
next and foll alt row, ending with RS facing
for next row.
Right sleeve only
Cast off 3 sts at beg and dec 1 st at end of
next row. 9 sts.
Dec 1 st at end (front neck edge) of next row
and at same edge of foll 4 rows, **and at same
time** dec 1 st at end (back raglan edge) of 2nd
and foll alt row, ending with RS facing for
next row.
Both sleeves
Next row (RS): K2tog and fasten off.

MAKING UP
Press as described on the information page.
Join both front and right back raglan seams
using back stitch, or mattress stitch if preferred.
Neckband
With RS facing, using 4½mm (US 7) needles,
pick up and knit 9 sts from top of left sleeve,
8 [8: 10: 10: 12] sts down left side of front neck,
27 sts from front neck, 8 [8: 10: 10: 12] sts up
right side of front neck, 9 sts from top of right
sleeve, then 36 [36: 38: 38: 40]sts from back neck.
97 [97: 103: 103: 109]sts.
Beg with row 2, work in rib as given for back
for 9cm, ending with RS facing for next row.
Cast off loosely in rib.
See information page for finishing instructions.

ANICE SHAWL

Sharon Miller

● ● ●

SIZE
Completed shawl measures 57cm (22½in) x 200cm (78½in)

YARN
Rowan Kidsilk Haze
5 x 25g balls
(photographed in Cream 634)

NEEDLES
1 pair 5mm (no 6) (US 8) needles

TENSION
18 sts and 26 rows to 10cm (4in) measured over pattern using 5mm (US 8) needles, after pressing.

LOWER BORDER
Using 5mm (US 8) needles and oddment of waste yarn, cast on 11 sts.
Break off waste yarn and join in main yarn.
Row 1 (RS): P1, yrn, P1, yon, K2tog tbl, yfwd, K2tog tbl, P2, K2tog, yfwd, K1. 12 sts.
Row 2 and every foll alt row: Purl.
Row 3: P1, yrn, P3, yon, K2tog tbl, yfwd, K2tog tbl, P1, K2tog, yfwd, K1. 13 sts.
Row 5: P1, yrn, P5, yon, K2tog tbl, yfwd, K2tog tbl, K2tog, yfwd, K1. 14 sts.
Row 7: K2tog tbl, yfwd, K2tog tbl, P1, K2tog, yfwd, K2tog, yfrn, P2, K2tog, yfwd, K1. 13 sts.
Row 9: K2tog tbl, yfwd, sl 1, K2tog, psso, yfwd, K2tog, yfrn, P3, K2tog, yfwd, K1. 12 sts.
Row 11: K2tog tbl, P1, K2tog, yfrn, P4, K2tog, yfwd, K1. 11 sts.
Row 12: As row 2.
These 12 rows form patt.

Rep last 12 rows 10 times more, then row 1 once again, ending after a RS row. 12 sts.
Do NOT break yarn.

MAIN SECTION
With 12 sts of lower border on right needle, with RS facing and using right needle, pick up and knit 66 sts evenly along straight row-end edge of lower border, unravel waste yarn used for cast-on and K these 11 sts. 89 sts on right needle.
Next row (WS): P11, place marker on needle, K4, inc in next st, (K6, inc in next st) 8 times, K5, place second marker on needle (there will be the 12 sts of the lower border beyond this marker) and turn.
Next row: K75 and turn.
Next row: K75 and turn.
Next row (RS): P2, K2tog, yfwd, K5, (K6, yfwd, sl 1, K2tog, psso, yfwd, K5) 4 times, K6, yfwd, K2tog tbl, P2, slip marker onto right needle, K1, yfwd, K2tog tbl, P2, K2tog, yfwd, K2tog, yfrn, P1, yrn, P1. 99 sts.
Next row: Purl.
Sts between markers form centre section, with sts beyond markers forming side borders.
Place centre section chart
Keeping original 12 sts from lower border correct in patt as set by lower border, cont in patt as follows:
Row 1 (RS): Lower border patt to first marker, slip marker onto right needle, work next 75 sts as row 1 of chart, slip marker onto right needle, K1, yfwd, K2tog tbl, P1, K2tog, yfwd, K2tog, yfrn, P3, yrn, P1.
Row 2 and every foll alt row: Purl.
Row 3: Lower border patt to first marker, slip marker onto right needle, work next 75 sts as row 3 of chart, slip marker onto right needle, K1, yfwd, K2tog tbl, K2tog, yfwd, K2tog, yfrn, P5, yrn, P1.
Row 5: Lower border patt to first marker, slip marker onto right needle, work next 75 sts as row 5 of chart, slip marker onto right needle, K1, yfwd, K2tog tbl, P2, yon, K2tog tbl, yfwd, K2tog tbl, P1, K2tog, yfwd, K2tog.
Row 7: Lower border patt to first marker, slip marker onto right needle, work next 75 sts as row 7 of chart, slip marker onto right needle, K1, yfwd, K2tog tbl, P3, yon, K2tog tbl, yfwd, sl 1, K2tog, psso, yfwd, K2tog.
Row 9: Lower border patt to first marker, slip marker onto right needle, work next 75 sts as row 9 of chart, slip marker onto right needle, K1, yfwd, K2tog tbl, P4, yon, K2tog tbl, P1, K2tog.
Row 11: Lower border patt to first marker, slip marker onto right needle, work next 75 sts as row 11 of chart, slip marker onto right needle, K1, yfwd, K2tog tbl, P2, K2tog, yfwd, K2tog, yfrn, P1, yrn, P1.
Row 12: As row 2.
These 12 rows form patt for border at ends of RS rows.
Now keeping border patt sts beyond markers correct as now set and working centre sts

between markers foll chart, repeating the 60 row patt repeat, cont as follows:
Work chart rows 13 to 60.
Now rep chart rows 1 to 60, 6 times more, then chart rows 1 to 58 again, ending with RS facing for next row.
Next row (RS): Lower border patt to first marker and slip these sts onto a holder, K75 and turn.
Next row: K75.
Next row: K75 and turn.
Next row: K75.
Next row: K4, K2tog, (K6, K2tog) 8 times, K5, slip marker onto right needle, patt to end.
(66 sts now in centre section.)
Work top border
Next row (WS): P to within 1 st of marker, P2tog (this is last st of border with first st of centre section) and turn.
Next row: Patt to end.
Next row: P to last st of border, P2tog (this is last st of border with next st of centre section) and turn.
Rep last 2 rows until all sts of centre section have been used up. 11 sts.
Break yarn, leaving a fairly long end.

MAKING UP
Graft 11 sts left on needle together with 11 sts of border up other side of work left on holder.
Pin out to measurement given, cover with damp cloths and leave to dry naturally.

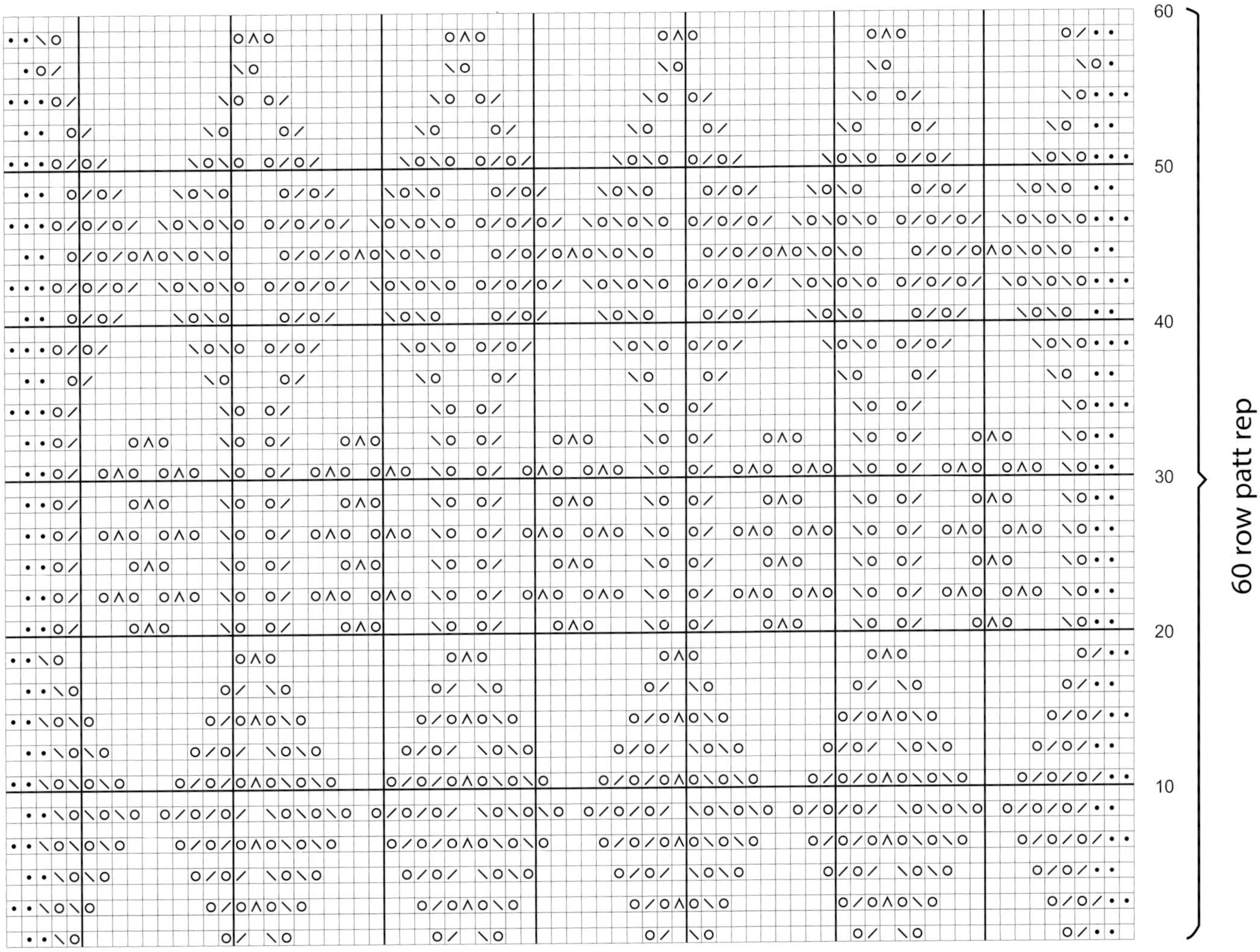

60 row patt rep

60
50
40
30
20
10

Key

☐ K on RS
P on WS

• P on RS

O yfwd

╱ K2tog

╲ sl1, K1, psso

∧ sl1, K2tog, psso

63

CARLOTTA

Kim Hargreaves

● ● ●

SIZE

XS	S	M	L	XL	
To fit bust					
81	86	91	97	102	cm
32	34	36	38	40	in

YARN

Rowan Yorkshire Tweed 4ply, 4ply Soft and Kidsilk Haze

A YTwd Sheer 267					
10	10	11	12	12	x 25gm
B YTwd Blessed 269					
1	1	1	1	1	x 25gm
C *KHaze Blushes 583					
1	1	1	1	1	x 25gm
D YTwd Foxy 275					
1	1	1	1	1	x 25gm
E *KHaze Liqueur 595					
1	1	1	1	1	x 25gm
F YTwd M Wine 279					
1	1	1	1	1	x 25gm
H Soft Black 383					
1	1	1	1	1	x 50gm
J *KHaze Meadow 581					
1	1	1	1	1	x 25gm
L Soft Leafy 367					
1	1	1	1	1	x 50gm
M YTwd Highlandr 266					
1	1	1	1	1	x 25gm
N Soft Military 388					
1	1	1	1	1	x 50gm

*Use Kid Silk Haze DOUBLE throughout.

NEEDLES

1 pair 2¼mm (no 13) (US 1) needles
1 pair 3mm (no 11) (US 2/3) needles

EXTRAS

Approx 1,400 x 01006 beads and 2.50 m of 4cm wide ribbon

TENSION

28 sts and 40 rows to 10cm (4in) measured over stocking stitch using 3mm (US 2/3) needles.

SPECIAL ABBREVIATIONS

Bead 1 = place a bead by bringing yarn to front (RS) of work and slipping bead up next to st just worked, slip next st purlwise from left needle to right needle and take yarn back to back (WS) of work, leaving bead sitting in front of slipped st on RS. Do not place beads on edge sts of rows as this will interfere with seaming and picking up sts.

Beading note: Before starting to knit, thread beads onto yarn. To do this, thread a fine sewing needle (one that will easily pass through the beads) with sewing thread. Knot ends of thread and then pass end of yarn through this loop. Thread a bead onto sewing thread and then gently slide it along and onto knitting yarn. Continue in this way until required number of beads are on yarn.

BACK

Cast on 97 (103: 111: 117: 125) sts using 2¼mm (US 1) needles and yarn M.
Break off yarn M and join in yarn A.
Row 1 (RS): K1, *P1, K1, rep from * to end.
Row 2: P1, *K1, P1, rep from * to end.
These 2 rows form rib.
Cont in rib for a further 26 rows, ending with a WS row.
Change to 3mm (US 2/3) needles.
Beg with a K row, work in st st for 2 rows.
Next row (eyelet row) (RS): Inc in first st, K6 (0: 4: 7: 2), *K2tog, yfwd, K7, rep from * to last 9 (3: 7: 10: 5) sts, K2tog, yfwd, K6 (0: 4: 7: 2), inc in last st.
99 (105: 113: 119: 127) sts.

Cont in st st for a further 7 rows, ending with a WS row.
Patt as folls:
Row 1 (RS): K4 (1: 5: 2: 6), bead 1, *K5, bead 1, rep from * to last 4 (1: 5: 2: 6) sts, K4 (1: 5: 2: 6).
Row 2 and every foll alt row: Purl.
Row 3: K2, M1, K to last 2 sts, M1, K2.
101 (107: 115: 121: 129) sts.
Rows 5 and 7: Knit.
Row 9: K2 (5: 3: 6: 4), bead 1, *K5, bead 1, rep from * to last 2 (5: 3: 6: 4) sts, K2 (5: 3: 6: 4).
Row 11: Knit.
Row 13: As row 3.
103 (109: 117: 123: 131) sts.
Row 15: Knit.
Row 16: Purl.
These 16 rows form patt and start side seam shaping.★★
Cont in patt, shaping side seams by inc 1 st at each end of 7th and every foll 10th row to 109 (115: 123: 129: 137) sts, then on every foll 8th row until there are 115 (121: 129: 135: 143) sts, taking inc sts into patt.
Cont straight until back measures 29 (30: 30: 31: 31) cm, ending with a WS row.
Shape armholes
Keeping patt correct, cast off 4 (5: 5: 6: 6) sts at beg of next 2 rows. 107 (111: 119: 123: 131) sts.
Dec 1 st at each end of next 7 (7: 9: 9: 11) rows, then on foll 2 (3: 3: 4: 4) alt rows.
89 (91: 95: 97: 101) sts.
Cont straight until armhole measures 18 (18: 19: 19: 20) cm, ending with a WS row.
Shape shoulders and back neck
Cast off 7 (7: 8: 8: 9) sts at beg of next 2 rows. 75 (77: 79: 81: 83) sts.
Next row (RS): Cast off 7 (7: 8: 8: 9) sts, patt until there are 12 sts on right needle and turn, leaving rem sts on a holder.
Work each side of neck separately.
Cast off 4 sts at beg of next row.
Cast off rem 8 sts.

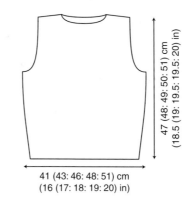

41 (43: 46: 48: 51) cm
(16 (17: 18: 19: 20) in)

47 (48: 49: 50: 51) cm
(18.5 (19: 19.5: 19.5: 20) in)

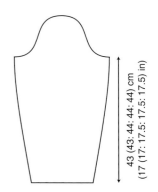

43 (43: 44: 44: 44) cm
(17 (17: 17.5: 17.5: 17.5) in)

With RS facing, rejoin yarn to rem sts, cast off centre 37 (39: 39: 41: 41) sts, patt to end. Complete to match first side, reversing shapings.

FRONT

Work as given for back to ★★, ending with a WS row.

Cont in patt, shaping side seams by inc 1 st at each end of 7th and foll 10th row, taking inc sts into patt. 107 (113: 121: 127: 135) sts.

Work a further 3 rows, ending after patt row 4 and with a WS row.

Place chart

Next row (RS): Patt 15 (18: 22: 25: 29) sts, work next 77 sts as row 1 of chart, patt to end.

Next row: Patt 15 (18: 22: 25: 29) sts, work next 77 sts as row 2 of chart, patt to end.

These 2 rows set position of chart.

Working rem 78 rows of chart and then completing front in patt, cont as follows:

Inc 1 st at each end of 5th and every foll 8th row until there are 115 (121: 129: 135: 143) sts, taking inc sts into patt.

Cont straight until front matches back to beg of armhole shaping, ending with a WS row.

Shape armholes

Keeping patt correct, cast off 4 (5: 5: 6: 6) sts at beg of next 2 rows. 107 (111: 119: 123: 131) sts.

Dec 1 st at each end of next 7 (7: 9: 9: 11) rows, then on foll 2 (3: 3: 4: 4) alt rows.

89 (91: 95: 97: 101) sts.

Cont straight until 20 (20: 20: 22: 22) rows less have been worked than on back to start of shoulder shaping, ending with a WS row.

Shape neck

Next row (RS): Patt 34 (34: 36: 37: 39) sts and turn, leaving rem sts on a holder.

Work each side of neck separately.

Dec 1 st at neck edge of next 8 rows, then on foll 4 (4: 4: 5: 5) alt rows. 22 (22: 24: 24: 26) sts.

Work 3 rows, ending with a WS row.

Shape shoulder

Cast off 7 (7: 8: 8: 9) sts at beg of next and foll alt row.

Work 1 row. Cast off rem 8 sts.

With RS facing, rejoin appropriate yarn to rem sts, cast off centre 21 (23: 23: 23: 23) sts, patt to end. Complete to match first side, reversing shapings.

SLEEVES (both alike)

Cast on 65 (65: 67: 69: 69) sts using 2¼mm (US 1) needles and yarn M.

Break off yarn M and join in yarn A.

Work in rib as given for back for 22 rows, ending with a WS row.

Change to 3mm (US 2/3) needles.

Patt as folls:

Row 1 (RS): Knit.

Row 2 and every foll alt row: Purl.

Row 3: K2, M1, K to last 2 sts, M1, K2. 67 (67: 69: 71: 71) sts.

Row 5: Knit.

Row 7: K3 (3: 4: 5: 5), bead 1, ★K5, bead 1, rep from ★ to last 3 (3: 4: 5: 5) sts, K3 (3: 4: 5: 5).

Row 9: Knit.

Row 11: (K2, M1) 0 (0: 0: 0: 1) times, K to last 0 (0: 0: 0: 2) sts, (M1, K2) 0 (0: 0: 0: 1) times. 67 (67: 69: 71: 73) sts.

Row 13: (K2, M1) 0 (1: 1: 1: 0) times, K to last 0 (2: 2: 2: 0) sts, (M1, K2) 0 (1: 1: 1: 0) times. 67 (69: 71: 73: 73) sts.

Row 15: (K2, M1) 1 (0: 0: 0: 0) times, K4 (1: 2: 3: 3), bead 1, ★K5, bead 1, rep from ★ to last 6 (1: 2: 3: 3) sts, K4 (1: 2: 3: 3), (M1, K2) 1 (0: 0: 0: 0) times. 69 (69: 71: 73: 73) sts.

Row 16: Purl.

These 16 rows form patt and start sleeve shaping.

Cont in patt, shaping sides by inc 1 st at each end of 11th (7th: 7th: 7th: 3rd) and every foll 12th (10th: 10th: 10th: 8th) row to 81 (73: 83: 85: 81) sts, then on every foll 14th (12th: 12th: 12th: 10th) row until there are 87 (89: 93: 95: 99) sts, taking inc sts into patt.

Cont straight until sleeve measures 43 (43: 44: 44: 44) cm, ending with a WS row.

Shape top

Keeping patt correct, cast off 4 (5: 5: 6: 6) sts at beg of next 2 rows.

79 (79: 83: 83: 87) sts.

Dec 1 st at each end of next 5 rows, then on foll 2 alt rows, then on every foll 4th row until 49 (49: 53: 53: 57) sts rem.

Work 1 row, ending with a WS row.

Dec 1 st at each end of next and every foll alt row to 41 sts, then on foll 3 rows, ending with a WS row. 35 sts.

Cast off 4 sts at beg of next 2 rows.

Cast off rem 27 sts.

MAKING UP

PRESS as described on the information page.

Join right shoulder seam using back stitch, or mattress stitch if preferred.

Neckband

With RS facing, using 2¼mm (US 1) needles and yarn A, pick up and knit 24 (24: 24: 26: 26) sts down left side of neck, 21 (23: 23: 23: 23) sts from front, 24 (24: 24: 26: 26) sts up right side of neck, then 44 (46: 46: 48: 48) sts from back. 113 (117: 117: 123: 123) sts.

Beg with row 2 of rib as given for back work 6 rows. Cast off in rib. See information page for finishing instructions, setting in sleeves using the set-in method. Thread ribbon through eyelet holes above ribbing.

Key

A

B

C used double

D

E used double

F

H

J used double

L

M

N

Bead 1

E V I A
Sarah Dallas

● ●

SIZE

	XS	S	M	L	XL	
To fit bust						
	81	86	91	97	102	cm
	32	34	36	38	40	in
A	Ice Water 239					
	2	2	2	2	3	x 50gm
B	Muddy 302					
	1	1	1	1	1	x 50gm
C	Zing 300					
	12	12	13	14	14	x 50gm

YARN

Rowan Handknit DK Cotton
A   Ice Water 239
B   Muddy 302
C   Zing 300

NEEDLES

1 pair 3¼mm (no 10) (US 3) needles
1 pair 4mm (no 8) (US 6) needles

TENSION

20 sts and 28 rows to 10cm (4in) measured over stocking stitch using 4mm (US 6) needles.

BACK

Cast on 106 (112: 118: 124: 130) sts using 3¼mm
(US 3) needles and yarn A.
Work in garter st for 6 rows, ending with a WS row.
Change to 4mm (US 6) needles.

Row 7 (RS): Knit.
Row 8: K7, P5 (3: 1: 4: 2), *K2, P3, rep from
* to last 9 (7: 10: 13: 11) sts, K0 (0: 2: 2: 2),
P2 (0: 1: 4: 2), K7.
Rep last 2 rows 8 times more.
All sizes
Break off yarn A and join in yarn B.
Using yarn B, work in garter st for 4 rows,
ending with a WS row. Break off yarn B, join in
yarn C and complete back using yarn C only.
Starting and ending rows as indicated, working
rows 1 and 2 once only and then repeating the
10 row repeat throughout, work in patt foll chart
as folls: Cont straight until back measures
36 (37: 37: 38: 38) cm, ending with a WS row.
Shape armholes
Keeping chart correct, cast off 7 sts at beg of
next 2 rows. 92 (98: 104: 110: 116) sts.
Cont straight until armhole measures
23 (23: 24: 24: 25) cm, ending with a WS row.
Shape shoulders and back neck
Next row (RS): Cast off 9 (9: 10: 11: 12) sts,
patt until 19 (21: 23: 24: 26) sts on right needle
and turn, leaving rem sts on a holder.
Work each side of neck separately.
Dec 1 st at beg of next row.
Cast off 9 (9: 10: 11: 12) sts at beg and dec 1 st at
end of next row.
Work 1 row. Cast off rem 8 (10: 11: 11: 12) sts.
With RS facing, rejoin yarn to rem sts, cast off
centre 28 (30: 32: 34: 36: 38: 38: 40: 40) sts, patt
to end. Complete to match first side,
reversing shapings.

FRONT

Work as for back until 18 (18: 18: 20: 20) rows
less have been worked than on back to start of
shoulder shaping, ending with a WS row.
Shape neck
Next row (RS): Patt 34 (36: 39: 42: 45) sts and
turn, leaving rem sts on a holder.
Work each side of neck separately.

Dec 1 st at neck edge of next 4 rows, then on
foll 3 (3: 3: 4: 4) alt rows, then on foll 4th row.
26 (28: 31: 33: 36) sts.
Work 3 rows, ending with a WS row.
Shape shoulder
Cast off 9 (9: 10: 11: 12) sts at beg of next and
foll alt row.
Work 1 row. Cast off rem 8 (10: 11: 11: 12) sts.
With RS facing, rejoin yarn to rem sts, cast off
centre 24 (26: 26: 26: 26) sts, patt to end.
Complete to match first side, reversing shapings.

SLEEVES (both alike)

Cast on 50 (50: 52: 52: 52) sts using 3¼mm
(US 3) needles and yarn B.
Work in garter st for 6 rows, ending with a
WS row.
Break off yarn B, join in yarn C and complete
sleeve using yarn C only.
Change to 4mm (US 6) needles.
Row 1 (RS): Knit.
Row 2: P4 (4: 5: 5: 5), *K2, P8, rep from * to
last 6 (6: 7: 7: 7) sts, K2, P4 (4: 5: 5: 5).
These 2 rows form patt.
Cont in patt, shaping sides by inc 1 st at each
end of next and every 6th row to
84 (84: 84: 84: 76) sts, then on every foll 4th row
until there are 92 (92: 96: 96: 100) sts, taking inc
sts into patt.
Cont straight until sleeve measures
50 (50: 51: 51: 51) cm, ending with a WS row.
Cast off.

MAKING UP

PRESS as described on the information page.
Join right shoulder seam using back stitch, or
mattress st if preferred.
Neckband
With RS facing, using 3¼mm (US 3) needles
and yarn C for ladies version or yarn A for
child's version, pick up and knit
22 (22: 22: 24: 24) sts down left side of neck,

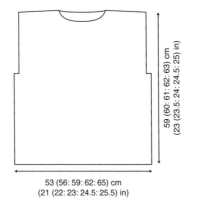

59 (60: 61: 62: 63) cm
(23 (23.5: 24: 24.5: 25) in)

53 (56: 59: 62: 65) cm
(21 (22: 23: 24.5: 25.5) in)

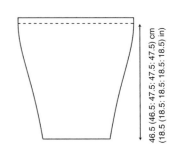

46.5 (46.5: 47.5: 47.5: 47.5) cm
(18.5 (18.5: 18.5: 18.5: 18.5) in)

24 (26: 26: 26: 26) sts from front,
22 (22: 22: 24: 24) sts up right side of neck, then
44 (46: 46: 48: 48) sts from back.
112 (116: 116: 122: 122) sts.
Work in garter st for 2 rows, ending with a
RS row. Cast off knitwise (on WS).
See information page for finishing instructions,
setting in sleeves using the square set-in method
and leaving side seams open for first 24 rows.

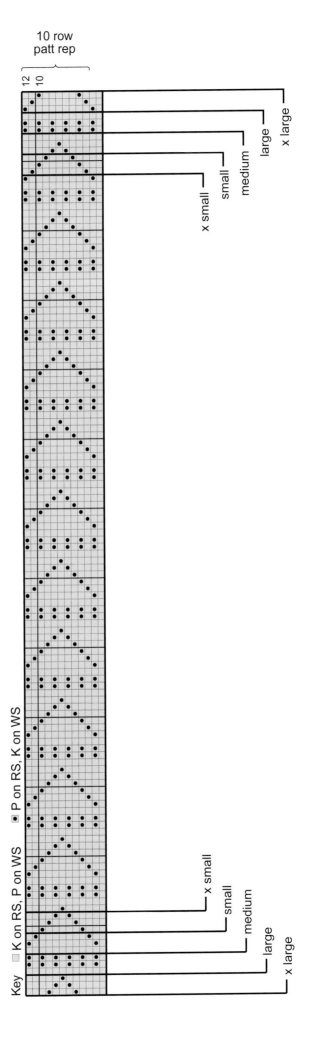

FICKLE

Louisa Harding

● ● ●

SIZE

S M L

YARN

Long version

A Fox Tweed Cricket 851

13 13 14 x 50gm

B Kid Silk Natural★ 977

2 2 2 x 25gm

C Kid Silk Holly★ 990

1 1 1 x 25gm

Cropped version

A D.D.K. 680

10 10 11 x 50gm

B Silk/Wool Pine★ 860

2 2 2 x 20gm

C Silk/Wool Moss Green★ 852

1 1 1 x 20gm

★USE DOUBLE THROUGHOUT

NEEDLES

1 pair 3¼mm (no 10) (US 3)
1 pair 4mm (no 8) (US 6)
Cable needle

TENSION

23 sts and 32 rows to 10cm (4in) measured over rev st st and cable patt using 4mm (US 6) needles.

Special note

From chart row 57 on back and fronts and chart row 37 on sleeve, all background sts are worked in rev st st.

N.B. Do not work any incomplete heart motifs, cont in 4 st cable patt only.

Fickle (Cropped version)

BACK

Cast 116 (126 : 136) sts using 3¼ mm (US 3) needles and yarn A,

Work 40 rows in patt from chart for back ending with a WS row.

Change to 4mm (US 6) needles and joining in and breaking off colours as required, cont in patt until chart row 70 has been completed.

Use separate lengths of yarn for each area of contrast colour. Link one colour to the next by twisting them around each other where they meet on the WS to avoid gaps.

Shape armholes

Cast off 5 sts at beg next 2 rows 106 (116 : 126) sts.

★Work 74 more rows without further shaping ending with a WS row.

Shape shoulders and back neck

Cast off 11 (13 : 14) sts at beg of next row, patt 31 (34 : 38) sts, turn and leave rem sts on a holder.

Work each side of neck separately.

Cast off 4 sts at beg next row.

Cast off 11 (13 : 15) at beg next row.

Cast off 4 sts at beg next row.

Cast off rem 12 (13 : 15) sts.

With RS facing, return to rem sts, leave centre 22 sts on a holder and patt to end.

Work 1 row.

Complete to match first side, reversing all shaping.

FRONT

Work as given for back to★

Cont without further shaping until chart row 122 has been completed ending with a WS row

Shape front neck

Next row: Patt 49 (54 : 59) sts, turn and leave rem sts on a holder.

Work each side of neck separately.

Cast off 4 sts at beg next row and foll alt row.

Dec 1 st at neck edge on next 2 rows and every foll alt row 5 times 34 (39 : 44) sts.)

Cont without further shaping until front matches back to shoulder shaping, ending with a WS row.

Shape shoulder

Cast off 11 (13 : 14) sts at beg next row and 11(13 : 15) sts at beg foll alt row.

Work 1 row.

Cast off rem 12 (13 : 15) sts.

With RS facing, return to rem sts, leave centre 8 sts on a holder and patt to end.

Work 1 row.

Complete to match first side reversing all shaping.

SLEEVES

Cast on 54 sts using 3¼ mm (US 3) needles and yarn A.

Work 20 rows in patt from chart for sleeve ending with a WS row.

Change to 4mm (US 6) needles and joining and breaking off colours as required, cont in patt until 160 chart rows have been completed and **at the same time** shape sides by increasing 1 st at each end of next row and every foll 5th row until there are 110 sts.

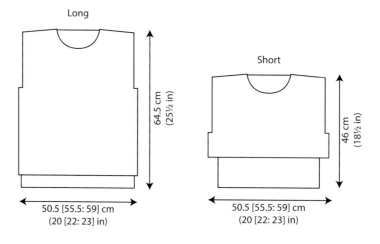

Long

64.5 cm (25½ in)

50.5 [55.5: 59] cm (20 [22: 23] in)

Short

46 cm (18½ in)

50.5 [55.5: 59] cm (20 [22: 23] in)

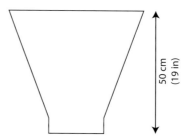

50 cm (19 in)

Take extra sts into rev st st as they occur.
Cast off evenly.

Fickle (Long version)
BACK
Cast on 100 (110 : 120) sts using 4mm (US 6)
needles and yarn A.

Row 1: P0 (1 : 2), (K2, P2) 3 (4 : 5) times, ★K4,
(P2, K2) three times, P2, rep from ★ three times
more, K4, (P2, K2) 3 (4 : 5) times, P0 (1 : 2).

Row 2: K0 (1 : 2), (P2, K2) 3 (4 : 5) times,
★P4 (K2, P2) three times, K2, rep from ★ three
times more, P4, (K2, P2) 3 (4 : 5) times, K0 (1 : 2).
Repeat these two rows once more.

Row 5: P0 (1 : 2), (K2, P2) 3 (4 : 5) times,★C4F,
(P2, K2) three times, P2, rep from ★ three times
more, C4F, (P2, K2) 3 (4 : 5) times, P0 (1 : 2).

Rows 6 and 8: Work as row 2.

Rows 7 and 9: Work as row 1.

Row 10 (inc): K0 (1 : 2), (P2,K2) 3 (4 : 5)
times, ★ P4, K1, M1, K1, (P2, K1, M1, K1) three
times, rep from ★ three times more, P4, (K2,
P2) 3 (4 : 5) times K0 (1:2). 116 (I26 : 136)
sts.). Then joining in and breaking off colours
as required, and beginning at chart row 41, cont
in patt from chart. Use separate lengths of yarn
for each area of contrast colour. Link one colour
to the next by twisting them around each other
where they meet on the WS to avoid gaps.
Cont until chart row 160 has been completed.★★

Shape armholes
Complete as given for the cropped sweater back.

FRONT
Work as given for back to ★★

Shape armholes
Cast off 5 sts at beg next 2 rows 106 (116 : 126) sts.)
Cont without further shaping until chart row
212 has been completed.

Shape front neck and shoulders
Complete as given for cropped sweater front.

SLEEVES (both alike)
Work as given for cropped sweater sleeves.

MAKING UP
Use backstitch on all main knitting and an edge
to edge to on all ribs, unless stated otherwise.
Press all pieces (except ribbing) on WS using a
warm iron over a damp cloth.
Join right shoulder seam.

Neckband
With RS facing, 3¼mm (US 3) needles and
yarn A, pick up and K 28 sts down left front
neck, then P2, K4, P2 from holder, pick up and
K 28 sts up right front neck, 8 sts down right
back neck, neck, then P9, K4, P9 from holder,
pick up and K 8 sts up left back neck. (102 sts.)

Row 1 (WS): P1, K2, P4★ (K2, P2) twice. K2,
P4, ★, rep from ★ to ★ once more, K2, P1, K2,
P4, rep from ★ to ★ four times, K2.

Row 2: P2, C4F★ (P2, K2) twice, P2, C4F, ★,
rep from ★ to ★ four times more, P2, K1, P2,
C4F, rep from ★ to ★ twice, P2, K1.

Rows 3 and 5: As row 1.

Row 4: P2, K4, ★(P2, K2) twice, P2, K4 ★rep
from ★ to ★ four times more, P2, K1, P2, K4,
rep from ★ to ★ twice, P2, K1.

Row 6: As row 4.
These 6 rows form the pattern
N.B For the long version repeat these 6 rows
once more.
For the cropped version repeat these 6 rows
twice more.

Both long and cropped versions:
Rep rows 1 to 3.
Cast off loosely and evenly in rib.
Join left shoulder and neckband seams.
Set sleeve head into armhole, the straight sides at
the top of the sleeve to form a neat right angle
to cast off sts at back and front.
Join side and sleeve seams.
Press seams.

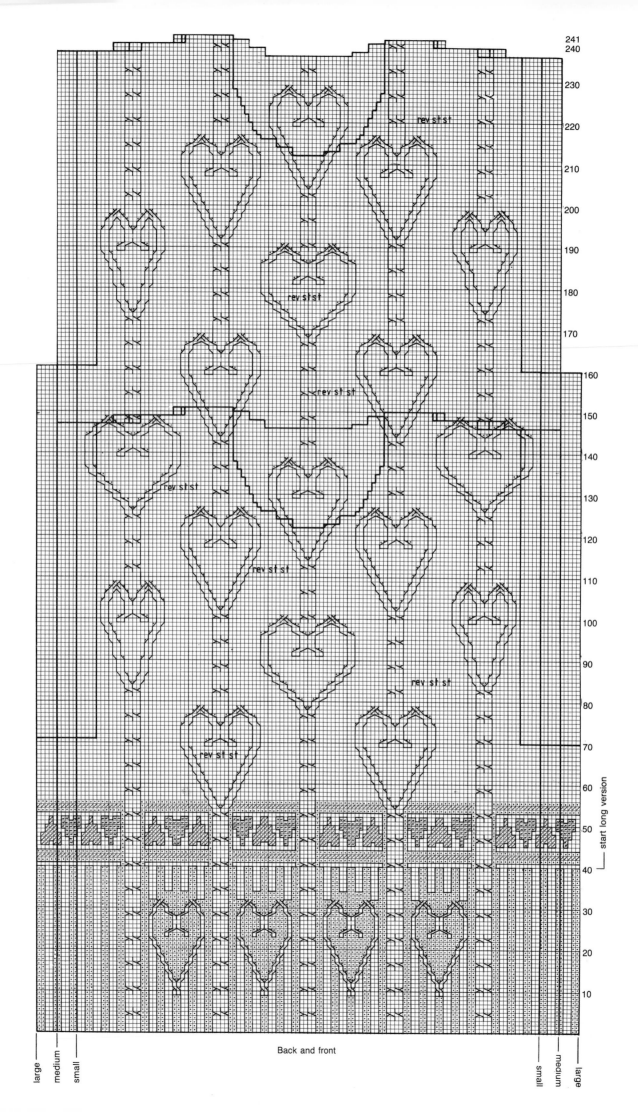

Back and front

large medium small

rev st st

start long version

Key

☐ = K on RS, P on WS

● = P on RS, K on WS

⋋⋎ = C4F-slip next 2 sts onto a cable needle and hold at front of work,K2, then K2 from cable needle.

⋋⋎ (RS) = C2F-slip next st onto a cable needle and hold at front of work, K1, then K1 from cable needle.

⋋⋎ (WS) = C2F-slip next st onto a cable needles and hold at front (WS) of work, P1, then P1, from cable needle.

⋎⋏ (RS) = C2B-slip next st onto a cable needle and hold at back of work, K1, then K1 from cable needle.

⋎⋏ (WS) = C2B-slip next st onto a cable needle and hold at back (RS) of work, P1, then P1 from cable needle.

╲● (RS) = T2F-slip next st onto cable needle and hold at front of work, P1, then K1 from cable needle.

╲● (WS) = T2F-slip next st onto a cable needle and hold at front (WS) of work, P1, then K1 from cable needle.

●╱╱ (RS) = T2B-slip next st onto a cable needle and hold at back of work, K1, then P1 from cable needle.

●╱╱ (WS) = T2B-slip next st onto a cable needle and hold at back (RS) of work, K1, then P1 from cable needle.

●⋎╱ = T3L-slip next 2 sts onto a cable needle and hold at back of work, K1, then P2 from cable needle.

╲╲● = T3R-slip next st onto a cable needle and hold at front of work P2, then K1 from cable needle.

●╱╱ = T3B-slip next st onto a cable needle and hold at back of work, K2, then P1 from cable needle.

╲╲● = T3F-slip next 2 sts onto a cable needle and hold at front of work, P1, then K2 from cable needle.

●●╱╱ = T4B-slip next 2 sts onto a cable needle and hold at back of work K2 then P2 from cable needle.

╲╲●● = T4F-slip next 2 sts onto a cable needle and hold at front of work, P2, then K2 from cable needle.

╱ = Using yarn B (double), K on RS, P on WS.

∿ = Using yarn C (double), K on RS, P on WS.

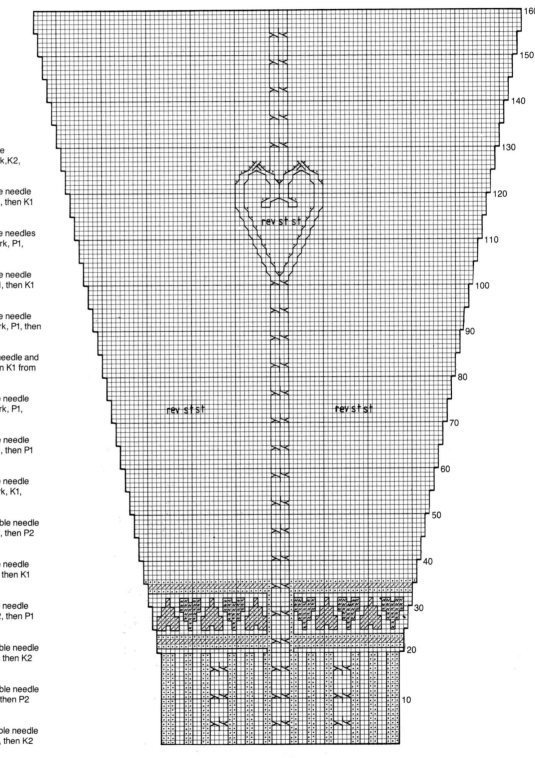

Sleeve

FLORA

Kim Hargreaves

● ●

SIZE

XS (S: M: L: XL)
To fit bust
81 (86: 91: 97: 102)cm
32 (34: 36: 38: 40)in

YARN

Rowan 4ply Cotton

4 (4: 4: 4: 5) x 50g balls of Rowan 4ply Cotton in
Cheeky 133 (A)
4 (4: 4: 4: 4) x 50g balls of Rowan 4ply Cotton in
Aegean 129 (B)
1 (1: 1: 1: 1) x 50g ball of Rowan 4ply Cotton in
Zest 134 (C)

NEEDLES

1 pair 2¼mm (no 13) (US 1) needles
1 pair 2¾mm (no 12) (US 2) needles
1 pair 3mm (no 11) (US 2/3) needles

TENSION

28 sts and 38 rows to 10cm (4in) measured over
stocking stitch using 3mm (US 2/3) needles.

BACK

Using 2¼mm (US 1) needles and yarn C, cast on
105 [113: 121: 129: 137] sts.
★★Beg with a K row, work in st st for 10 rows, ending
with RS facing for next row.
Row 11 (eyelet row) (RS): ★K2tog, yfwd, rep from ★
to last st, K1.
Row 12: Purl.
Break off yarn C and join in yarn A.
Change to 2¾mm (US 2) needles.
Beg with a K row, work in striped st st as follows:
Using yarn A, work 2 rows.
Join in yarn B.

Using yarn B, work 2 rows.
Last 4 rows form striped st st.
Cont in striped st st for a further 6 rows, ending
with RS facing for next row.
Change to 3mm (US 2/3) needles.★★
Cont in striped st st, shaping side seams by inc
1 st at each end of 5th and every foll 16th row
until there are 115 [123: 131: 139: 147] sts.
Cont straight until back measures
27 [28: 28: 29: 29]cm **from eyelet row**, ending
with RS facing for next row.
Shape armholes
Keeping stripes correct, cast off 4 [5: 5: 6: 6] sts
at beg of next 2 rows.
107 [113: 121: 127: 135] sts.
Dec 1 st at each end of next 5 [7: 7: 9: 9] rows,
then on foll 3 [3: 5: 5: 7] alt rows.
91 [93: 97: 99: 103] sts.
Cont straight until armhole measures
20 [20: 21: 21: 22]cm, ending with RS facing for
next row.
Shape shoulders and back neck
Cast off 7 [7: 7: 7: 8] sts at beg of next 2 rows.
77 [79: 83: 85: 87] sts.
Next row (RS): Cast off 7 [7: 7: 7: 8] sts, K
until there are 10 [10: 12: 12: 12] sts on right
needle and turn, leaving rem sts on a holder.
Work each side of neck separately.
Cast off 4 sts at beg of next row.
Cast off rem 6 [6: 8: 8: 8] sts.
With RS facing, rejoin appropriate yarn to rem
sts, cast off centre 43 [45: 45: 47: 47] sts, K to end.
Complete to match first side, reversing shapings.

FRONT

Work as given for back until 24 [24: 24: 26: 26]
rows less have been worked to start of shoulder
shaping, ending with RS facing for next row.
Shape neck
Next row (RS): K33 [33: 35: 36: 38] and turn,
leaving rem sts on a holder.
Work each side of neck separately.

Keeping stripes correct, dec 1 st at neck edge of
next 10 rows, then on foll 2 [2: 2: 3: 3] alt rows,
then on foll 4th row. 20 [20: 22: 22: 24] sts.
Work 5 rows, ending with RS facing for
next row.
Shape shoulder
Cast off 7 [7: 7: 7: 8] sts at beg of next and foll
alt row.
Work 1 row.
Cast off rem 6 [6: 8: 8: 8] sts.
With RS facing, rejoin appropriate yarn to rem
sts, cast off centre 25 [27: 27: 27: 27] sts,
K to end.
Complete to match first side, reversing shapings.

SLEEVES

Using 2¼mm (US 1) needles and yarn C, cast
on 65 [65: 67: 69: 69] sts.
Work as given for back from ★★ to ★★.
Cont in striped st st, shaping sides by inc 1 st at
each end of 7th and every foll 12th [10th: 10th:
10th: 10th] row to 75 [91: 89: 91: 75] sts, then
on every foll 10th [8th: 8th: 8th: 8th] row until
there are 91 [93: 97: 99: 103] sts.
Cont straight until sleeve measures approx
43 [43: 44: 44: 44]cm **from eyelet row**, ending
after same stripe row as on back to beg of
armhole shaping and with RS facing for
next row.
Shape top
Keeping stripes correct, cast off 4 [5: 5: 6: 6] sts
at beg of next 2 rows. 83 [83: 87: 87: 91] sts.
Dec 1 st at each end of next 5 rows, then on foll
3 alt rows, then on every foll 4th row until
53 [53: 57: 57: 61] sts rem.
Work 1 row, ending with RS facing for
next row.
Dec 1 st at each end of next and every foll alt
row to 45 sts, then on foll 5 rows, ending with
RS facing for next row.
Cast off rem 35 sts.

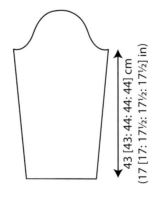

43 [43: 44: 44: 44] cm
(17 [17: 17½: 17½: 17½] in)

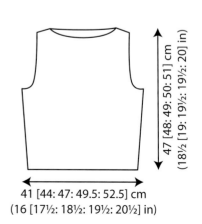

47 [48: 49: 50: 51] cm
(18½ [19: 19½: 19½: 20] in)

41 [44: 47: 49.5: 52.5] cm
(16 [17½: 18½: 19½: 20½] in)

MAKING UP

Press as described on the information page.
Join both shoulder seams using back stitch, or
mattress stitch if preferred.

Neck binding

Using 2¼mm (US 1) needles and yarn C, cast
on 8 sts.

Row 1 (RS): Using yarn C, knit.

Row 2: Using yarn C, inc purlwise in first st,
P5, P2tog. 8 sts.

Join in yarn B.

Row 3: Using yarn B, knit.

Row 4: Using yarn B, inc purlwise in first st,
P5, P2tog. 8 sts.

Rep last 4 rows until binding, when slightly
stretched, fits around entire neck edge, ending
after row 4.

Cast off.

Join ends of binding, then sew one edge of
binding to neck edge, placing binding seam at
left shoulder. Fold binding in half to inside and
stitch in place.

See information page for finishing instructions,
setting in sleeves using the set-in method. Fold
first 10 rows of sleeves and body to inside along
eyelet row and stitch in place.

SIZE

	XS	S	M	L	XL	
To fit bust	81	86	91	97	102	cm
	32	34	36	38	40	in

YARN

Rowan Cotton Glace
Multi coloured cardigan

		XS	S	M	L	XL	
A Oyster	730	10	11	11	12	12	x 50gm
B Butter	795	1	1	1	1	1	x 50gm
C Terracotta	786	2	2	2	2	2	x 50gm
D Blood Orange	445	2	2	3	3	3	x 50gm
E Black	727	1	1	1	1	1	x 50gm

Alternative colourway (not photographed)

		XS	S	M	L	XL	
A Oyster	730	10	11	11	12	12	x 50gm
B Butter	795	1	1	1	1	1	x 50gm
C Bubbles	724	2	2	2	2	2	x 50gm
D Crushed Rose	793	2	2	3	3	3	x 50gm
E Black	727	1	1	1	1	1	x 50gm

One colour cardigan

	8	8	9	9	10 x 50gm

(photographed in Glee 799)

NEEDLES

1 pair 2¾mm (no 12) (US 2) needles
1 pair 3¼mm (no 10) (US 3) needles

BUTTONS - 5

TENSION

23 sts and 32 rows to 10cm (4in) measured over patterned stocking stitch using 3¼mm (US 3) needles.

Multi coloured cardigan
BACK

Cast on 107 (113: 119: 125: 131) sts using 2¾mm (US 2) needles and yarn C.
Break off yarn C and join in yarn A.
Knit 3 rows.
Row 4 (WS): P1 (0: 1: 0: 1), ★K1, P1, rep from ★ to last 0 (1: 0: 1: 0) st, K0 (1: 0: 1: 0).
Row 5: As row 4.
These 2 rows form moss st.
Work a further 15 rows in moss st.
Change to 3¼mm (US 3) needles.
Using the **intarsia** technique described on the information page and starting and ending rows as indicated, cont in patt foll chart for back, which is worked entirely in st st, as folls:
Work 2 rows.
Place markers on 26th (29th: 32nd: 35th: 38th) st in from each end of row.
Row 3 (dec) (RS): K2tog, patt to within 1 st of marked st, K3tog tbl, patt to within 1 st of second marked st, K3tog, patt to last 2 sts, K2tog.
Work 7 rows.
Rep last 8 rows twice more and then row 3 (the dec row) again. 83 (89: 95: 101: 107) sts.
Work 15 rows, ending with chart row 42.
Row 43 (inc) (RS): Inc in first st, ★patt to marked st, M1, K marked st, M1, rep from ★ once more, patt to last st, inc in last st.
Work 11 rows.
Rep last 12 rows twice more and then row 43 (the inc row) again. 107 (113: 119: 125: 131) sts.
Work 13 (17: 17: 21: 21) rows, ending with chart row 92 (96: 96: 100: 100).
(Work measures 35 (36: 36: 37: 37) cm.)
Shape armholes
Keeping chart correct, cast off 3 (4: 4: 5: 5) sts at beg of next 2 rows. 101 (105: 111: 115: 121) sts.
Dec 1 st at each end of next 5 (5: 7: 7: 9) rows, then on foll 6 (7: 7: 8: 8) alt rows.
79 (81: 83: 85: 87) sts.
Cont straight until chart row
156 (160: 164: 168: 170) has been completed,

ending with a WS row.
(Armhole measures 20 (20: 21: 21: 22) cm.)
Shape shoulders and back neck
Cast off 8 sts at beg of next 2 rows.
63 (65: 67: 69: 71) sts.
Next row (RS): Cast off 8 sts, patt until there are 11 (11: 12: 12: 13) sts on right needle and turn, leaving rem sts on a holder.
Work each side of neck separately.
Cast off 4 sts at beg of next row.
Cast off rem 7 (7: 8: 8: 9) sts.
With RS facing, rejoin yarn to rem sts, cast off centre 25 (27: 27: 29: 29) sts, patt to end.
Work to match first side, reversing shapings.

LEFT FRONT
Centre front panel
Cast on 28 sts using 2¾mm (US 2) needles and yarn C.
Break off yarn C and join in yarn A.
Knit 3 rows.
Row 4 (WS): ★K1, P1, rep from ★ to end.
This row sets position of moss st.
Row 5: P1, K1, pick up loop lying between needles and P then K into back of this loop, moss st to end.
Work 5 rows.
Rep last 6 rows once more. 32 sts.
Break yarn and leave sts on a holder.
Side panel
Cast on 21 (24: 27: 30: 33) sts using 2¾mm (US 2) needles and yarn C.
Break off yarn C and join in yarn A.
Knit 3 rows.
Row 4 (WS): ★P1, K1, rep from ★ to last 1 (0: 1: 0: 1) st, P1 (0: 1: 0: 1).
This row sets position of moss st.
Row 5: Moss st to last 2 sts, pick up loop lying between needles and K then P into back of this loop, K1, P1.
Work 5 rows.
Rep last 6 rows once more.
25 (28: 31: 34: 37) sts.

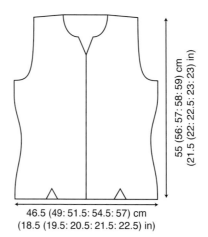

55 (56: 57: 58: 59) cm
(21.5 (22: 22.5: 23: 23) in)

46.5 (49: 51.5: 54.5: 57) cm
(18.5 (19.5: 20.5: 21.5: 22.5) in)

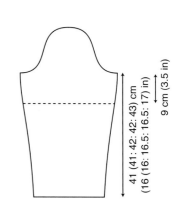

41 (41: 42: 42: 43) cm
(16 (16: 16.5: 16.5: 17) in)

9 cm (3.5 in)

Join panels

Row 17 (RS): Moss st across first
24 (27: 30: 33: 36) sts of side panel, (P1, K1) into
next st, then moss st across 32 sts of centre front
panel. 58 (61: 64: 67: 70) sts.
Work 2 rows.
Row 20 (WS): Moss st 6 sts and slip these sts
onto a holder for button band, M1, moss st to
end. 53 (56: 59: 62: 65) sts.
Change to 3¼mm (US 3) needles.
Cont in patt foll chart for fronts as folls:
Work 2 rows.
Place marker on 26th (29th: 32nd: 35th: 38th) st
in from side seam.
Row 3 (dec) (RS): K2tog, patt to within 1 st
of marked st, K3tog tbl, patt to end.
Work 7 rows.
Rep last 8 rows twice more and then row 3
(the dec row) again.
41 (44: 47: 50: 53) sts.
Work 15 rows, ending with chart row 42.
Row 43 (inc) (RS): Inc in first st, patt to
marked st, M1, K marked st, M1, patt to end.
Work 11 rows.
Rep last 12 rows twice more and then row
43 (the inc row) again.
53 (56: 59: 62: 65) sts.
Work 13 (17: 17: 21: 21) rows, ending with
chart row 92 (96: 96: 100: 100). (Front matches
back to beg of armhole shaping.)

Shape armhole
Keeping chart correct, cast off 3 (4: 4: 5: 5) sts at
beg of next row.
50 (52: 55: 57: 60) sts.
Work 1 row.
Dec 1 st at armhole edge of next
5 (5: 7: 7: 8) rows, then on foll
5 (3: 2: 0: 0) alt rows. 40 (44: 46: 50: 52) sts.
Work 1 (1: 1: 1: 0) row, ending with chart
row 110.

Shape front slope
Dec 1 st at armhole edge of next and foll
0 (3: 4: 7: 8) alt rows **and at same time** dec
1 st at neck edge on next and every foll 6th row.
38 (38: 39: 39: 40) sts.
Dec 1 st at neck edge on every foll 6th row
from previous dec until 35 (35: 36: 36: 37) sts
rem.
Work 6 (4: 8: 4: 6) rows, ending with chart row
135 (139: 143: 145: 147).

Shape neck
Cast off 3 sts at beg of next row.
32 (32: 33: 33: 34) sts.
Dec 1 st at neck edge of next 5 (5: 5: 3: 3) rows,
then on foll 3 (3: 3: 5: 5) alt rows, then on foll
4th row. 23 (23: 24: 24: 25) sts.
Work 5 rows, ending with chart row
156 (160: 164: 168: 170).

Shape shoulder
Cast off 8 sts at beg of next and foll alt row.
Work 1 row.
Cast off rem 7 (7: 8: 8: 9) sts.

RIGHT FRONT

Side panel
Cast on 21 (24: 27: 30: 33) sts using 2¾mm
(US 2) needles and yarn C.
Break off yarn C and join in yarn A.
Knit 3 rows.
Row 4 (WS): P1 (0: 1: 0: 1), ★K1, P1, rep
from ★ to end.
This row sets position of moss st.
Row 5: P1, K1, pick up loop lying between
needles and P then K into back of this loop,
moss st to end.
Work 5 rows.
Rep last 6 rows once more.
25 (28: 31: 34: 37) sts.
Break yarn and leave sts on a holder.

Centre front panel
Cast on 28 sts using 2¾mm (US 2) needles and
yarn C.
Break off yarn C and join in yarn A.
Knit 3 rows.
Row 4 (WS): ★P1, K1, rep from ★ to end.
This row sets position of moss st.
Row 5: Moss st to last 2 sts, pick up loop lying
between needles and K then P into back of this
loop, K1, P1.
Work 5 rows. Rep last 6 rows once more.
32 sts.

Join panels
Row 17 (RS): Moss st across first 31 sts of
centre front panel,
(P1, K1) into next st, then moss st across
25 (28: 31: 34: 37) sts of side panel.
58 (61: 64: 67: 70) sts.
Work 2 rows.
Row 20 (WS): Moss st to last 6 sts, M1
and turn, leaving rem 6 sts on a holder for
buttonhole band. 53 (56: 59: 62: 65) sts.
Change to 3¼mm (US 3) needles.
Cont in patt foll chart for fronts as folls:
Work 2 rows.
Place marker on 26th (29th: 32nd: 35th: 38th) st
in from side seam.
Row 3 (dec) (RS): Patt to within 1 st of
marked st, K3tog, patt to last 2 sts, K2tog.
Complete to match left front,
reversing shapings.

LEFT SLEEVE

Cast on 49 (49: 49: 53: 53) sts using 2¾mm
(US 2) needles and yarn C.
Break off yarn C and join in yarn A.
Knit 3 rows.
Work 17 rows in moss st, inc 1 st at each end
of 6th and foll 8th row. 53 (53: 53: 57: 57) sts.
Change to 3¼mm (US 3) needles.
Cont in patt foll chart for sleeve as folls:
Work 4 rows.
Inc 1 st at each end of next and every foll
8th row until there are 77 (79: 81: 83: 85) sts,
taking inc sts into patt. Cont straight until
chart row 112 (112: 116: 116: 118) has been
completed, ending with a WS row.

Shape top
Keeping chart correct, cast off 3 (4: 4: 5: 5) sts at
beg of next 2 rows. 71 (71: 73: 73: 75) sts.
Dec 1 st at each end of next 5 rows, then on foll
3 alt rows, then on every foll 4th row until
45 (45: 47: 47: 49) sts rem.
Work 1 row.
Dec 1 st at each end of next and foll
2 (2: 3: 3: 4) alt rows, then on foll 3 rows.
33 sts.
Cast off 6 sts at beg of next 2 rows, ending with
chart row 156 (156: 162: 162: 166).
Cast off rem 21 sts.

RIGHT SLEEVE

Work as given for left sleeve but reversing chart
by reading odd numbered K rows from left to
right, and even numbered P rows from right
to left.

One colour cardigan

BACK and FRONTS
Work as given for multi coloured cardigan
but using same colour throughout.

SLEEVES
Cast on 71 (73: 75: 77: 79) sts using 2¾mm
(US 2) needles.
Knit 3 rows.
Work 17 rows in moss st, inc 1 st at each end
of 4th and every foll 6th row.
77 (79: 81: 83: 85) sts.
Change to 3¼mm (US 3) needles.
Beg with a K row, cont in st st until sleeve
measures 9 cm, ending with a WS row.

Shape top
Cast off 3 (4: 4: 5: 5) sts at beg of next 2 rows.
71 (71: 73: 73: 75) sts.
Dec 1 st at each end of next 5 rows, then on
foll 3 alt rows, then on every foll 4th row until
45 (45: 47: 47: 49) sts rem.
Work 1 row.
Dec 1 st at each end of next and foll
2 (2: 3: 3: 4) alt rows, then on foll 3 rows, ending
with a WS row. 33 sts.
Cast off 6 sts at beg of next 2 rows.
Cast off rem 21 sts.

MAKING UP
PRESS all pieces as described on the info page.
Multi coloured cardigan
Join shoulder seams using back stitch, or
mattress stitch if preferred.
Button band
Slip 6 sts left on holder for button band onto
2¾mm (US 2) needles and rejoin yarn A with
RS facing.
Cont in moss st as set until band, when slightly
stretched, fits up left front opening edge to start
of neck shaping, ending with a WS row.
Break yarn and leave sts on a holder.
Slip stitch band in place.
Mark positions for 5 buttons on this band
– lowest button level with beg of chart, top
button 2 cm below start of front slope shaping
and rem 3 buttons evenly spaced between.

Buttonhole band

Work as given for button band, rejoining yarn with WS facing and with the addition of 5 buttonholes to correspond with positions marked for buttons worked as folls:

Buttonhole row (RS): Moss st 2 sts, yrn (to make a buttonhole), work 2 tog, moss st 2 sts. When band is completed, ending with a WS row, do NOT break off yarn.

Slip stitch band in place.

Neckband

With RS facing, using 2¾mm (US 2) needles and yarn A, moss st across 6 sts of buttonhole band, pick up and knit 29 (29: 29: 31: 31) sts up right side of neck, 33 (35: 35: 37: 37) sts from back, 29 (29: 29: 31: 31) sts down left side of neck, then moss st across 6 sts of button band. 103 (105: 105: 111: 111) sts.

Work in moss st as set by front bands for 5 rows.

Cast off in moss st.

See information page for finishing instructions, setting in sleeves using the set-in method.

One colour cardigan

Work as given for multi coloured cardigan but using same colour throughout

BACK

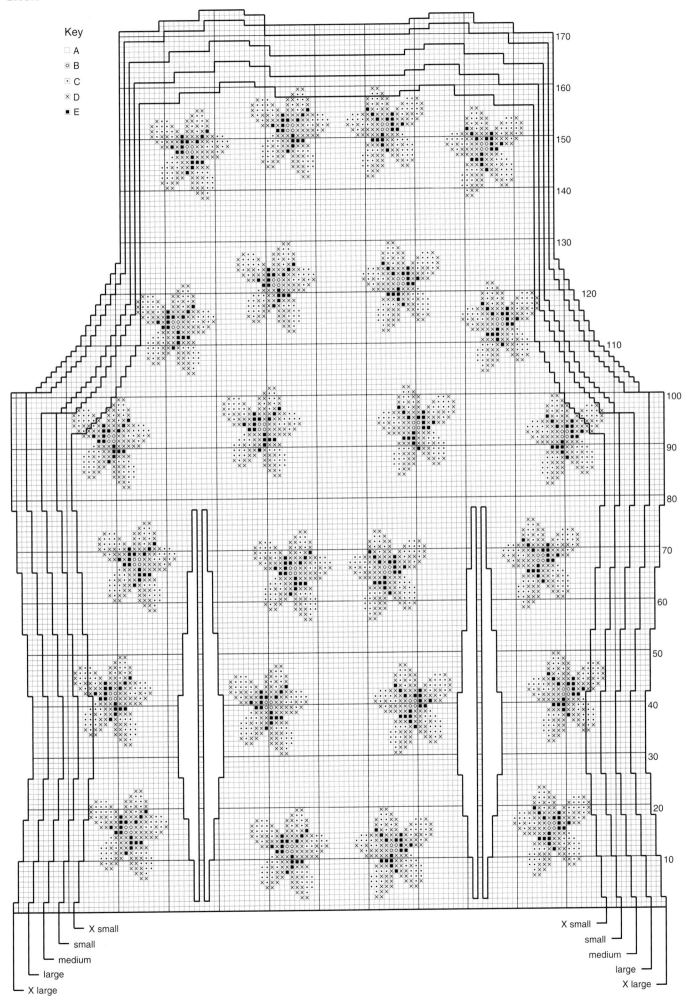

Key
□ A
⊙ B
⊡ C
⊠ D
■ E

170
160
150
140
130
120
110
100
90
80
70
60
50
40
30
20
10

X small
small
medium
large
X large

X small
small
medium
large
X large

79

FRONT

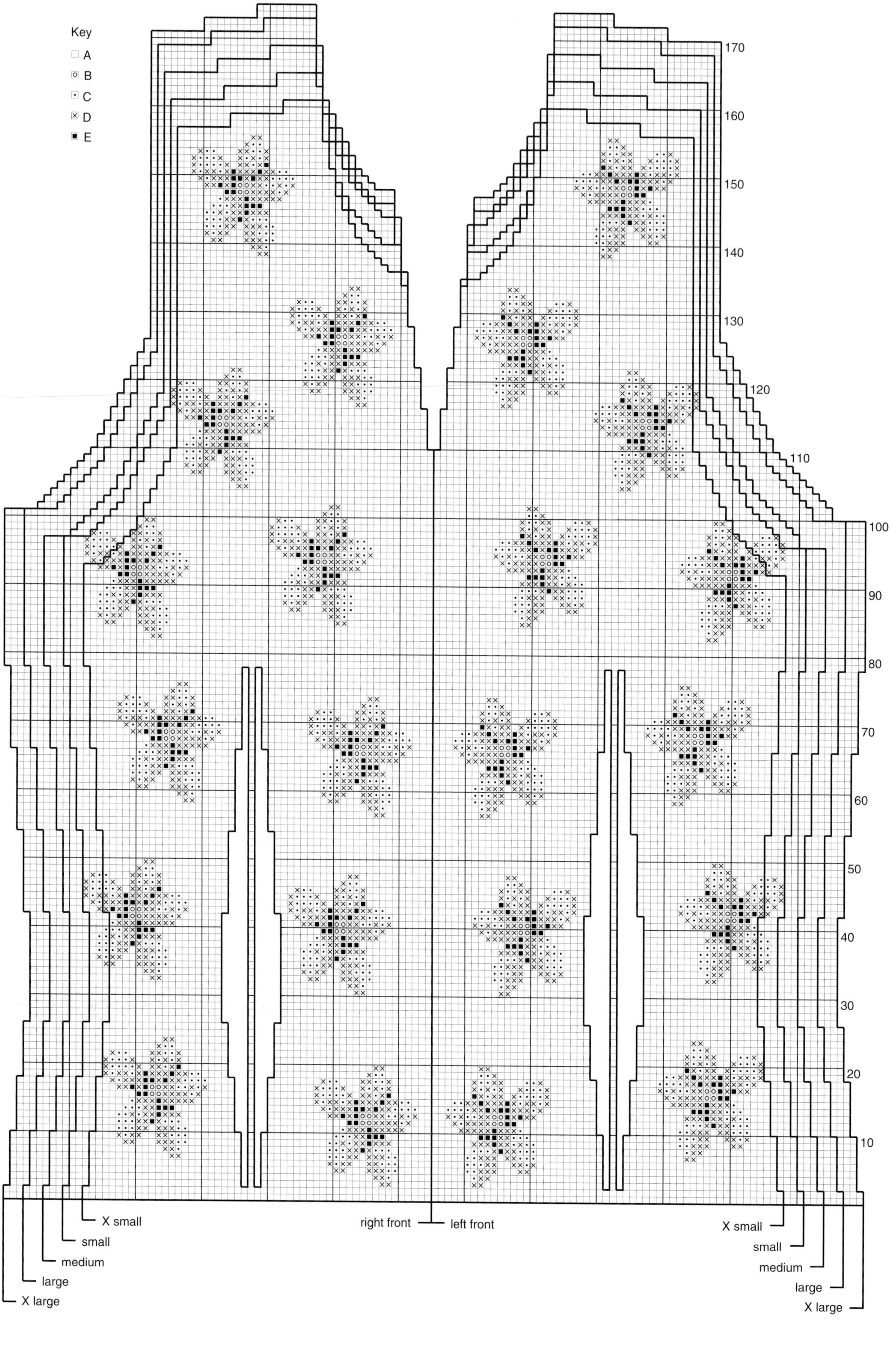

Key
□ A
⊙ B
⊡ C
⊠ D
■ E

170
160
150
140
130
120
110
100
90
80
70
60
50
40
30
20
10

X small
small
medium
large
X large

right front — left front

X small
small
medium
large
X large

80

SLEEVE

Key
A
B
C
D
E

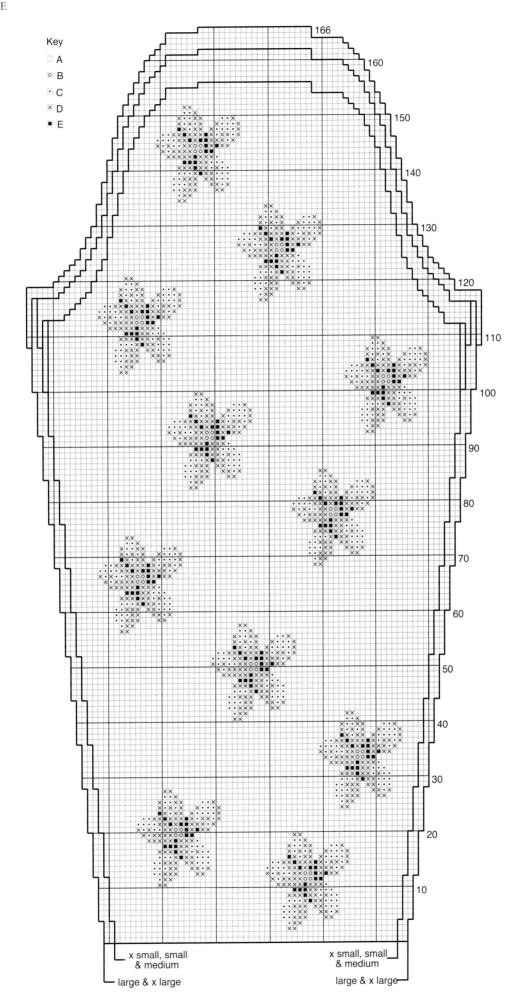

166
160
150
140
130
120
110
100
90
80
70
60
50
40
30
20
10

x small, small
& medium

large & x large

x small, small
& medium

large & x large

81

FRANZISKA

Galina Carroll

SIZE

	S	M	L	XL	XXL	
To fit bust						
	81-86	91-97	102-107	112-117	122-127	cm
	32-34	36-38	40-42	44-46	48-50	in

YARN

Felted Tweed

A Mineral 181						
	12	13	14	15	16	x 50gm
B Bilberry 151						
	2	2	2	2	2	x 50gm
C Jaffa 188						
	2	2	2	2	2	x 50gm
D Watery 152						
	1	1	1	1	1	x 50gm

NEEDLES

1 pair 3¼mm (no 10) (US 3) needles

TENSION

26 sts and 28 rows to 10cm (4in) measured over main chart patt, 25 sts and 30 rows to 10cm (4in) measured over yoke patt, both using 3¼mm (US 3) needles.

BACK

Using 3¼mm (US 3) needles and yarn A cast on 213 [227: 243: 257: 275] sts.
Work in g st for 8 rows, ending with RS facing for next row.
Beg and ending rows as indicated, using the **fairisle** technique as described on the information page and repeating the 8 st patt repeat 26 [28: 30: 32: 34] times across each row, cont in patt from chart, which is worked entirely in st st beg with a K row, as folls:
Work chart rows 1 to 96, ending with RS facing for next row.
Break off contrasts and cont using yarn A **only**.
Next row (RS): Knit.
Next row: P11 [9: 12: 10: 10], P2tog, (P25 [21: 22: 24: 26], P2tog) 7 [9: 9: 9: 9] times, P11 [9: 13: 11: 11]. 205 [217: 233: 247: 265] sts.
Joining in yarn B when required, now work in yoke patt as folls:
Row 1 (RS): Using yarn A, knit.
Row 2: Using yarn A P2 [2: 2: 3: 2], using yarn B P1, *using yarn A P3, using yarn B P1, rep from * to last 2 [2: 2: 3: 2] sts, using yarn A P2 [2: 2: 3: 2].
Row 3: Using yarn A, knit.
Row 4: Using yarn A, purl.
Rows 5 and 6: As rows 3 and 4.
Row 7: Using yarn A K4 [4: 4: 1: 4], using yarn B K1, *using yarn A K3, using yarn B K1, rep from * to last 4 [4: 4: 1: 4] sts, using yarn A K4 [4: 4: 1: 4].
Row 8: As row 4.
Rows 9 and 10: As rows 3 and 4.
These 10 rows form yoke patt.
Cont in yoke patt until back meas 71 [73: 75: 77: 79] cm, ending with RS facing for next row.

Shape shoulders

Keeping patt correct, cast off 10 [11: 12: 13: 14] sts at beg of next 6 rows, ending with RS facing for next row. 145 [151: 161: 169: 181] sts.

Shape back neck

Next row (RS): Cast off 11 [11: 12: 13: 15] sts, patt until there are 37 [40: 43: 46: 49] sts on right needle and turn, leaving rem sts on a holder.
Work each side of neck separately.
Dec 1 st at neck edge of next 4 rows **and at same time** cast off 11 [12: 13: 14: 15] sts at beg of 2nd and foll alt row.
Work 1 row.
Cast off rem 11 [12: 13: 14: 15] sts.
With RS facing, slip centre 49 [49: 51: 51: 53] sts onto a holder, rejoin yarns and patt to end.
Complete to match first side, reversing shapings.

FRONT

Work as given for back until
12 [12: 14: 14: 16] rows less have been worked than on back to beg of shoulder shaping, ending with RS facing for next row.

Shape front neck

Next row (RS): Patt 86 [92: 100: 107: 116] sts and turn, leaving rem sts on a holder.
Work each side of neck separately.
Keeping patt correct, dec 1 st at neck edge of next 8 rows, then on foll 1 [1: 2: 2: 3] alt rows.
77 [83: 90: 97: 105] sts.
Work 1 row, ending with RS facing for next row.

Shape shoulder

Cast off 10 [11: 12: 13: 14] sts at beg of next and foll 2 [3: 3: 3: 2] alt rows, then 11 [12: 13: 14: 15] sts at beg of foll 3 [2: 2: 2: 3] alt rows **and at same time** dec 1 st at neck edge of next and foll alt row, then on foll 4th row.
Work 1 row.
Cast off rem 11 [12: 13: 14: 15] sts.
With RS facing, slip centre 33 sts onto a holder, rejoin yarns and patt to end.
Complete to match first side, reversing shapings.

SLEEVES

Using 3¼mm (US 3) needles and yarn A cast on 50 [50: 54: 54: 58] sts.
Row 1 (RS): K2, *P2, K2, rep from * to end.
Row 2: P2, *K2, P2, rep from * to end.
These 2 rows form rib.
Cont in rib, shaping sides by inc 1 st at each end of 5th [3rd: 3rd: 3rd: 3rd] and every foll 8th [6th: 6th: 6th: 6th] row to 78 [62: 64: 88: 92] sts, then on every foll – [8th: 8th: 8th: 8th] row until there are – [82: 86: 92: 96] sts, taking inc sts into rib.
Cont straight until sleeve meas 40 [41: 42: 42: 42] cm, ending with RS facing for next row.
Cast off **loosely** in rib.

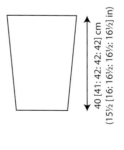

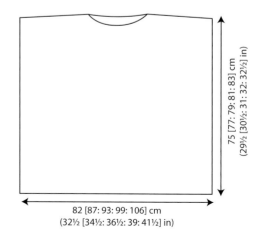

40 [41: 42: 42: 42] cm
(15½ [16: 16½: 16½: 16½] in)

75 [77: 79: 81: 83] cm
(29½ [30½: 31: 32: 32½] in)

82 [87: 93: 99: 106] cm
(32½ [34½: 36½: 39: 41½] in)

MAKING UP

Press as described on the information page.
Join right shoulder seam using back stitch, or
mattress stitch if preferred.

Collar

With RS facing, using 3¼mm (US 3) needles
and yarn A, pick up and knit 23 [23: 26: 26: 27] sts
down left side of front neck, K across 33 sts on
front holder, pick up and knit 23 [23: 26: 26: 27] sts
up right side of front neck, and 5 sts down right
side of back neck, K across 49 [49: 51: 51: 53] sts
on back holder, then pick up and knit 5 sts
up left side of back neck.
138 [138: 146: 146: 150] sts.
Beg with row 1, work in rib as given for sleeves
for 46 cm, ending with RS facing for next row.
Cast off **loosely** in rib.
Join collar and left shoulder seam, reversing
collar seam for last 25 cm (for turn-back).
Mark points along side seam edges 16 [17: 18:
19: 20] cm either side of shoulder seams
(to denote base of armholes).
See information page for finishing
instructions, setting in sleeves using the
straight cast-off method.

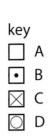

key
- ☐ A
- ⊡ B
- ⊠ C
- ⊙ D

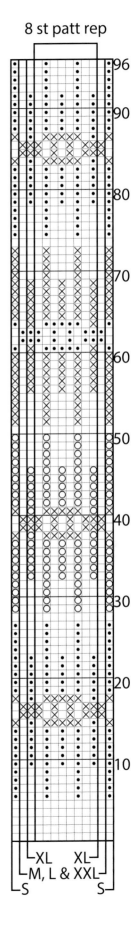

GUISELEY

Sarah Hatton

● ● ●

SIZE

S (M: L: XL: XXL)
To fit bust
81-86 (91-97: 102-107:112-117:122-127)cm
32-34 (36-38: 40-42: 44-46: 48-50)in

YARN

Rowan Cocoon
6 (7: 7: 8: 9) x 100g balls
(photographed in Seascape 813)

NEEDLES

1 pair 6mm (no 4) (US 10) needles
1 pair 7mm (no 2) (US 10½) needles
6mm (no 4) (US 10) circular needle
Cable needle

TENSION

16 sts and 17 rows to 10cm (4in) measured over pattern
using 7mm (US 10½) needles.

SPECIAL ABBREVIATIONS

Cr2R = slip next st onto cable needle and leave at back
of work, K1, then P1 from cable needle; **Cr2L** = slip
next st onto cable needle and leave at front of work,
P1, then K1 from cable needle; **C2B** = slip next st onto
cable needle and leave at back of work, K1, then K1
from cable needle; **C3F** = slip next st onto cable needle
and leave at front of work, K1, P1, then K1 from
cable needle.

BACK

Using 7mm (US 10½) needles, cast on
79 (87: 97: 107: 117) sts.
Row 1 (RS): K1, *P1, K1, rep from * to end.
Row 2: As row 1.
These 2 rows form moss st.
Work in moss st for a further 10 rows, ending
with RS facing for next row.
Now place chart as follows:
Row 13 (RS): Moss st 9 sts, work next
60 (68: 78: 88: 98) sts as row 1 of chart,
moss st 10 sts.
Row 14: Moss st 10 sts, work next
60 (68: 78: 88: 98) sts as row 2 of chart, moss st 9 sts.
These 2 rows set the sts – centre sts in patt from
chart with edge sts still in moss st.
Cont as set for a further 4 rows, dec 1 st at beg
of last row and ending with RS facing for
next row. 78 (86: 96: 106: 116) sts.
Now working all sts from chart and now
repeating chart rows 7 to 18 throughout, cont
as follows:
Cont straight until work measures
36 (37: 38: 39: 40)cm, ending with RS facing for
next row.
Shape for cap sleeves
Keeping patt correct, inc 1 st at each end of next
and 2 foll 4th rows, then on foll alt row, taking
inc sts into rev st st. 86 (94: 104: 114: 124) sts.
Place markers at each end of last row to denote
base of armhole openings.★★
Cont straight until work measures
25 (26: 27: 28: 29)cm **from markers**, ending
with RS facing for next row.
Shape shoulders and back neck
Next row (RS): Cast off 12 (14: 16: 18: 20) sts,
patt until there are 15 (17: 19: 22: 24) sts on
right needle and turn, leaving rem sts on
a holder.
Work each side of neck separately.
Cast off 3 sts at beg of next row.
Cast off rem 12 (14: 16: 19: 21) sts.
With RS facing, rejoin yarn to rem sts,
cast off centre 32 (32: 34: 34: 36) sts, patt to end.
Complete to match first side, reversing shapings.

FRONT

Work as given for back to ★★.
Work 1 row, ending with RS facing for
next row.
Divide for neck
Next row (RS): Patt 34 (38: 43: 48: 53) sts and
turn, leaving rem sts on a holder.
Work each side of neck separately.
Keeping patt correct, dec 1 st at neck edge of
2nd and foll 3 (2: 3: 2: 3) alt rows, then on every
foll 4th row until 24 (28: 32: 37: 41) sts rem.
Cont straight until front matches back to beg
of shoulder shaping, ending with RS facing for
next row.
Shape shoulder
Cast off 12 (14: 16: 18: 20) sts at beg of next row.
Work 1 row.
Cast off rem 12 (14: 16: 19: 21) sts.
With RS facing, rejoin yarn to rem sts, cast off
centre 18 sts, patt to end.
Complete to match first side, reversing shapings.

MAKING UP

Press as described on the information page.
Join both shoulder seams using back stitch, or
mattress stitch if preferred.
Collar
With RS facing and using 6mm (US 10) circular
needle, beg and ending at either end of centre
front cast-off sts, pick up and knit
45 (47: 49: 51: 53) sts up right front slope,
39 (38: 40: 42: 44) sts from back, then
45 (47: 49: 51: 53) sts down left front slope.
129 (132: 138: 144: 150) sts.
Row 1 (WS): K1, *P1, K2, rep from * to last
2 sts, P1, K1.
Row 2: K2, *P2, K1, rep from * to last st, K1.
These 2 rows form rib.
Work in rib for a further 8 rows, ending with
WS facing for next row.
Keeping rib correct, cont as follows:
Row 11 (WS): Rib 96 (97: 101: 105: 109),
wrap next st (by slipping next st from left needle
onto right needle, taking yarn to opposite side of
work between needles, and then slipping same

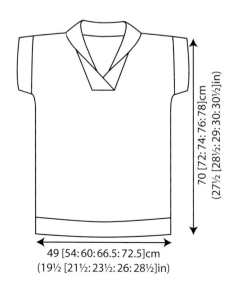

70 [72:74:76:78]cm
(27½ [28½: 29: 30: 30½]in)

49 [54: 60: 66.5: 72.5]cm
(19½ [21½: 23½: 26: 28½]in)

st back onto left needle – when working back across wrapped sts work the wrapped st and the wrapping loop tog as 1 st) and turn.

Row 12: Rib 63 (62: 64: 66: 68), wrap next st and turn.

Row 13: Rib 59 (58: 60: 62: 64), wrap next st and turn.

Row 14: Rib 55 (54: 56: 58: 60), wrap next st and turn.

Row 15: Rib 51 (50: 52: 54: 56), wrap next st and turn.

Row 16: Rib 47 (46: 48: 50: 52), wrap next st and turn.

Row 17: Rib 43 (42: 44: 46: 48), wrap next st and turn.

Row 18: Rib 39 (38: 40: 42: 44), wrap next st and turn.

Row 19: Rib 35 (34: 36: 38: 40), wrap next st and turn.

Row 20: Rib 31 (30: 32: 34: 36), wrap next st and turn.

Row 21: Rib to end.

Now working across all sts, cont as follows:

Row 22 (RS): K2, (P2, K1) 11 (11: 12: 13: 13) times, (P1, M1P, P1, K1) 20 (21: 21: 21: 23) times, (P2, K1) 11 (11: 12: 13: 13) times, K1. 149 (153: 159: 165: 173) sts.

Row 23: K1, P1, (K2, P1) 11 (11: 12: 13: 13) times, (K3, P1) 20 (21: 21: 21: 23) times, (K2, P1) 11 (11: 12: 13: 13) times, K1.

Row 24: K2, (P2, K1) 11 (11: 12: 13: 13) times, (P3, K1) 20 (21: 21: 21: 23) times, (P2, K1) 11 (11: 12: 13: 13) times, K1.

Rep last 2 rows twice more.

Cast off in patt.

Lay right front end of collar over left front end and neatly sew row-end edges of collar to cast-off sts at base of neck.

Armhole borders (both alike)

With RS facing and using 6mm (US 10) needles, pick up and knit 82 (85: 88: 91: 94) sts evenly along armhole opening edge between markers.

Row 1 (WS): P1, ★K2, P1, rep from ★ to end.

Row 2: K1, ★P2, K1, rep from ★ to end.

These 2 rows form rib.

Work in rib for a further 9 rows, ending with RS facing for next row.

Cast off in rib.

See information page for finishing instructions, leaving side seams open for first 18 rows.

12 row patt rep

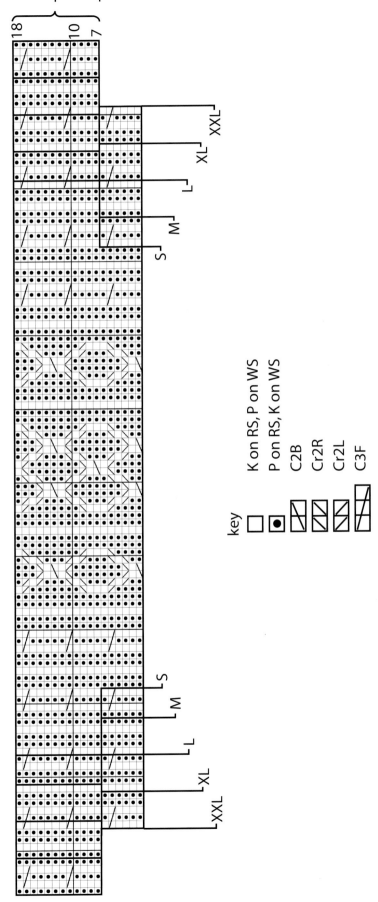

key

K on RS, P on WS

P on RS, K on WS

C2B

Cr2R

Cr2L

C3F

KINTYRE

Marie Wallin

● ● ●

SIZE

S (M: L: XL: XXL)
To fit bust
81-86 (91-97: 102-107: 112-117: 122-127)cm
32-34 (36-38: 40-42: 44-46: 48-50)in

YARN

**Rowan Wool Cotton, Rowan Kidsilk Haze
and Rowan Pure Wool DK**

2(3: 3: 3: 4) x 50g balls of Rowan Wool Cotton in
Mocha 965 (A)
1 (1: 1: 1: 2: 2) x 25g balls of ★Rowan Kidsilk Haze in
Blackcurrant 641 (B)
2(2: 2: 2: 3: 3) x 50g balls of Rowan Wool Cotton in
Deepest Olive 907 (C)
2 (2: 2: 2: 3) x 25g balls of ★Rowan Kidsilk Haze in
Fudge 658 (D)
1 (1: 1: 1: 1) x 50g ball of Rowan Wool Cotton in Ship
Shape 955 (E)
2 (2: 2: 2: 2) x 50g balls of Rowan Pure Wool DK in
Ox Blood 049 (F)
1 (1: 1: 1: 1) x 25g ball of ★Rowan Kidsilk Haze in
Brick 649 (G)
1 (1: 1: 1: 1) x 25g ball of ★Rowan Kidsilk Haze in
Liqueur 595 (H)
4 (5: 5: 6: 6) x 50g balls of Rowan Wool Cotton in
Coffee Rich 956 (I)
0 (0: 1: 1: 1) x 50g ball of Rowan Wool Cotton in
Windbreak 984 (J)
★Use Rowan Kidsilk Haze DOUBLE throughout

NEEDLES

1 pair 3¼mm (no 10) (US 3) needles

TENSION

27 sts and 27 rows to 10cm (4in) measured
over patterned stocking stitch using
3¼mm (US 3) needles.

BACK

Using 3¼mm (US 3) needles and yarn E,
cast on 113 (127: 143: 159: 179) sts.
Row 1 (RS): K1, ★P1, K1, rep from ★
to end.
Row 2: As row 1.
These 2 rows form moss st.
Work in moss st for a further 2 rows,
ending with RS facing for next row.
Beg and ending rows as indicated and
using the fairisle technique as described
on the information page, cont in patt from
chart for body, which is worked entirely in
st st beg with a K row, as follows:
Work 4 (4: 6: 6: 8) rows, ending with RS
facing for next row.
Keeping patt correct, dec 1 st at each end
of next and 2 foll 6th rows, then on 2 foll
4th rows. 103 (117: 133: 149: 169) sts.
Work 17 rows, ending with RS facing
for next row.
Inc 1 st at each end of next and 4 foll 8th
rows, taking inc sts into patt.
113 (127: 143: 159: 179) sts.
Cont straight until chart row
90 (94: 96: 98: 102) has been completed,
ending with RS facing for next row.
Back should measure approx
35 (36: 37: 38: 39)cm.

Shape armholes

Keeping patt correct, cast off
5 (6: 7: 8: 9) sts at beg of next 2 rows.
103 (115: 129: 143: 161) sts.
Dec 1 st at each end of next
5 (7: 7: 9: 13) rows, then on foll
3 (5: 8: 8: 9) alt rows.
87 (91: 99: 109: 117) sts.
Cont straight until chart row
138 (146: 150: 154: 162) has been
completed, ending with RS facing for
next row. Armhole should measure approx
18 (19: 20: 21: 22)cm.

Shape shoulders and back neck
Next row (RS): Cast off
7 (7: 8: 10: 11) sts, patt until there are
16 (18: 20: 23: 25) sts on right needle and
turn, leaving rem sts on a holder.
Work each side of neck separately.
Dec 1 st at neck edge of next 3 rows,
ending with RS facing for next row, **and
at same time** cast off 7 (7: 8: 10: 11) sts at
beg of 2nd row.
Cast off rem 6 (8: 9: 10: 11) sts.
With RS facing, rejoin yarns to rem sts,
cast off centre 41 (41: 43: 43: 45) sts, patt
to end.
Complete to match first side,
reversing shapings.

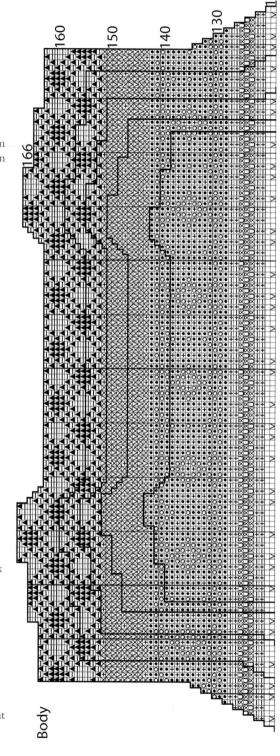

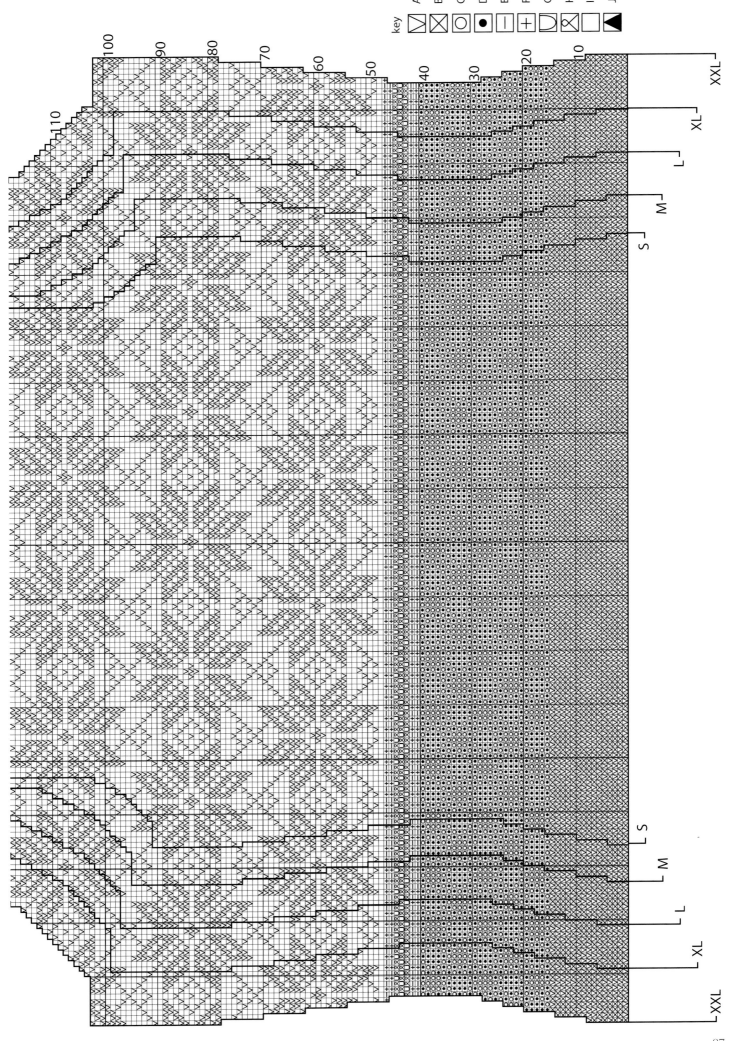

FRONT

Work as given for back until
18 (18: 20: 20: 22) rows less have been worked
than on back to beg of shoulder shaping, ending
after chart row 120 (128: 130: 134: 140) and with
RS facing for next row.

Shape front neck
(Note: Front neck shaping is NOT shown
on chart.)
Next row (RS): Patt 31 (33: 37: 42: 46) sts and
turn, leaving rem sts on a holder.
Work each side of neck separately.
Keeping patt correct, dec 1 st at neck edge of
next 6 rows, then on foll 5 (5: 6: 6: 7) alt rows.
20 (22: 25: 30: 33) sts.
Work 1 row, ending with RS facing for
next row.
Shape shoulder
Cast off 7 (7: 8: 10: 11) sts at beg of next and foll
alt row.
Work 1 row.
Cast off rem 6 (8: 9: 10: 11) sts.
With RS facing, rejoin yarns to rem sts, cast off
centre 25 sts, patt to end.
Complete to match first side, reversing shapings.

SLEEVES

Using 3¼mm (US 3) needles and yarn C, cast on
49 (51: 53: 55: 57) sts.
Work in moss st as given for back for 4 rows,
ending with RS facing for next row.
Beg and ending rows as indicated and using the
fairisle technique as described on the information
page, cont in patt from chart for sleeve, which
is worked entirely in st st beg with a K row, as
follows:
Inc 1 st at each end of 3rd and every foll 4th row to
65 (69: 75: 83: 91) sts, then on every foll 6th row
until there are 91 (95: 99: 103: 107) sts, taking inc
sts into patt.
Cont straight until chart row 114 (118: 120:
120: 120) has been completed, ending with
RS facing for next row. Sleeve should
measure approx 44 (45: 46: 46: 46)cm.
Shape top
Keeping patt correct, cast off 5 (6: 7: 8: 9) sts at
beg of next 2 rows.
81 (83: 85: 87: 89) sts.
Dec 1 st at each end of next 5 rows, then on
every foll alt row until 59 sts rem, then on foll 15
rows, ending with RS facing for next row. 29 sts.
Cast off 5 sts at beg of next 2 rows.
Cast off rem 19 sts.

MAKING UP

Press as described on the information page.
Join right shoulder seam using back stitch, or
mattress stitch if preferred.
Neckband
With RS facing, using 3¼mm (US 3) needles
and yarn I, pick up and knit 18 (18: 20: 20: 22) sts
down left side of neck, 25 sts from front,
18 (18: 20: 20: 22) sts up right side of neck, then
48 (48: 50: 50: 52) sts from back.
109 (109: 115: 115: 121) sts.

Work in moss st as given for back for 4 rows,
ending with WS facing for next row.
Cast off in moss st (on WS).
See information page for finishing instructions,
setting in sleeves using the set-in method.

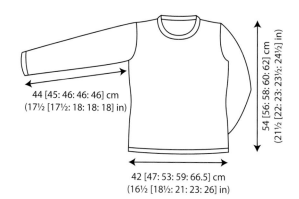

44 [45: 46: 46: 46] cm
(17½ [17½: 18: 18: 18] in)

54 [56: 58: 60: 62] cm
(21½ [22: 23: 23½: 24½] in)

42 [47: 53: 59: 66.5] cm
(16½ [18½: 21: 23: 26] in)

Sleeves

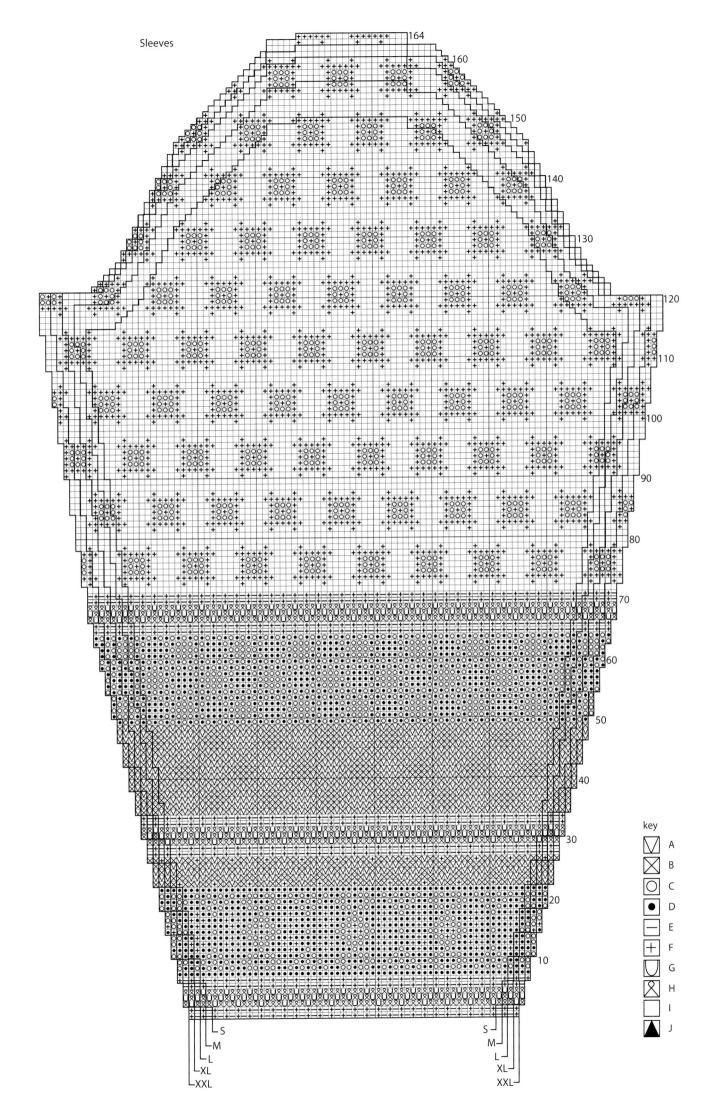

164
160
150
140
130
120
110
100
90
80
70
60
50
40
30
20
10

S
M
L
XL
XXL

S
M
L
XL
XXL

key

A
B
C
D
E
F
G
H
I
J

89

LIDIYA
Kaffe Fasett

● ● ●

SIZE

	S	M	L	XL	XXL	
To fit bust						
	81-86	91-97	102-107	112-117	122-127	cm
	32-34	36-38	40-42	44-46	48-50	in

YARN
Felted Tweed

A Phantom 153						
2	2	2	2	2	x 50gm	
B Ginger 154						
1	1	1	1	1	x 50gm	
C Melody 142						
1	1	1	1	1	x 50gm	
D Avocado 161						
2	2	2	2	3	x 50gm	
E Watery 152						
1	1	1	1	1	x 50gm	
F Rage 150						
1	1	2	2	2	x 50gm	
G Bilberry 151						
2	2	2	2	2	x 50gm	
H Gilt 160						
1	2	2	2	2	x 50gm	
I Paisley 171						
3	3	4	4	4	x 50gm	
J Seasalter 178						
1	1	1	1	2	x 50gm	
K Maritime 167						
1	1	1	1	2	x 50gm	

NEEDLES
1 pair 3¼mm (no 10) (US 3) needles
1 pair 3¾mm (no 9) (US 5) needles

TENSION
25 sts and 29 rows to 10cm (4in) measured over patterned st st using 3¾mm (US 5) needles.

BACK
Using 3¼mm (US 3) needles and yarn G cast on 137 [149: 165: 179: 197] sts.
Row 1 (RS): K1, ★P1, K1, rep from ★ to end.
Row 2: As row 1.
These 2 rows form moss st.
Work in moss st for a further 4 rows, ending with RS facing for next row.
Change to 3¾mm (US 5) needles.
Beg and ending rows as indicated, using the fairisle technique as described on the information page and repeating the 100 row patt rep throughout, now work in patt from chart, which is worked entirely in st st beg with a K row, as folls:
Work 42 rows, ending with RS facing for next row.
Keeping patt correct, dec 1 st at each end of next and 4 foll 16th rows.
127 [139: 155: 169: 187] sts.
Work 25 rows, ending with RS faacing for next row.
Inc 1 st at each end of next and 4 foll 8th rows, taking inc sts into patt.
137 [149: 165: 179: 197] sts.
Cont straight until back meas 63 [64: 65: 66: 67] cm, ending with RS facing for next row.
Shape armholes
Keeping patt correct, cast off 6 [7: 8: 9: 10] sts at beg of next 2 rows.
125 [135: 149: 161: 177] sts.
Dec 1 st at each end of next 3 [5: 7: 9: 11] rows, then on foll 3 [3: 5: 5: 7] alt rows.
113 [119: 125: 133: 141] sts.
Cont straight until armhole meas 22 [23: 24: 25: 26] cm, ending with RS facing for next row.

Shape back neck and shoulders
Next row (RS): Patt 43 [46: 48: 52: 55] sts and turn, leaving rem sts on a holder.
Work each side of neck separately.
Cast off 4 sts at beg of next row, then 10 [11: 12: 13: 14] sts at beg of foll row.
Rep last 2 rows once more.
Cast off 4 sts at beg of next row, ending with RS facing for next row.
Cast off rem 11 [12: 12: 14: 15] sts.
With RS facing, rejoin yarns to rem sts, cast off centre 27 [27: 29: 29: 31] sts, patt to end.
Complete to match first side, reversing shapings.

FRONT
Work as given for back until 30 [30: 32: 32: 34] rows less have been worked than on back to beg of shoulder shaping (shoulder is 2 rows higher than beg of back neck shaping), ending with RS facing for next row.
Shape front neck
Next row (RS): Patt 43 [46: 49: 53: 57] sts and turn, leaving rem sts on a holder.
Work each side of neck separately.
Keeping patt correct, dec 1 st at neck edge of next 6 rows, then on foll 3 [3: 4: 4: 5] alt rows, then on 3 foll 4th rows. 31 [34: 36: 40: 43] sts.
Work 5 rows, ending with RS facing for next row.
Shape shoulder
Cast off 10 [11: 12: 13: 14] sts at beg of next and foll alt row.
Work 1 row.
Cast off rem 11 [12: 12: 14: 15] sts.
With RS facing, rejoin yarns to rem sts, cast off centre 27 sts, patt to end.
Complete to match first side, reversing shapings.

SLEEVES
Using 3¼mm (US 3) needles and yarn G cast on 51 [53: 57: 57: 59] sts.
Work in moss st as given for back for 6 rows, ending with RS facing for next row.
Change to 3¾mm (US 5) needles.
Beg and ending rows as indicated, now work in patt from chart, shaping sides by inc 1 st at each end of next and foll 4 [4: 3: 7: 9] alt rows, then

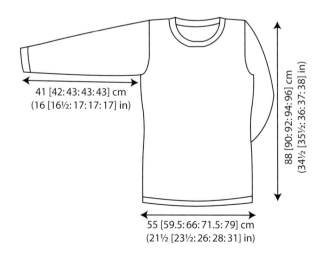

41 [42: 43: 43: 43] cm
(16 [16½: 17: 17: 17] in)

88 [90: 92: 94: 96] cm
(34½ [35½: 36: 37: 38] in)

55 [59.5: 66: 71.5: 79] cm
(21½ [23½: 26: 28: 31] in)

on every foll 4th row until there are
105 [109: 113: 117: 121] sts, taking inc sts
into patt.
Cont straight until sleeve meas
41 [42: 43: 43: 43] cm, ending with RS facing
for next row.

Shape top
Keeping patt correct, cast off 6 [7: 8: 9: 10] sts at
beg of next 2 rows. 93 [95: 97: 99: 101] sts.
Dec 1 st at each end of next 3 rows, then on
every foll alt row to 77 sts, then on foll 7 rows,
ending with RS facing for next row. 63 sts.
Cast off 14 sts at beg of next 2 rows.
Cast off rem 35 sts.

MAKING UP
Press as described on the information page.
Join right shoulder seam using back stitch, or
mattress stitch if preferred.

Neckband
With RS facing, using 3¼mm (US 3) needles
and yarn G, pick up and knit
35 [35: 37: 37: 39] sts down left side of neck,
27 sts from front, 35 [35: 37: 37: 39] sts up
right side of neck, then 56 [56: 58: 58: 60] sts
from back. 153 [153: 159: 159: 165] sts.
Work in moss st as given for back for 5 rows,
ending with RS facing for next row.
Cast off in moss st.
See information page for finishing instructions,
setting in sleeves using the set-in method.

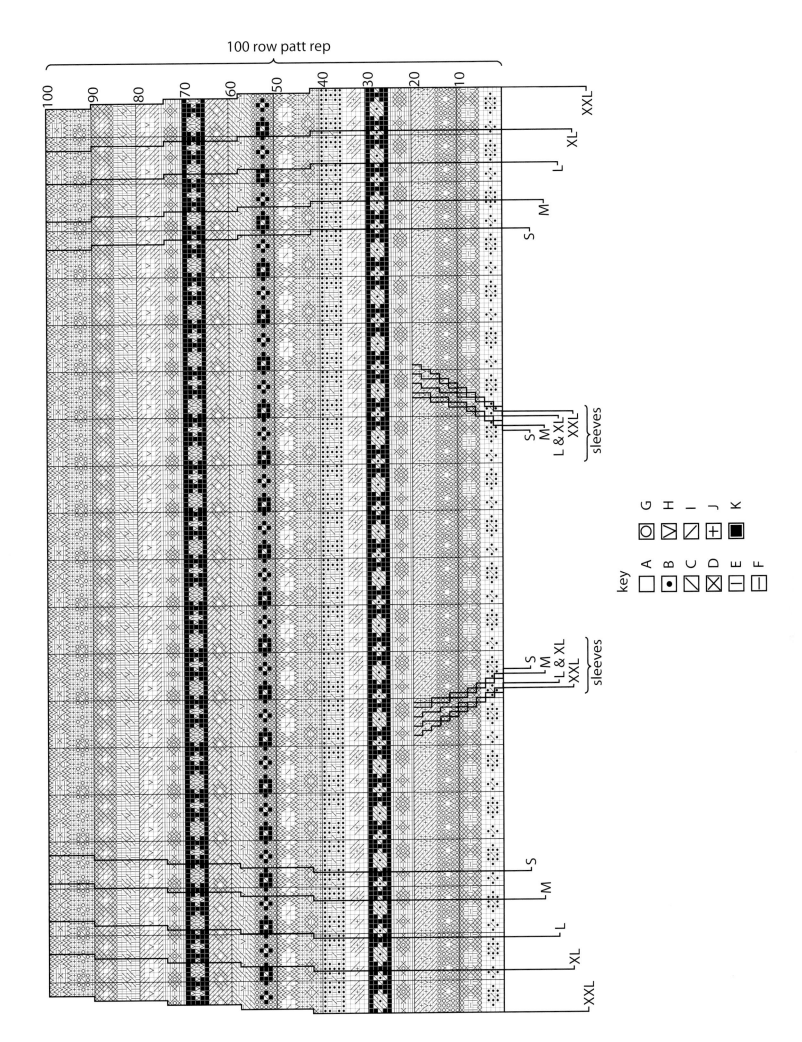

100 row patt rep

key
A ☐   G ⊡
B ⊙   H ⊻
C ⊠   I ⬚
D ⊠   J ⊞
E ☐   K ■
F ▤

93

MIST

Kim Hargreaves

● ●

YARN

Rowan Felted Tweed

1st	2nd	3rd	4th	5th		
7	7	7	8	8	x	50gm

(photographed in Bonny 137)

NEEDLES

1 pair 3¾mm (no 9) (US 5) needles.

BUTTONS - 2

TENSION

22 sts and 38 rows to 10cm (4in) measured over moss st using 3¾mm (US 5) needles.

Pattern note: As row end edges of fronts form actual finished edges of garment, it is important these edges are kept neat. Therefore, all new balls of yarn should be joined in at marked side seam or armhole edges of rows.

BACK

Cast on 89 (95: 101: 107: 113) sts using 3¾mm (US 5) needles.

Row 1 (RS): K1, *P1, K1, rep from * to end.

This row forms moss st.

Cont in moss st, shaping side seams by inc 1 st at each end of 16th row and every foll 14th row until there are 99 (105: 111: 117: 123) sts, taking inc sts into moss st.

Cont without further shaping until back measures 24 (25: 25: 26: 26) cm, ending with a WS row.

Shape armholes

Keeping patt correct, cast off 4 (4: 5: 5: 6) sts at beg of next 2 rows. 91 (97: 101: 107: 111) sts.

Dec 1 st at each end of next 5 (7: 7: 9: 9) rows, then on foll 6 (6: 7: 7: 8) alt rows.

69 (71: 73: 75: 77) sts.

Cont without further shaping until armhole measures 20 (20: 21: 21: 22) cm, end with a WS row.

Shape shoulders and back neck

Keeping patt correct, cast off 6 (6: 7: 6: 7) sts at beg of next 2 rows. 57 (59: 59: 63: 63) sts.

**Next row (RS): Cast off 6 (6: 7: 6: 7) sts, patt until there are 10 (11: 10: 11: 10) sts on right needle, wrap next st (by slipping next st from left needle to right needle, take yarn to opposite side of work between needles, and then slip same st back onto left needle), turn and patt to end. Cast off 6 (7: 6: 7: 6) sts at beg of next row, patt to end.

45 (46: 46: 50: 50) sts.

Rep from ** once more. 33 (33: 33: 37: 37) sts.

Work 1 row, thus ending with a **RS** row.

Cast off rem 33 (33: 33: 37: 37) sts.

LEFT FRONT

Cast on 62 (65: 68: 71: 74) sts using 3¾mm (US 5) needles.

Row 1 (RS): *K1, P1, rep from * to last 0 (1: 0: 1: 0) st, K0 (1: 0: 1: 0).

This row sets position of moss st as given for back.

Place marker at beg of last row to denote base of side seam.

Patt 2 rows, thus ending with a **RS** row.

Next row: Patt 6 (8: 10: 12: 14) sts, wrap next st, turn and patt to end.

Next row: Patt 16 (18: 20: 22: 24) sts, wrap next st, turn and patt to end.

Next row: Patt 26 (28: 30: 32: 34) sts, wrap next st, turn and patt to end.

Next row: Patt 36 (38: 40: 42: 44) sts, wrap next st, turn and patt to end.

Next row: Patt 46 (48: 50: 52: 54) sts, wrap next st, turn and patt to end.

Next row: Patt 56 (58: 60: 62: 64) sts, wrap next st, turn and patt to end.

Next row: Patt to end.

Patt a further 12 rows, thus ending with a WS row.

***Cont in moss st, shaping side seams by inc 1 st at marked side seam edge of next and every foll 14th row until there are 67 (70: 73: 76: 79) sts, taking inc sts into moss st. Cont without further shaping until left front measures 24 (25: 25: 26: 26) cm **from marker**, ending at side seam.

Shape armhole

Keeping patt correct, cast off 4 (4: 5: 5: 6) sts at beg of next row. 63 (66: 68: 71: 73) sts.

Work 1 row.

Dec 1 st at armhole edge of next 5 (7: 7: 9: 9) rows, then on foll 6 (6: 7: 7: 8) alt rows. 52 (53: 54: 55: 56) sts.***

Cont without further shaping until 40 rows less have been worked than on back to start of shoulder and back neck shaping, thus ending with a WS row.

Shape neck

Next row (RS) (dec): Patt to last 6 sts, work 3 tog, patt 3 sts.

Work 1 row.

Rep last 2 rows 13 (13: 13: 15: 15) times more. 24 (25: 26: 23: 24) sts.

Next row (RS) (dec): Patt to last 6 sts, work 3 tog, patt 3 sts.

Work 3 rows.

Rep last 4 rows 2 (2: 2: 1: 1) times more. 18 (19: 20: 19: 20) sts.

Shape shoulder

Keeping patt correct, cast off 6 (6: 7: 6: 7) sts at beg of next and foll alt row.

Work 1 row. Cast off rem 6 (7: 6: 7: 6) sts.

RIGHT FRONT

Cast on 62 (65: 68: 71: 74) sts using 3¾mm (US 5) needles.

Row 1 (RS): K0 (1: 0: 1: 0), *P1, K1, rep from * to end.

This row sets position of moss st as given for back.

Place marker at end of last row to denote base of side seam. Patt 2 rows, thus ending with a **RS** row.

Next row: Patt 6 (7: 8: 9: 10) sts, wrap next st, turn and patt to end.

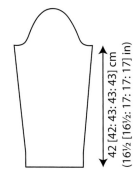

42 [42: 43: 43: 43] cm (16½ [16½: 17: 17: 17] in)

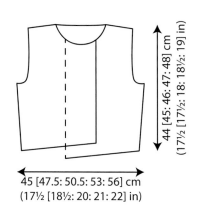

44 [45: 46: 47: 48] cm (17½ [17½: 18: 18½: 19] in)

45 [47.5: 50.5: 53: 56] cm (17½ [18½: 20: 21: 22] in)

Next row: Patt 16 (17: 18: 19: 20) sts, wrap next st, turn and patt to end.

Next row: Patt 26 (27: 28: 29: 30) sts, wrap next st, turn and patt to end.

Next row: Patt 36 (37: 38: 39: 40) sts, wrap next st, turn and patt to end.

Next row: Patt 46 (47: 48: 49: 50) sts, wrap next st, turn and patt to end.

Next row: Patt 56 (57: 58: 59: 60) sts, wrap next st, turn and patt to end.

Next row: Patt to end.

Work as given for left front from ★★★ to ★★★.
Cont without further shaping until 42 rows less have been worked than on back to start of shoulder and back neck shaping, thus ending with a WS row.

Next row (RS) (buttonhole row): Patt 5 sts, cast off 2 sts, patt to end.

Next row: Patt to end, casting on 2 sts over those cast-off on previous row.

Shape neck

Next row (RS) (dec): Patt 3 sts, work 3 tog, patt to end. Work 1 row.
Rep last 2 rows 13 (13: 13: 15: 15) times more.
24 (25: 26: 23: 24) sts.

Next row (RS) (dec): Patt 3 sts, work 3 tog, patt to end.
Work 3 rows.
Rep last 4 rows 2 (2: 2: 1: 1) times more.
18 (19: 20: 19: 20) sts.
Work 1 row, thus ending at armhole edge.

Shape shoulder

Keeping patt correct, cast off 6 (6: 7: 6: 7) sts at beg of next and foll alt row.
Work 1 row. Cast off rem 6 (7: 6: 7: 6) sts.

SLEEVES (both alike)
Cast on 41 (43: 45: 47: 49) sts using 3¾mm (US 5) needles.
Cont in moss st as given for back, shaping sleeve seam by inc 1 st at each end of 9th and every foll 8th row to 61 (63: 51: 53: 55) sts, then on every foll 10th row until there are 71 (73: 75: 77: 79) sts, taking inc sts into moss st.
Cont without further shaping until sleeve measures 42 (42: 43: 43: 43) cm, ending with a WS row.

Shape top

Keeping patt correct, cast off 4 (4: 5: 5: 6) sts at beg of next 2 rows.63 (65: 65: 67: 67) sts.
Dec 1 st at each end of next 3 rows, then on foll 2 alt rows. 53 (55: 55: 57: 57) sts.
Work 3 rows, thus ending with a WS row.
Dec 1 st at each end of next and every foll 4th row until 35 (39: 35: 39: 35) sts rem, then on every foll alt row until 33 sts rem.
Dec 1 st at each end of next 5 rows, thus ending with a WS row. 23 sts. Cast off 4 sts at beg of next 2 rows. Cast off rem 15 sts.

MAKING UP
PRESS all pieces as described on the info page.
See information page for finishing instructions, setting in sleeves using the set-in method.
Sew one button onto left front to correspond with buttonhole in right front. Make button loop along edge of left front and sew other button to inside of right front to fasten inner edge.

RAPUNZEL
Jean Moss

●●●●

SIZE

	XS	S	M	L	XL	
To fit bust	81	86	91	97	102	cm
	32	34	36	38	40	in

YARN

Rowan Kid Classic and Lurex Shimmer

A Kid	Crystal 840	8	8	9	9	10	x 50gm
B *LurexPewter 333	3	3	3	4	4	x 25gm

*Use Lurex Shimmer **DOUBLE** throughout

NEEDLES

1 pair 4½mm (no 7) (US 7) needles
2 double-pointed 4½mm (no 7) (US 7) needles
3.00mm (no 11) (US D/3) crochet hook
Cable needle

BUTTONS

6

TENSION

20 sts and 30 rows to 10cm (4in) measured over moss stitch using 4½mm (US 7) needles.

SPECIAL ABBREVIATIONS

C4F = Cable 4 front Slip next 2 sts onto cable needle and leave at front of work, K2, then K2 from cable needle.

Cr3L = Cross 3 left Slip next 2 sts onto cable needle and leave at front of work, P1, then K2 from cable needle.

Cr3R = Cross 3 right Slip next st onto cable needle and leave at back of work, K2, then P1 from cable needle.

CROCHET ABBREVIATIONS

Dc = double crochet; **ch** = chain; **ss** = slip stitch.

BACK

Cast on 104 (108: 114: 118: 124) sts using 4½mm (US 7) needles and yarn A.
Starting and ending rows as indicated, cont in patt from chart for back as folls:
Dec 1 st at each end of 7th and every foll 4th row until 86 (90: 96: 100: 106) sts rem.
Work 9 rows, ending after chart row 48 and with a **WS** row.
Row 49 (RS): Patt 41 (43: 46: 48: 51) sts, slip next 4 sts onto a holder and, in their place, pick up and knit 4 sts from behind these sts, patt to end. 86 (90: 96: 100: 106) sts.
Join in yarn B.
Using the **fairisle** technique as described on the information page, cont in patt from chart, working rows 50 to 74 once only and then repeating rows 75 to 78 throughout (these 4 rows form 2 colour moss st), until back measures 37 (38: 38: 39: 39) cm, ending with a WS row.

Shape armholes

Keeping patt correct, cast off 4 (5: 5: 6: 6) sts at beg of next 2 rows. 78 (80: 86: 88: 94) sts.
Dec 1 st at each end of next 1 (1: 3: 3: 5) rows, then on foll 3 alt rows. 70 (72: 74: 76: 78) sts.
Cont straight until armhole measures 19 (19: 20: 20: 21) cm, ending with a **WS** row.

Shape shoulders

Cast off 6 (7: 7: 7: 8) sts at beg of next 4 rows, then 7 (6: 7: 8: 7) sts at beg of foll 2 rows.
Leave rem 32 sts on a holder.

LEFT FRONT

Cast on 52 (54: 57: 59: 62) sts using 4½mm (US 7) needles and yarn A.
Starting and ending rows as indicated and repeating the 10 row patt repeat, cont in chevron patt from chart for lower left front as folls:
Dec 1 st at beg of 7th and every foll 4th row until 43 (45: 48: 50: 53) sts rem.
Work 33 (33: 35: 35: 37) rows, ending with a **WS** row.
Join in yarn B.

Using the **fairisle** technique as described on the information page and keeping centre front sts correct in chevron patt, cont in patt from chart for middle left front, working rows 1 to 24 once only and then repeating rows 25 to 28 throughout (these 4 rows form 2 colour moss st), until left front matches back to beg of armhole shaping, ending with a **WS** row.

Shape armhole

Keeping side edge sts correct in 2 colour moss st patt as set, working rows 1 to 32 once only and then repeating rows 33 to 42 throughout, cont in patt from chart for upper left front as folls:
Cast off 4 (5: 5: 6: 6) sts at beg of next row.
39 (40: 43: 44: 47) sts.
Work 1 row.
Dec 1 st at armhole edge of next 1 (1: 3: 3: 5) rows, then on foll 3 alt rows. 35 (36: 37: 38: 39) sts.
Cont straight until left front matches back to start of shoulder shaping, ending with a **WS** row.

Shape shoulder

Cast off 6 (7: 7: 7: 8) sts at beg of next and foll alt row, then 7 (6: 7: 8: 7) sts at beg of foll alt row.
Work 1 row, ending with a WS row.
Leave rem 16 sts on a holder.

RIGHT FRONT

Cast on 52 (54: 57: 59: 62) sts using 4½mm (US 7) needles and yarn A.
Starting and ending rows as indicated and repeating the 10 row patt repeat, cont in chevron patt from chart for lower right front as folls:
Dec 1 st at end of 7th and every foll 4th row until 43 (45: 48: 50: 53) sts rem.
Complete to match left front, reversing shapings and foll charts for right front.

SLEEVES (both alike)

Cast on 68 (68: 70: 72: 72) sts using 4½mm (US 7) needles and yarn A.
Starting and ending rows as indicated and using the **fairisle** technique as described on the information page, cont in patt from chart for sleeve, working rows 1 to 48 once only and

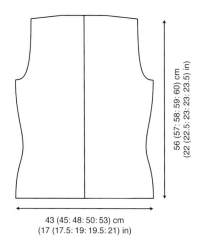

43 (45: 48: 50: 53) cm
(17 (17.5: 19: 19.5: 21) in)

56 (57: 58: 59: 60) cm
(22 (22.5: 23: 23: 23.5) in)

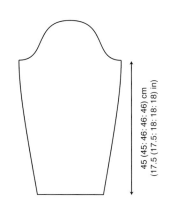

45 (45: 46: 46: 46) cm
(17.5 (17.5: 18: 18: 18) in)

then repeating rows 49 to 68 throughout, as folls:

Dec 1 st at each end of 9th and every foll 8th row until 58 (58: 60: 62: 62) sts rem. Work 5 rows, ending with a WS row. Inc 1 st at each end of next and every foll 6th row to 78 (74: 78: 80: 76) sts, then on every foll 4th row until there are 80 (82: 84: 86: 88) sts, taking inc sts into patt. Cont straight until sleeve measures 45 (45: 46: 46: 46) cm, ending with a WS row.

Shape top
Keeping patt correct, cast off 4 (5: 5: 6: 6) sts at beg of next 2 rows.
72 (72: 74: 74: 76) sts.
Dec 1 st at each end of next and every foll alt row to 42 sts, then on foll row, ending with a WS row. 40 sts.
Cast off 3 sts at beg of next 2 rows, 4 sts at beg of foll 2 rows, then 5 sts at beg of next 2 rows.
Cast off rem 16 sts.

MAKING UP
PRESS as described on the information page.
Join both shoulder seams using back stitch, or mattress st if preferred.
Collar
With RS facing, using 4½mm (US 7) needles and yarn A, patt across 16 sts from right front holder, cont in chevron patt as set by right front sts across first 16 sts from back holder, patt across rem 16 sts from back holder in chevron patt as set by sts on left front holder, then patt across 16 sts from left front holder. 64 sts.
Cont in chevron patt as now set until collar measures 12 cm.
Cast off in patt.
Fold collar in half to inside and neatly slip stitch in place.
Cord trim
Slip 2 sts nearest left side seam from centre back holder onto one double-pointed 4½mm (US 7) needle and rejoin yarn A with RS facing.
Row 1 (RS): Inc in first st, K1, ★without turning work slip these 3 sts to opposite end of needle and bring yarn to opposite end of work pulling it quite tightly across back of these 3 sts★★, using other double-pointed needle K these 3 sts again; rep from ★ until cord is long enough to travel along line between chevron and 2 colour moss st patt to side seam and across front to front opening edge, up front opening edge to point where chevron patt begins again, along line between chevron patt and 2 colour moss st to neck point and then across to centre back neck, slip stitching cord in place as you go along.
Cast off.
Slip other 2 sts from centre back holder onto one double-pointed 4½mm (US 7) needle and make and attach second cord in same way, inc st at end of first row.
Join ends of cords at centre back neck.
Mark positions for 6 button loops along right front opening edge – top loop just below point where cord trim starts to follow chevron patt away from front opening edge, lowest loop

15 cm up from cast-on edge and rem 4 loops evenly spaced between.
Crochet edging
Using 3.00mm (US D/3) hook and yarn B, rejoin yarn at base of one sleeve seam and, placing sts evenly along edge, work around cast-on edge of sleeve as folls: ★3 dc, 3 ch, 1 ss into same place as last dc, rep from ★ to end.
Fasten off.
Starting and ending at folded edges of collar, work crochet edging down left front opening edge, across cast-on edge and up right front opening edge in same way, ensuring the 3 ch loops correspond with positions marked for button loops. Attach buttons to left front to correspond with button loops, positioning buttons 3 sts in from finished edge.
See information page for finishing instructions, setting in sleeves using the set-in method.

Key
■ A - K on RS, P on WS
▪ A - P on RS, K on WS
◉ B - K on RS, P on WS
▨ C4F
▨ Cr3L
▧ Cr3R

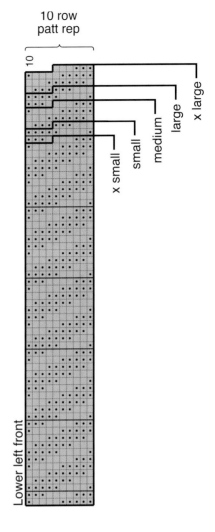

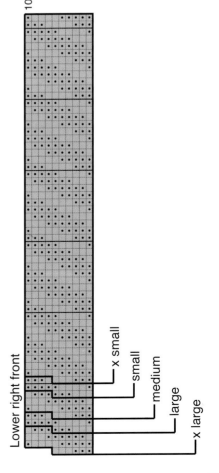

Back chart

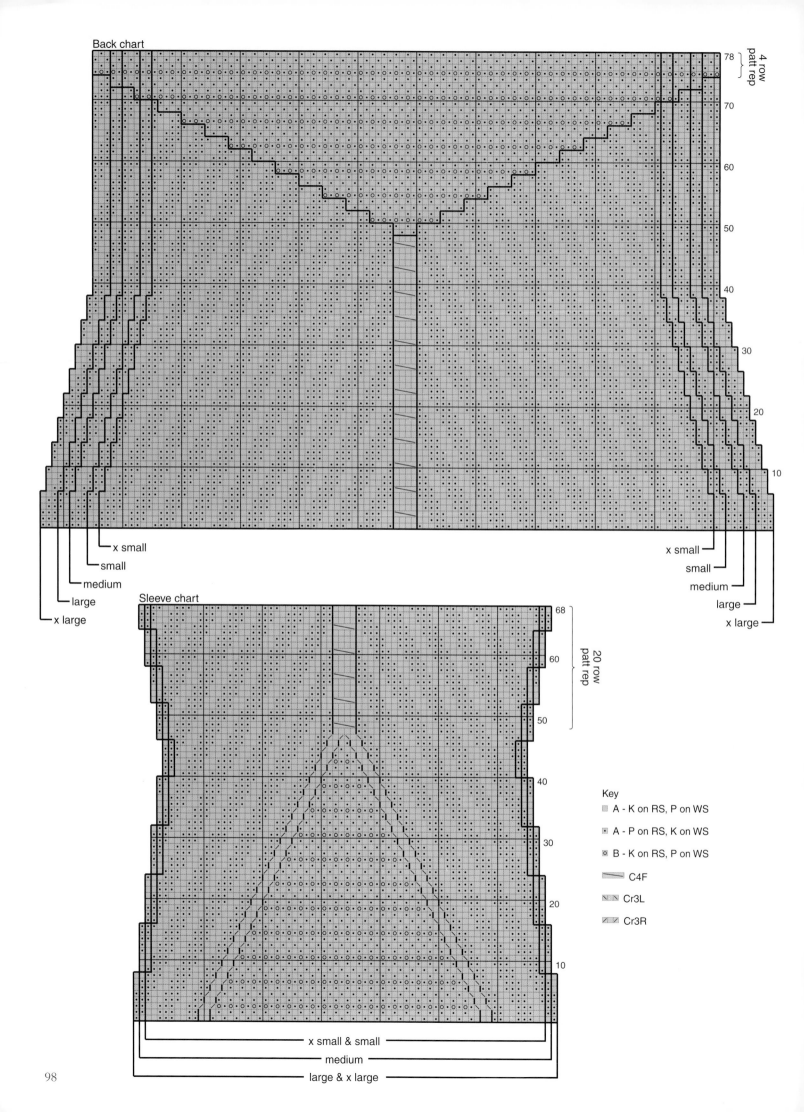

4 row
patt rep

78

70

60

50

40

30

20

10

x small
small
medium
large
x large

x small
small
medium
large
x large

Sleeve chart

20 row
patt rep

68

60

50

40

30

20

10

Key

A - K on RS, P on WS

A - P on RS, K on WS

B - K on RS, P on WS

C4F

Cr3L

Cr3R

x small & small
medium
large & x large

Upper right front

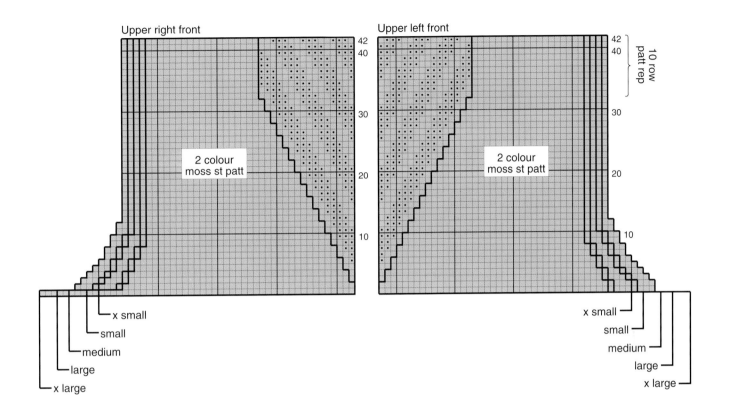

2 colour
moss st patt

42
40

30

20

10

x small
small
medium
large
x large

Upper left front

2 colour
moss st patt

42
40

30

20

10

10 row
patt rep

x small
small
medium
large
x large

Middle right front

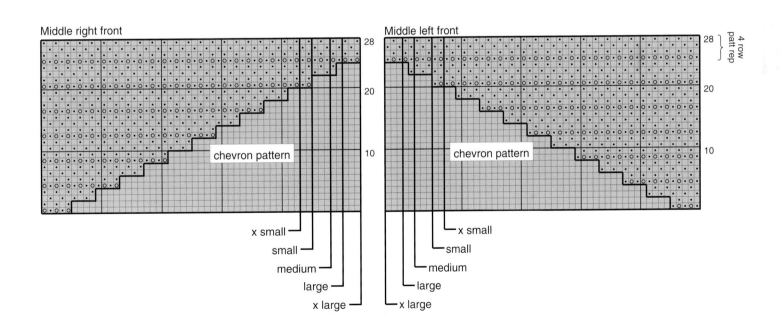

chevron pattern

28

20

10

x small
small
medium
large
x large

Middle left front

chevron pattern

28

20

10

4 row
patt rep

x small
small
medium
large
x large

RESTFUL

Martin Storey

• • •

SIZE
S (M: L: XL: XXL)
To fit bust
81-86 (91-97: 102-107: 112-117: 122-127)cm
31-33¾ (35¾-38¼: 40¼-42¼: 44-46: 48-50)in

YARN
Rowan Purelife Organic Cotton DK
18 (19: 21: 23: 26) x 50g balls
(photographed in Light Brazilwood 997)

NEEDLES
1 pair 2¾mm (no 12) (US 2) needles
1 pair 3¾mm (no 9) (US 5) needles
2¾mm (no 12) (US 2) circular needle
2 double-pointed 2¾mm (no 12) (US 2) needles
Cable needle

TENSION
29 sts and 30 rows to 10cm (4in) measured over pattern
using 3¾mm (US 5) needles.

SPECIAL ABBREVIATIONS
C5BP = slip next 3 sts onto cable needle and leave at
back of work, Tw2, then P3 from cable needle; **C5FP**
= slip next 2 sts onto cable needle and leave at front of
work, P3, then Tw2 from cable needle; **C5BK** = slip
next 3 sts onto cable needle and leave at back of work,
Tw2, then K3 from cable needle; **C5FK** = slip next 2
sts onto cable needle and leave at front of work, K3,
then Tw2 from cable needle; **C7F** = slip next 3 sts onto
cable needle and leave at front of work, K4, then K3
from cable needle; **Tw2** = K2tog leaving sts on

left needle, K first st again and slip both sts off
left needle together.

BACK
Using 2¾mm (US 2) needles, cast on
111 (123: 137: 151: 167) sts.
Beg with a K row, work in st st for 11 rows,
ending with **WS** facing for next row.
Row 12 (WS): Knit (to form fold line).
Beg with a K row, work in st st for 11 rows,
ending with **WS** facing for next row.
Row 24 (WS): P1 (3: 2: 1: 1), M1, (P4, M1)
27 (29: 33: 37: 41) times, P2 (4: 3: 2: 2).
139 (153: 171: 189: 209) sts.
Change to 3¾mm (US 5) needles.
Beg and ending rows as indicated and repeating
the 24 row patt rep throughout, now work in
patt from chart for body as follows:
Cont straight until back measures
58 (59: 60: 61: 62)cm **from fold line row**,
ending with RS facing for next row.
Shape armholes
Keeping patt correct, cast off 3 sts at beg of next
2 rows. 133 (147: 165: 183: 203) sts.
Dec 1 st at each end of next and foll 5 alt rows.
121 (135: 153: 171: 191) sts.
Cont straight until armhole measures
23 (24: 25: 26: 27)cm, ending with RS facing
for next row.
Shape shoulders and back neck
Cast off 12 (14: 17: 20: 23) sts at beg of next
2 rows. 97 (107: 119: 131: 145) sts.
Next row (RS): Cast off 12 (14: 17: 20: 23) sts,
patt until there are 16 (19: 21: 24: 26) sts on
right needle and turn, leaving rem sts on
a holder.
Work each side of neck separately.
Cast off 4 sts at beg of next row.
Cast off rem 12 (15: 17: 20: 22) sts.
With RS facing, rejoin yarn to rem sts, cast off
centre 41 (41: 43: 43: 47) sts, patt to end.
Complete to match first side, reversing shapings.

LEFT FRONT
Using 2¾mm (US 2) needles, cast on
53 (59: 67: 73: 81) sts.
Beg with a K row, work in st st for 11 rows,

ending with **WS** facing for next row.
Row 12 (WS): Knit (to form fold line).
Beg with a K row, work in st st for 6 rows,
ending with RS facing for next row.
Row 19 (RS): K to last 9 sts, K2tog, yfwd
(to make eyelet hole for cord), K7.
Work a further 4 rows, ending with **WS** facing
for next row.
Row 24 (WS): P2 (3: 5: 2: 2), M1, (P4, M1)
12 (13: 14: 17: 19) times, P3 (4: 6: 3: 3).
66 (73: 82: 91: 101) sts.
Change to 3¾mm (US 5) needles.
Beg and ending rows as indicated, now work in
patt from chart for body as follows:
Cont straight until 40 rows less have been
worked than on back to beg of armhole shaping,
ending with RS facing for next row.
Shape front slope
Keeping patt correct, dec 1 st at end of next and
9 foll 4th rows. 56 (63: 72: 81: 91) sts.
Work 3 rows, ending with RS facing for
next row.
Shape armhole
Keeping patt correct, cast off 3 sts at beg and dec
1 (0: 1: 0: 1) st at end of next row.
52 (60: 68: 78: 87) sts.
Work 1 row.
Dec 1 st at armhole edge of next and foll 5 alt
rows **and at same time** dec 1 st at front slope
edge of 5th (next: 5th: next: 3rd) and
1 (1: 1: 1: 2) foll 6th (6th: 6th: 6th: 4th) rows.
44 (52: 60: 70: 78) sts.
Dec 1 st at front slope edge only on
6th (2nd: 6th: 2nd: 6th) and 7 (8: 8: 9: 9) foll
6th rows. 36 (43: 51: 60: 68) sts.
Cont straight until left front matches back to
beg of shoulder shaping, ending with RS facing
for next row.
Shape shoulder
Cast off 12 (14: 17: 20: 23) sts at beg of next and
foll alt row.
Work 1 row.
Cast off rem 12 (15: 17: 20: 22) sts.

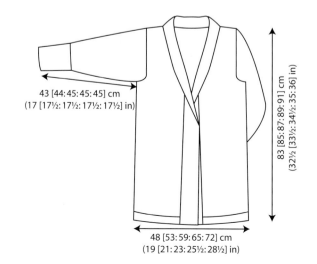

43 [44: 45: 45: 45] cm
(17 [17½: 17½: 17½: 17½] in)

83 [85: 87: 89: 91] cm
(32½ [33½: 34½: 35: 36] in)

48 [53: 59: 65: 72] cm
(19 [21: 23: 25½: 28½] in)

RIGHT FRONT

Using 2¾mm (US 2) needles, cast on
53 (59: 67: 73: 81) sts.
Beg with a K row, work in st st for 11 rows,
ending with **WS** facing for next row.
Row 12 (WS): Knit (to form fold line).
Beg with a K row, work in st st for 6 rows,
ending with RS facing for next row.
Row 19 (RS): K7, yfwd, K2tog (to make eyelet
hole for cord), K to end.
Work a further 4 rows, ending with **WS** facing
for next row.
Row 24 (WS): P2 (3: 5: 2: 2), M1,
(P4, M1) 12 (13: 14: 17: 19) times, P3 (4: 6: 3: 3).
66 (73: 82: 91: 101) sts.
Change to 3¾mm (US 5) needles.
Beg and ending rows as indicated, now work in
patt from chart for body as follows:
Cont straight until 40 rows less have been
worked than on back to beg of armhole shaping,
ending with RS facing for next row.
Shape front slope
Keeping patt correct, dec 1 st at beg of next and
9 foll 4th rows. 56 (63: 72: 81: 91) sts.
Complete to match left front, reversing shapings.

SLEEVES (both alike)

Using 2¾mm (US 2) needles, cast on 74 (78: 82:
82: 82) sts.
Row 1 (RS): K2, *P2, K2, rep from * to end.
Row 2: P2, *K2, P2, rep from * to end.
These 2 rows form rib.
Work in rib for a further 39 rows, ending with
WS facing for next row.
Row 42 (WS): Rib 1 (6: 8: 8: 5), M1,
(rib 3, M1) 24 (22: 22: 22: 24) times, rib 1
(6: 8: 8: 5). 99 (101: 105: 105: 107) sts.
Change to 3¾mm (US 5) needles.
Beg and ending rows as indicated and repeating
the 24 row patt rep throughout, now work in
patt from chart for sleeves as follows:
Inc 1 st at each end of 3rd (3rd: 3rd: 3rd: next)
and every foll 6th (4th: 4th: 4th: 4th) row to
125 (113: 119: 137: 149) sts, then on every foll
– (6th: 6th: 6th: –) row until there are –
(131: 137: 143: –) sts, taking inc sts into rev st st.
Cont straight until sleeve measures
43 (44: 45: 45: 45)cm, ending with RS facing
for next row.
Shape top
Keeping patt correct, cast off 3 sts at beg of next
2 rows. 119 (125: 131: 137: 143) sts.
Dec 1 st at each end of next and foll 5 alt rows,
then on foll row, ending with RS facing for
next row.
Cast off rem 105 (111: 117: 123: 129) sts.

MAKING UP

Press as described on the information page.
Join both shoulder seams using back stitch, or
mattress stitch if preferred.
Front bands and collar
With RS facing and using 2¾mm (US 2)
circular needle, beg and ending at fold line rows,
pick up and knit 116 (119: 122: 125: 128) sts up
right front opening edge to beg of front slope
shaping, 104 (107: 111: 114: 117) sts up right
front slope, 40 (40: 42: 42: 46) sts from back,
104 (107: 111: 114: 117) sts down left front slope
to beg of front slope shaping, then
116 (119: 122: 125: 128) sts down left front
opening edge. 480 (492: 508: 520: 536) sts.
Row 1 (WS): K1, P2, *K2, P2, rep from
* to last st, K1.
Row 2: K3, *P2, K2, rep from * to last st, K1.
These 2 rows form rib.
Work in rib for a further 11 rows, ending with
RS facing for next row.
Row 14 (RS): Rib 260 (266: 275: 281: 291)
wrap next st (by slipping next st from left needle
onto right needle, taking yarn to opposite side
of work between needles and then slipping same
st back onto left needle – when working back
across wrapped sts, work the wrapped st and the
wrapping loop tog as one st) and turn.
Row 15: Rib 40 (40: 42: 42: 46), wrap next st
and turn.
Row 16: Rib 45 (45: 47: 47: 51), wrap next st
and turn.
Row 17: Rib 50 (50: 52: 52: 56), wrap next st
and turn.
Row 18: Rib 55 (55: 57: 57: 61), wrap next st
and turn.
Row 19: Rib 60 (60: 62: 62: 66), wrap next st
and turn.
Cont in this way, working an extra 5 sts on every
row before wrapping next st and turning, until
the foll row has been worked:
Next row (WS): Rib 250 (260: 262: 272: 276),
wrap next st and turn.
Next row: Rib to end.
Now work 12 rows in rib across all sts, ending
with **WS** facing for next row.
Cast off in rib (on **WS**).
See information page for finishing instructions,
setting in sleeves using the shallow set-in
method. Around lower edge, fold first 11 rows to
inside along fold line row and sew in place.
Cord
Using double-pointed 2¾mm (US 2) needles,
cast on 3 sts.
Row 1 (RS): K3, *without turning slip these 3
sts to opposite end of needle and bring yarn to
opposite end of work pulling it quite tightly
across WS of work, K these 3 sts again, rep from
* until cord is 180 (190: 200: 210: 220)cm long.
Cast off.
Thread cord through casing around lower edge
and tie ends at front as in photograph.

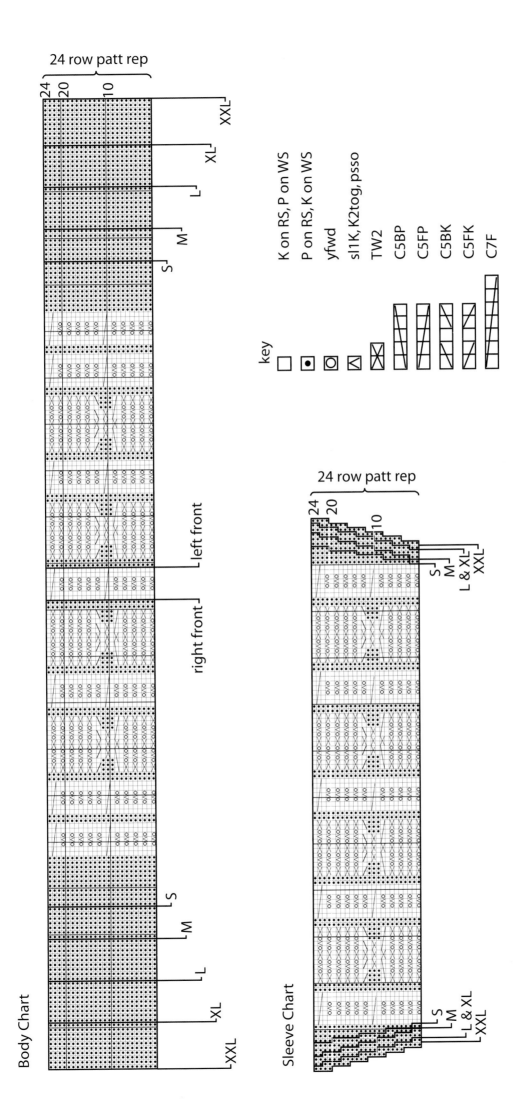

Body Chart

Sleeve Chart

24 row patt rep

key

K on RS, P on WS

P on RS, K on WS

yfwd

sl1K, K2tog, psso

TW2

C5BP

C5FP

C5BK

C5FK

C7F

SNOWBERRY

Sasha Kagan

• • •

SIZE

XS(S: M: L: XL)
To fit bust
81 (86: 91: 97: 102)cm
32 (34: 36: 38: 40)in

YARN

**Rowan Rowanspun DK and Rowan
Rowanspun 4ply**

6 (6: 7: 7: 8) x 50g balls of Rowan Rowanspun DK in
Mouse 749 (A)

1(1: 1: 1: 1) x 50g ball of Rowan Rowanspun DK in S
Almond 746 (B)

1(1: 1: 1: 1) x 50g ball of Rowan Rowanspun DK in
Lavender 733 (C)

1(1: 1: 1: 1) x 50g ball of Rowan Rowanspun DK in
Punch 731(D)

1 (1: 2: 2: 2) x 25g balls of ***Rowan Rowanspun 4ply**
in Spiced Orange 705 (E)

2 (2: 2: 2: 2) x 25g balls of ***Rowan Rowanspun 4ply**
in Burgundy 710 (F)

1(1: 1: 1: 1) x 50g ball of Rowan Rowanspun DK in
Catkin 747 (G)

1 (1: 2: 2: 2) x 25g balls of ***Rowan Rowanspun 4ply**
in Jade712 (H)

***Use Rowan Rowanspun 4ply DOUBLE
throughout.**

NEEDLES

1 pair 3mm (no 11) (US 2/3) needles
1 pair 3¾mm (no 9) (US 5) needles

BUTTONS

7

TENSION

24 sts and 32 rows to 10cm (4in) measured over
stocking stitch using 3¾mm (US 5) needles.

BACK

Using 3mm (US 2/3) needles and yarn A, cast
on 123 (129: 135: 141: 147) sts.
Row 1 (RS): K1, *P1, K1, rep from * to end.
Row 2: As row 1.
These 2 rows form moss st.
Work in moss st for a further 16 rows, ending
with a **WS** row.
Change to 3¾mm (US 5) needles.
Beg with a K row, work in st st for 2 rows,
ending with a **WS** row.
Place border chart
Using the intarsia technique as described on
the information page and starting and ending
rows as indicated, work in patt foll border chart,
which is worked entirely in st st, as follows:
Work 12 rows, ending with chart row 12 and a
WS row.
Break off all contrasts and cont in st st, beg with
a K row, using yarn A only as follows:
Cont straight until back measures
28 (29: 29: 30: 30)cm, ending with a **WS** row.
Shape armholes
Cast off 6 sts at beg of next 2 rows.
111 (117: 123: 129: 135) sts.
Place yoke chart
Using the intarsia technique as described on the
information page and starting and ending rows
as indicated, cont in patt from chart, which is
worked entirely in st st, as follows:
Work 64 rows, ending with a **WS** row.
Break off all contrasts and cont in st st, beg with
a K row, using yarn A only as follows:
Cont straight until armhole measures
23 (23: 24: 24: 25)cm, ending with a **WS** row.
Shape shoulders and back neck
Cast off 12 (13: 14: 14: 15) sts at beg of next
2 rows. 87 (91: 95: 101: 105) sts.
Next row (RS): Cast off 12 (13: 14: 14: 15) sts,
K until there are 16 (16: 17: 19: 20) sts on right
needle and turn, leaving rem sts on a holder.
Work each side of neck separately.
Cast off 4 sts at beg of next row.

Cast off rem 12 (12: 13: 15: 16) sts.
With RS facing, rejoin yarn to rem sts, cast off
centre 31 (33: 33: 35: 35) sts, K to end.
Complete to match first side, reversing shapings.

LEFT FRONT

Using 3mm (US 2/3) needles and yarn A, cast
on 67 (71: 73: 77: 79) sts.
Work in moss st as given for back for 17 rows,
ending with a RS row.
Row 18 (WS): Moss st 7 sts and slip these sts
onto a holder, M1, moss st to last 1 (0: 1: 0: 1) st,
(inc in last st) 1 (0: 1: 0: 1) times.
62 (65: 68: 71: 74) sts.
Change to 3¾mm (US 5) needles.
Beg with a K row, work in st st for 2 rows,
ending with a **WS** row.
Place border chart
Starting and ending rows as indicated, work in
patt foll border chart as follows:
Work 12 rows, ending with chart row 12 and a
WS row.
Break off all contrasts and cont in st st, beg with
a K row, using yarn A only as follows:
Cont straight until left front matches back to
beg of armhole shaping, ending with a WS row.
Shape armhole
Cast off 6 sts at beg of next row.
56 (59: 62: 65: 68) sts.
Work 1 row, ending with a WS row.
Place yoke chart
Starting and ending rows as indicated, cont in
patt from chart as follows:
Cont straight until 19 (19: 19: 21: 21) rows
less have been worked than on back to start of
shoulder shaping, ending with a **RS** row.
Shape neck
Keeping chart correct until chart row 64 has
been completed and then cont using yarn A
only, cast off 8 (9: 9: 9: 9) sts at beg of next row,
then 4 sts at beg of foll alt row.
44 (46: 49: 52: 55) sts.
Dec 1 st at neck edge of next 4 rows, then on
foll 4 (4: 4: 5: 5) alt rows. 36 (38: 41: 43: 46) sts.
Work 4 rows, ending with a **WS** row.
Shape shoulder
Cast off 12 (13: 14: 14: 15) sts at beg of next and
foll alt row.
Work 1 row.
Cast off rem 12 (12: 13: 15: 16) sts.

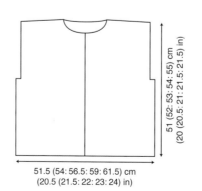

51.5 (54: 56.5: 59: 61.5) cm
(20.5 (21.5: 22: 23: 24) in)

51 (52: 53: 54: 55) cm
(20 (20.5: 21: 21.5: 21.5) in)

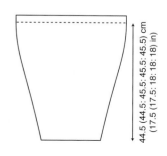

44.5 (44.5: 45.5: 45.5: 45.5) cm
(17.5 (17.5: 18: 18: 18) in)

RIGHT FRONT

Using 3mm (US 2/3) needles and yarn A, cast on 67 (71: 73: 77: 79) sts.

Work in moss st as given for back for 10 rows, ending with a WS row.

Row 11 (RS): K1, P1, K2tog, yfwd (to make a buttonhole), moss st to end.

Work in moss st for a further 6 rows, ending with a **RS** row.

Row 18 (WS): (Inc in first st)

1 (0: 1: 0: 1) times, moss st to last 7 sts, M1 and turn, leaving last 7 sts on a holder.

62 (65: 68: 71: 74) sts.

Change to 3¾mm (US 5) needles and complete to match left front, foll chart for right front and reversing shapings.

SLEEVES (both alike)

Using 3mm (US 2/3) needles and yarn A, cast on 53 (53: 55: 57: 57) sts.

Work in moss st as given for back for 16 rows, ending with a **WS** row.

Cont in moss st, inc 1 st at each end of next and foll 6th row.

57 (57: 59: 61: 61) sts.

Work 1 row, ending with a **WS** row.

Change to 3¾mm (US 5) needles.

Beg with a K row, work in st st for 2 rows, ending with a **WS** row.

Place border chart

Starting and ending rows as indicated, work in patt foll border chart until chart row 12 has been completed and then cont using yarn A only **at the same time** inc 1 st at each end of 3rd and every foll 6th (6th: 6th: 6th: 4th) row to 69 (69: 67: 73: 119) sts, then on every foll 4th (4th: 4th: 4th: -) row until there are 107 (107: 113: 113: -) sts.

Cont straight until sleeve measures 47 (47: 48: 48: 48)cm, ending with a **WS** row.

Cast off.

MAKING UP

Press as described on the information page.

Join shoulder seams using back stitch, or mattress st if preferred.

Button band

Slip 7 sts left on left front holder onto 3mm (US 2/3) needles and rejoin yarn A with RS facing.

Cont in moss st as set until band, when slightly stretched, fits up left front opening edge to neck shaping, ending with a **WS** row.

Break yarn and leave sts on a holder.

Slip stitch band in position.

Mark positions for 7 buttons on this band – first to come level with buttonhole already worked in right front, last to come 1cm up from neck shaping and rem 5 buttons evenly spaced between.

Button band

Slip 7 sts left on right front holder onto 3mm (US 2/3) needles and rejoin yarn A with **WS** facing.

Cont in moss st as set until band, when slightly stretched, fits up right front opening edge to

neck shaping, ending with a **WS** row and with the addition of a further 5 buttonholes worked as follows:

Buttonhole row (RS): K1, P1, K2tog, yfwd (to make a buttonhole), K1, P1, K1.

Do NOT break off yarn.

Neckband

With RS facing, using 3mm (US 2/3) needles and yarn A, moss st across 7 sts of buttonhole band, pick up and knit 31 (32: 32: 34: 34) sts up right side of neck, 39 (41: 41: 43: 43) sts from front and 31 (32: 32: 34: 34) sts down left side of neck, then moss st across 7 sts of button band.

115 (119: 119: 125: 125) sts.

Work in moss st as set by front bands for 3 rows, ending with a **WS** row.

Row 4 (RS): K1, P1, K2tog, yfwd (to make 7th buttonhole), moss st to end.

Work in moss st for a further 3 rows.

Cast off in moss st.

Key

A
B
C
D

E
F
G
H

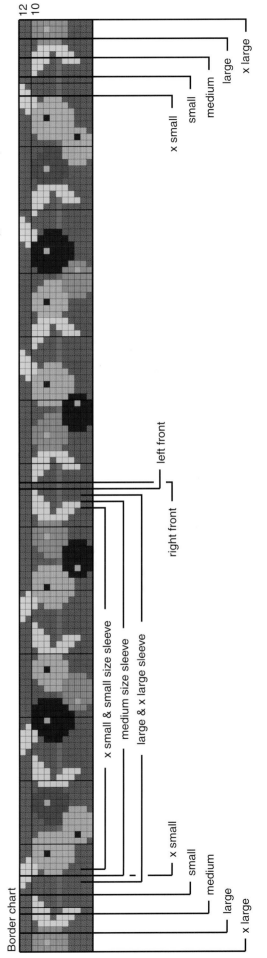

Border chart

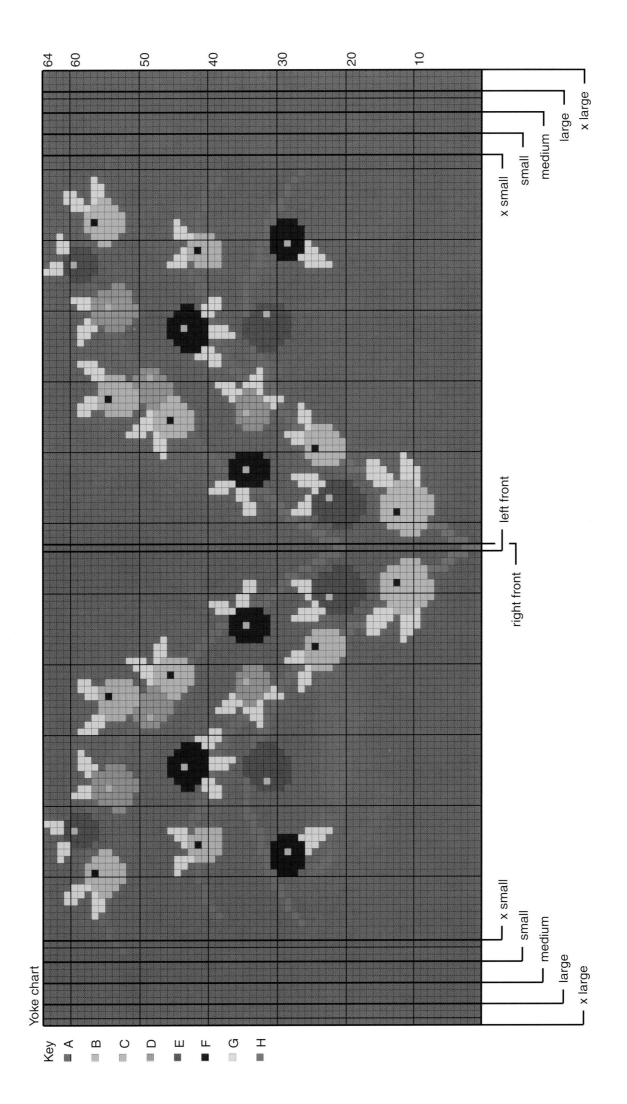

Yoke chart

Key
A
B
C
D
E
F
G
H

STRIVEN

Jennie Atkinson

● ● ● ●

SIZE
8 (10: 12: 14: 16: 18)
To fit bust
81 (86: 91: 97: 102: 107)cm
32 (34: 36: 38: 40: 42)in

YARN
Rowan Wool Cotton and Rowan Felted Tweed
7 (7: 8: 8: 9:10) x 50g balls of Rowan Wool Cotton in Gypsy 910 (A)
1 (1: 1: 1: 2:2) x 50g balls of Rowan Felted Tweed in Ginger 154 (B)
1 (1: 1: 1: 2: 2) x 50g balls of Rowan Felted Tweed in Rage 150 (C)
1 (1: 1: 1: 1: 1) x 50g ball of Rowan Felted Tweed in Treacle 145 (D)
1 (1: 1: 1: 1: 1) x 50g ball of Rowan Felted Tweed in Whisper 141 (E)
1 (1: 1: 1: 1: 1) x 50g ball of Rowan Felted Tweed in Gilt 160 (F)
1 (1: 1: 1: 1: 1) x 50g ball of Rowan Felted Tweed in Pine 158 (G)
1 (1: 1: 1: 1: 1) x 50g ball of Rowan Felted Tweed in Clover 162 (H)
1 (1: 1: 1: 1: 1) x 50g ball of Rowan Felted Tweed in Avocado 161 (I)

NEEDLES
1 pair 3¼mm (no 10) (US 3) needles
1 pair 3¾mm (no 9) (US 5) needles
1 pair 4mm (no 8) (US 6) needles

BUTTONS
6

TENSION
22 sts and 30 rows to 10cm (4in) measured over stocking stitch using 4mm (US 6) needles and yarn A.
27 sts and 46 rows to 10cm (4in) measured over pattern using 3¾mm (US 5) needles.

STRIPE SEQUENCE
Rows 1 and 2: Using yarn B.
Rows 3 and 4: Using yarn C.
Rows 5 and 6: Using yarn B.
Rows 7 and 8: Using yarn D.
Rows 9 and 10: Using yarn B.
Rows 11 and 12: Using yarn D.
Rows 13 to 18: As rows 1 to 6.
Rows 19 and 20: Using yarn C.
Rows 21 and 22: Using yarn E.
Rows 23 to 26: As rows 19 to 22.
Rows 27 and 28: Using yarn I.
Rows 29 and 30: Using yarn E.
Rows 31 and 32: Using yarn G.
Rows 33 and 34: Using yarn E.
Rows 35 to 38: As rows 19 to 22.
Rows 39 and 40: Using yarn C.
Rows 41 to 66: As rows 1 to 26.
Rows 67 and 68: Using yarn F.
Rows 69 and 70: Using yarn E.
Rows 71 and 72: Using yarn H.
Rows 73 to 80: As rows 33 to 40.
These 80 rows form stripe sequence.
(Note: As row 1 is a WS row, colour change falls after RS rows.)

Pattern note: When working patt on back and fronts, slip all sts purlwise with yarn at WS (back) of work.

BACK
Using 3¼mm (US 3) needles and yarn A, cast on 98 (102: 106: 114: 118: 126) sts.
Row 1 (RS): K2, ★P2, K2, rep from ★ to end.
Row 2: P2, ★K2, P2, rep from ★ to end.
These 2 rows form rib.
Work in rib for 12cm, ending with **WS** facing for next row.
Change to 3¾mm (US 5) needles.
Beg with row 1 and joining in and breaking off colours as required, cont in stripe sequence (as given above) as follows:
Next row (WS): P3 (1: 3: 7: 0: 4), inc in next st, (P4, inc in next st, P3, inc in next st)
10 (11: 11: 11: 13: 13) times, P4 (1: 3: 7: 0: 4).
119 (125: 129: 137: 145: 153) sts.
Using appropriate colour yarn, cont in patt as follows:
Row 1 (RS): P1, ★sl 1, P1, rep from ★ to end.
Row 2: Purl.
Row 3: P2, ★sl 1, P1, rep from ★ to last st, P1.
Row 4: Purl.
These 4 rows form patt.
Cont in patt and stripe sequence until back measures 30 (30: 29: 32: 31: 33)cm, ending with RS facing for next row.
Shape armholes
Keeping patt and stripes correct, cast off
6 (7: 7: 8: 8: 9) sts at beg of next 2 rows.
107 (111: 115: 121: 129: 135) sts.
Dec 1 st at each end of next 3 (3: 5: 5: 7: 7) rows, then on foll 5 (6: 4: 5: 5: 6) alt rows.
91 (93: 97: 101: 105: 109) sts.
Cont straight until armhole measures
14 (14: 15: 15: 16: 16)cm, ending with **RS** facing for next row.
Cast off.

LEFT FRONT
Using 3¼mm (US 3) needles and yarn A, cast on 43 (47: 47: 51: 55: 59) sts.
Row 1 (RS): K2, ★P2, K2, rep from ★ to last st, P1.
Row 2: K1, P2, ★K2, P2, rep from ★ to end.
These 2 rows form rib.
Work in rib for 12cm, ending with **WS** facing for next row.
Change to 3¾mm (US 5) needles.
Beg with row 1 and joining in and breaking off colours as required, cont in stripe sequence (as given above) as follows:
Next row (WS): P3 (3: 3: 0: 2: 4), inc in next st, [P3 (4: 3: 4: 4: 4), inc in next st]
9 (8: 10: 10: 10: 10) times, P3 (3: 3: 0: 2: 4).
53 (56: 58: 62: 66: 70) sts.
Cont in patt and stripe sequence as given for back until left front matches back to beg of armhole shaping, ending with **RS** facing for next row.

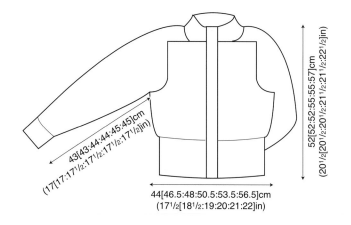

43[43:44:44:45:45]cm
(17[17:17½:17½:17½:17½]in)

52[52:52:55:55:57]cm
(20½[20½:20½:21½:21½:22½]in)

44[46.5:48:50.5:53.5:56.5]cm
(17½[18½:19:20:21:22]in)

Shape armhole

Keeping patt and stripes correct, cast off
6 (7: 7: 8: 8: 9) sts at beg of next row.
47 (49: 51: 54: 58: 61) sts.
Work 1 row.
Dec 1 st at armhole edge of next
3 (3: 5: 5: 7: 7) rows, then on foll
5 (6: 4: 5: 5: 6) alt rows.
39 (40: 42: 44: 46: 48) sts.
Cont straight until armhole measures
14 (14: 15: 15: 16: 16)cm, ending with RS facing
for next row.
Cast off.
Place marker on cast-off edge 3.5cm in from
front opening edge.

RIGHT FRONT

Using 3¼mm (US 3) needles and yarn A, cast on
43 (47: 47: 51: 55: 59) sts.
Row 1 (RS): P1, K2, *P2, K2, rep from
* to end.
Row 2: P2, *K2, P2, rep from * to last st, K1.
These 2 rows form rib.
Complete to match left front, reversing shapings.

SLEEVES (both alike)

Using 3¼mm (US 3) needles and yarn A, cast on
66 (66: 66: 66: 70: 70) sts.
Work in rib as given for back for 6cm, inc
0 (0: 1: 1: 0: 0) st at each end of last row and
ending with **RS** facing for next row.
66 (66: 68: 68: 70: 70) sts.
Change to 4mm (US 6) needles.
Row 1 (RS): P26 (26: 27: 27: 28: 28), (K2, P2)
3 times, K2, P to end.
Row 2: K26 (26: 27: 27: 28: 28), (P2, K2)
3 times, P2, K to end.
Row 3: P26 (26: 27: 27: 28: 28), C6F, P2, C6F,
P to end.
Row 4: As row 2.
Row 5: (Inc in first st) 0 (0: 0: 0: 0: 1) times,
P26 (26: 27: 27: 28: 27), (K2, P2) 3 times, K2,
P to last 0 (0: 0: 0: 0: 1) st, (inc in last st)
0 (0: 0: 0: 0: 1) times.
66 (66: 68: 68: 70: 72) sts.
Row 6: K26 (26: 27: 27: 28: 29), (P2, K2)
3 times, P2, K to end.
Row 7: (Inc in first st) 1 (1: 1: 1: 1: 0) times,
P25 (25: 26: 26: 27: 29), (K2, P2) 3 times, K2,
P to last 1 (1: 1: 1: 1: 0) st, (inc in last st)
1 (1: 1: 1: 1: 0) times.
68 (68: 70: 70: 72: 72) sts.
Row 8: K27 (27: 28: 28: 29: 29), (P2, K2)
3 times, P2, K to end.
Row 9: P27 (27: 28: 28: 29: 29), K2, P2, C6B,
P2, K2, P to end.
Row 10: As row 8.
Row 11: P27 (27: 28: 28: 29: 29), (K2, P2)
3 times, K2, P to end.
Row 12: As row 10.
These 12 rows form patt.
Cont in patt, shaping sides by inc 1 st at each
end of 3rd (3rd: 3rd: 3rd: 3rd: next) and every
foll 10th (8th: 8th: 8th: 8th: 8th) row to
86 (80: 78: 88: 88: 96) sts, then on every foll
– (10th: 10th: 10th: 10th: –) row until there are

– (88: 90: 92: 94: –) sts, taking inc sts into rev st st.
Cont straight until sleeve measures
43 (43: 44: 44: 45: 45)cm, ending with RS facing
for next row.

Shape top

Keeping patt correct, cast off 6 (7: 7: 8: 8: 9) sts at
beg of next 2 rows. 74 (74: 76: 76: 78: 78) sts.
Dec 1 st at each end of next 3 rows, then on
every foll alt row until 34 sts rem.

Shape saddle shoulder strap

Place markers at both ends of last row – these
markers correspond to armhole ends of back and
front cast-off edges.
Cont straight until saddle shoulder strap fits
across front cast-off edge from armhole to
marker, ending with **RS** facing for next row.

Left sleeve only

Next row (RS): P10 and turn, leaving rem sts
on a holder.
Work each side of neck separately.
Dec 1 st at end of 6th and foll 4th row. 8 sts.
Cont straight until this section, from marker, fits
across cast-off edge of back from armhole edge
to centre back, ending with **RS** facing for
next row.
Cast off.
With RS facing, rejoin yarn to rem sts, cast off
centre 14 sts dec 2 sts evenly, P to end. 10 sts.
Dec 1 st at neck (cast-off) edge of every row
until 2 sts rem, ending with **WS** facing for
next row.
Next row (WS): K2tog and fasten off.

Right sleeve only

Next row (RS): P10 and turn, leaving rem
sts on a holder.
Work each side of neck separately.
Dec 1 st at neck (cast-off) edge of every row
until 2 sts rem, ending with **WS** facing for
next row.
Next row (WS): K2tog and fasten off.
With RS facing, rejoin yarn to rem sts, cast off
centre 14 sts dec 2 sts evenly, P to end. 10 sts.
Dec 1 st at beg of 6th and foll 4th row. 8 sts.
Cont straight until this section, **from marker**,
fits across cast-off edge of back from armhole
edge to centre back, ending with **RS** facing for
next row.
Cast off.

MAKING UP

Press as described on the information page.
Join cast-off ends of back saddle shoulder straps.
Matching this seam to centre back, sew straight
row-end edge of back edge of saddle straps to
back cast-off edge, matching sleeve markers to
ends of cast-off edge. In same way, sew front
edges of saddle straps to front cast-off edges –
fasten off point of saddle strap will be
at front opening edge. Sew rest of sleeve top
into armhole.

Collar

With **RS** facing, using 3¼mm (US 3) needles
and yarn A, beg and ending at front opening
edges, pick up and knit 110 sts evenly all round
neck edge.
Beg with row 2, work in rib as given for back

for 9cm, ending with RS facing for next row.
Cast off in rib.

Button band

With RS facing, using 3¼mm (US 3) needles
and yarn A, beg at top of collar, pick up and knit
154 (154: 154: 162: 162: 170) sts evenly down
left front opening edge to cast-on edge.
Beg with row 2, work in rib as given for back
for 15 rows, ending with **RS** facing for next row.
Cast off in rib.

Buttonhole band

With **RS** facing, using 3¼mm (US 3) needles
and yarn A, beg at
cast-on edge, pick up and knit
154 (154: 154: 162: 162: 170) sts evenly up right
front opening edge to top of collar.
Beg with row 2, work in rib as given for back
for 7 rows, ending with RS facing for next row.
Row 8 (RS): Rib 6, *work 2tog, yrn (to make
a buttonhole), rib 29 (29: 29: 31: 31: 33), rep
from * 3 times more, work 2tog, yrn, rib 15,
work 2tog, yrn, rib 5.
Work in rib for a further 7 rows, ending with
RS facing for next row.
Cast off in rib.
See information page for finishing instructions.

Embroidery

Using photograph as a guide, swiss darn vertical
lines onto back and fronts using yarns D and I.

TILLIE
Louisa Harding

• • •

SIZE
S: M: L

YARN
Rowan 4ply Cotton & Fine Cotton Chenille

		S	M	L	
A	Tear 116	7	7	8	x 50gm
B	CornFlower 412	2	2	2	x 50gm

NEEDLES
1 pair 2¼mm (no 13) (US 1) needles
1 pair 3mm (no 11) (US 2/3) needles

BUTTONS
10 buttons

TENSION
30 sts and 32 rows to 10cm (4in) measured over fairisle pattern using 3mm (US 2/3) needles
28 sts and 38 rows to 10cm (4in) measured over lace pattern using 3mm (US 2/3) needles

BACK
Using 2¼mm (US 1) needles and yarn A, work picot cast on as folls:
★ Cast on 5 sts, cast off 2 sts, slip st on RH needle back onto LH needle★ (3 sts now on LH needle); rep from ★ to ★ until 123 (132: 141) sts on needle, cast on 2 (1: 0) sts. 125 (133: 141) sts.
Knit 4 rows.

Change to 3mm (US 2/3) needles, joining yarn B and using the FAIRISLE technique as described on the information page, work 26 rows in patt from chart for back which is worked in st st beg with a K row, inc 1 st at each end of chart rows 13 and 25 as indicated.
Cont in patt, rep the 26 row rep throughout and **at the same time** cont shaping sides by inc 1 st at each end of 11th and every foll 12th row to 135 (143: 151) sts.
Cont without shaping until work measures 24.5cm from cast on edge, ending with a WS row.
Shape armholes
Cast off 6 (6: 7) sts at beg of next 2 rows.
123 (131: 137) sts.
2nd and 3rd sizes only
Cast off – (4: 5) sts at beg of next 2 rows.
– (123: 127) sts.
All 3 sizes
Dec 1 st at each end of next 8 (6: 6) rows, 2 foll alt rows and 2 foll 4th rows.
99 (103: 107) sts.
Cont without shaping until work measures 21cm from beg of armhole shaping, ending with a WS row
Shape shoulders and back neck
Cast off 5 (6: 7) sts at beg of next row, patt 19 (20: 21) sts, turn and leave rem sts on a holder.
Work each side of neck separately
Cast off 4 sts at beg of next row, 5 (6: 7) sts at beg of foll row, then 4 sts at beg of next row.
Cast off rem 6 sts.
With RS facing, rejoin yarn to rem sts, cast off centre 51 sts, patt to end.
Complete to match first side, reversing shapings.

LEFT FRONT
Using 2¼mm (US 1) needles and yarn A, work picot cast on as folls: ★ Cast on 5 sts, cast off 2 sts, slip st on RH needle back onto LH needle★ (3 sts now on LH needle); rep from ★ to ★ until 63 (66: 69) sts on needle, cast on 0 (1: 2) sts. 63 (67: 71) sts.
Knit 4 rows.
Change to 3mm (US 2/3) needles joining in yarn B and work 26 rows in patt from chart for left front, inc 1 st at side edge on chart rows 13 and 25 as indicated.
Cont in patt, rep the 26 rows patt throughout until front matches back to beg of armhole shaping and **at the same time** inc 1 st at side edge on 11th and every foll 12th row to 68 (72: 76) sts, ending with a WS row.
Shape armhole
Cast off 6 (6: 7) sts at beg of next row.
62 (66: 69) sts.
Work 1 row.
2nd and 3rd sizes only
Cast off – (4: 5) sts at beg of next row.
– (62: 64) sts.
Work 1 row.
All 3 sizes
Dec 1 st at armhole edge on next 8 (6: 6) rows, 2 foll alt rows and 2 foll 4th rows. 50 (52: 54) sts.
Cont without shaping until front is 17 rows less than back to beg of shoulder shaping, ending with a RS row.
Shape front neck
Cast off 18 sts at beg of next row and 8 sts at beg of foll alt row. 24 (26: 28) sts.
Dec 1 st at neck edge on next 6 rows and 2 foll alt rows. 16 (18: 20) sts.
Cont without shaping until front matches back to beg of shoulder shaping, ending with a WS row.
Shape shoulder
Cast off 5 (6: 7) sts at beg of next row and foll alt row.
Work 1 row.
Cast off rem 6 sts.

RIGHT FRONT
Work as given for left front following chart for right front and reversing shapings.

SLEEVES
Using 2¼mm (US 1) needles and yarn A, work picot cast on as folls: ★ Cast on 5 sts, cast off 2 sts, slip st on RH needle back onto LH needle★ (3 sts now on LH needle); rep from ★ to ★ until 42 sts on needle.
Knit 4 rows.
Change to 3mm (US 2/3) needles and using yarn A throughout work in lace patt from chart for sleeve setting sts as folls:
Chart row 1 (RS): K1, ★yo, K3tog, yo, K2, yo, sl 1, K1, psso, yo, K3tog, yo, K1, yo, sl 1, K1, psso, yo, K3tog, yo, K2, yo, sl 1, K1, psso; rep from ★, K1.

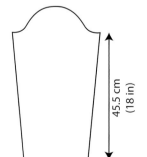

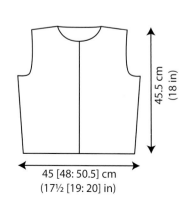

45.5 cm (18 in)

45.5 cm (18 in)

45 [48: 50.5] cm (17½ [19: 20] in)

Chart row 2 and all WS rows: Purl.

Chart row 3: K1, sl 1, K1, psso, yo, K4, yo, sl 1, K2tog, psso, yo, K3, yo, sl 1, K2tog, psso, yo, K4, yo, sl 1, K2tog, psso, yo, K4, yo, sl 1, K2tog, psso, yo, K3, yo, sl 1, K2tog, psso, yo, K6.

Chart row 5: K2, ★ (yo, sl 1, K1, psso) twice, K3, yo, sl 1, K1, psso, yo, K3tog, yo, K3, (K2tog, yo) twice, K1; rep from ★ to end.

Chart row 7: ★K3, (yo, sl 1, K1, psso) twice, K3, yo, sl 1, K2tog, psso, yo, K3, (K2tog, yo) twice; rep from ★, K2.

Chart row 9: K4, ★ (yo, sl 1, K1, psso) twice, K7, (K2tog, yo) twice, K5; rep from ★, end last rep K3.

Chart row 11: K5, ★(yo, sl 1, K1, psso) twice, K5, (K2tog, yo) twice, K7; rep from ★, end last rep K4.

Chart row 13: K6, ★ (yo, sl 1, K1, psso) twice, K3, (K2tog, yo) twice, K9; rep from ★, end last rep K5.

Chart row 15: K2, ★ yo, sl 1, K1, psso, K3, (yo, sl 1, K1,psso) twice, K1, (K2tog, yo) twice, K3, K2tog, yo, K1; rep from ★ to end.

Chart row 17: ★ (K3, yo, sl 1, K1, psso) twice, yo, sl 1, K2tog, psso, yo, K2tog, yo, K3, K2tog, yo; rep from ★, K2.

Chart row 19: K1,★yo, K3tog, yo, K1, yo, K3, K3tog, yo, K1, yo, sl 1, K2tog, psso, K3, yo, K1, yo, sl 1, K1, psso; rep from★, K1.

Chart row 20: Purl.

Cont in patt from chart inc 1 st at each end of next row, 9 foll 6th rows, then every foll 8th row to 82 sts.

Cont without shaping until chart row 170 has been completed, ending with a WS row.

Shape top

Keeping patt correct, cast off 4 sts at beg of next 2 rows and 3 sts at beg of foll 2 rows.

Dec 1 st at each end of next row, 1 foll alt row, 1 foll 4th row and 1 foll 6th row. 60 sts.

Work 7 rows.

Dec 1 st at each end of next row, 1 foll 8th row, 1 foll 6th row and 1 foll 4th row. 52 sts.

Work 1 row. Dec 1 st at each end of next row, 2 foll alt rows and 3 foll rows. 40 sts.

Cast off 4 sts at beg of next 4 rows.

Cast off rem 24 sts.

MAKING UP

Press all pieces as described on the info page.
Join both shoulder seams using back stitch.

Buttonhole band

With RS facing and using 2¼mm (US 1) needles and yarn A, pick up and knit 114 sts along right front edge.
Knit 1 row.

Next row (RS) (buttonhole): K1, (K2tog, (yon) twice, K2tog, K8)
9 times, K2tog, (yon) twice, K2tog, K1.
Knit 2 rows.

Next row (WS) (Picot cast off): Cast off 3 sts knitwise, (cast on
2 sts, cast off 5 sts knitwise) to end. Fasten off.

Button band

Work as given for buttonhole band omitting buttonholes.

Neckband

With RS facing and using 2¼mm (US 1) needles and yarn A, pick up and knit 46 sts up right front neck from centre front to shoulder, 8 sts down right back neck, 48 sts across back neck, 8 sts up left back neck to shoulder and 46 sts down left front to centre front. 156 sts.
Knit 3 rows.

Next row (RS) (dec): K10, (K2tog, K13) 9 times,K2tog, K9. 146 sts.

Next row (WS)(Picot cast off): Cast off 4 sts knitwise, (cast on 2 sts, cast off 5 sts knitwise) to last st, cast off 1 st. Fasten off.

See information page for finishing instructions, setting in sleeves using the set-in method.
Sew on buttons.

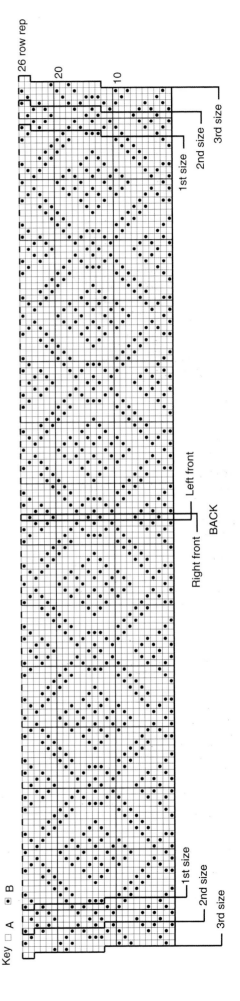

Key
◎ yarn over

☑ K2tog

◩ sl1, K1, psso

◭ K3tog

◮ sl1, K2tog, psso

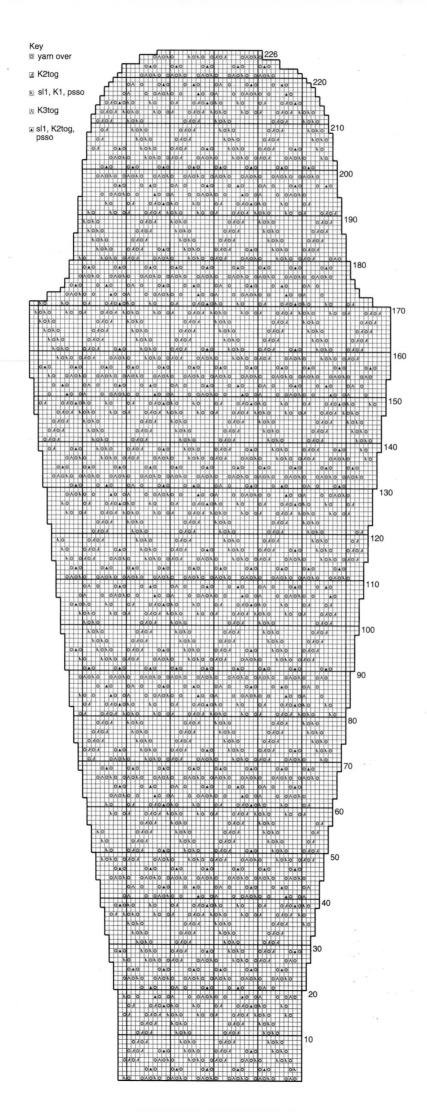

VALENTINA
Martin Storey

● ● ● ●

SIZE
S (M: L: XL: XXL)
To fit bust
81-86 (91-97: 102-107: 112-117: 122-127)cm
32-34 (36-38: 40-42: 44-46: 48-50)in

YARN
Rowan Kid Classic
8 (9: 10: 10: 11) x 50g balls of Rowan Kid Classic in Nightly 846 (A)
2 (3: 3: 3: 3) x 50g balls of Rowan Kid Classic in Straw 851 (B)
2 (2: 2: 2: 2) x 50g balls of Rowan Kid Classic in Crushed Velvet 825 (C)
2 (2: 2: 2: 3) x 50g balls of Rowan Kid Classic in Tea Rose 854 (D)
2 (2: 2: 2: 2) x 50g balls of Rowan Kid Classic in Royal 835 (E)
2 (2: 3: 3: 3) x 50g balls of Rowan Kid Classic in Lavender Ice 841 (F)
1 (1: 1: 1: 1) x 50g ball of Rowan Kid Classic in Earth 872 (G)
1 (1: 1: 1: 1) x 50g ball of Rowan Kid Classic in Teal 862 (H)

NEEDLES
1 pair 4mm (no 8) (US 6) needles
1 pair 5mm (no 6) (US 8) needles

TENSION
21 sts and 21 rows to 10cm (4in) measured over patterned stocking stitch using 5mm (US 8) needles.

BACK
Using 5mm (US 8) needles and yarn A, cast on 107 (117: 131: 143: 157) sts.
Beg and ending rows as indicated, using a combination of the fairisle and intarsia techniques as described on the information page and working chart rows 1 to 44 once only and then repeating chart rows 45 to 70 throughout, now work in patt from main chart, which is worked entirely in st st beg with a K row, as follows:
Work straight until back measures 71 (72: 73: 74: 75)cm, ending with **RS** facing for next row.
Shape armholes
Keeping patt correct, cast off 3 sts at beg of next 2 rows. 101 (111: 125: 137: 151) sts.
Dec 1 st at each end of next and foll 3 alt rows. 93 (103: 117: 129: 143) sts.
Cont straight until armhole measures 24 (25: 26: 27: 28)cm, ending with **RS** facing for next row.
Shape shoulders and back neck
Cast off 9 (10: 12: 14: 16) sts at beg of next 2 rows. 75 (83: 93: 101: 111) sts.
Next row (RS): Cast off 9 (10: 12: 14: 16) sts, patt until there are 12 (15: 17: 19: 21) sts on right needle and turn, leaving rem sts on a holder.
Work each side of neck separately.
Cast off 4 sts at beg of next row.
Cast off rem 8 (11: 13: 15: 17) sts.
With RS facing, rejoin yarns to rem sts, cast off centre 33 (33: 35: 35: 37) sts, patt to end.
Complete to match first side, reversing shapings.

LEFT FRONT
Using 5mm (US 8) needles and yarn A, cast on 49 (54: 61: 67: 74) sts.
Beg and ending rows as indicated, now work in patt from main chart as follows:
Work 1 row, ending with **WS** facing for next row.
Inc 1 st at beg of next row and at same edge on foll 4 rows, taking inc sts into patt.
54 (59: 66: 72: 79) sts.
Cont straight until left front matches back to beg of armhole shaping, ending with **RS** facing for next row.
Shape armhole
Keeping patt correct, cast off 3 sts at beg of next row. 51 (56: 63: 69: 76) sts.
Work 1 row.
Dec 1 st at armhole edge of next and foll 3 alt rows. 47 (52: 59: 65: 72) sts.
Cont straight until 33 (33: 35: 35: 37) rows less have been worked than on back to beg of shoulder shaping, ending with **WS** facing for next row.
Shape neck
Keeping patt correct, cast off 5 sts at beg of next row. 42 (47: 54: 60: 67) sts.
Dec 1 st at neck edge of next and foll 15 (15: 16: 16: 17) alt rows. 26 (31: 37: 43: 49) sts.
Work 1 row, ending with RS facing for next row.
Shape shoulder
Cast off 9 (10: 12: 14: 16) sts at beg of next and foll alt row.
Work 1 row.
Cast off rem 8 (11: 13: 15: 17) sts.

RIGHT FRONT
Using 5mm (US 8) needles and yarn A, cast on 49 (54: 61: 67: 74) sts.
Beg and ending rows as indicated, now work in patt from chart as follows:
Work 1 row, ending with **WS** facing for next row.
Inc 1 st at end of next row and at same edge on foll 4 rows, taking inc sts into patt.
54 (59: 66: 72: 79) sts.
Complete to match left front, reversing shapings.

SLEEVES (both alike)
Using 5mm (US 8) needles and yarn A, cast on 67 (69: 71: 71: 73) sts.
Beg and ending rows as indicated, now work in patt from main chart, shaping sides by inc 1 st at each end of 5th (5th: 5th: 3rd: 3rd) and every foll 4th (4th: 4th: alt: alt) row to 93 (99: 105: 75: 81) sts, then on every foll 6th (6th: 6th: 4th: 4th) row until there are 101 (105: 109: 113: 117) sts, taking inc sts into patt.

43 [44: 45: 45: 45] cm
(17 [17½: 17½: 17½: 17½] in)

100 [102: 104: 106: 108] cm
(39½ [40: 41: 41½: 42½] in)

51 [55.5: 62.5: 68: 75] cm
(20 [22: 24½: 27: 29½] in)

Cont straight until sleeve measures
41 (42: 43: 43: 43)cm, ending with RS facing
for next row.

Shape top

Keeping patt correct, cast off 3 sts at beg of next
2 rows. 95 (99: 103: 107: 111) sts.
Dec 1 st at each end of next and foll 2 alt rows,
then on foll row, ending with RS facing for
next row.
Cast off rem 87 (91: 95: 99: 103) sts.

MAKING UP

Press as described on the information page.
Join both shoulder seams using back stitch, or
mattress stitch if preferred.

Collar

Using 5mm (US 8) needles and yarn A, cast on
109 (109: 115: 115: 121) sts loosely.
Beg with a K row, work in st st as follows:
Work 1 row, ending with **WS** facing for
next row.
Inc 1 st at each end of next 3 rows, ending with
RS facing for next row.
115 (115: 121: 121: 127) sts.

Now place motif charts as follows:

Next row (RS): Inc in first st, K1 (1: 2: 2: 4),
work next 35 sts as row 1 of chart A,
K3 (3: 5: 5: 6), work next 35 sts as row 1 of
chart B, K3 (3: 5: 5: 6), work next 35 sts as
row 1 of chart C, K1 (1: 2: 2: 4), inc in last st.
Next row: Inc in first st, P2 (2: 3: 3: 5), work
next 35 sts as row 2 of chart C, P3 (3: 5: 5: 6),
work next 35 sts as row 2 of chart B,
P3 (3: 5: 5: 6), work next 35 sts as row 2 of chart
A, P2 (2: 3: 3: 5), inc in last st.
119 (119: 125: 125: 131) sts.
These 2 rows complete shaping and set position
of charts with st st using yarn A between and
at sides.
Cont as set until all 37 rows of charts have been
completed, ending with **WS** facing for next row.
Break off contrasts and, beg with a P row, cont
in st st using yarn A only as follows:
Work 7 rows, ending with RS facing for
next row.
Cast off 13 (13: 14: 14: 14) sts at beg of next
4 rows, then 13 (13: 13: 13: 15) sts at beg of
foll 2 rows.
Cast off rem 41 (41: 43: 43: 45) sts.
Sew shaped cast-off edge of collar to neck edge,
matching ends of collar to front opening edges.

Front opening and hem trim

Using 4mm (US 6) needles and yarn A, cast
on 7 sts.
Row 1 (RS): K2, ★P1, K1, rep from ★ to
last st, K1.
Row 2: K1, ★P1, K1, rep from ★ to end.
These 2 rows form rib.
Work in rib until trim, beg and ending at collar
seam and when slightly stretched, fits down
entire right front opening edge, across entire
lower edge and up entire left front opening edge,
ending with RS facing for next row.
Cast off in rib.
Slip stitch trim in place.

Collar trim

Using 4mm (US 6) needles and yarn A, cast on
7 sts.
Work in rib as given for front opening and hem
trim until this trim, beg and ending at collar
seam and when slightly stretched, fits around
entire outer edge of collar, ending with RS
facing for next row.
Cast off in rib.
Slip stitch trim in place, joining ends of trims at
collar seam.

Sleeve trims (both alike)

Using 4mm (US 6) needles and yarn A, cast on
7 sts.
Work in rib as given for front opening and hem
trim until this trim, when slightly stretched, fits
across cast-on edge of sleeve, ending with RS
facing for next row.
Cast off in rib.
Slip stitch trim in place.
See information page for finishing
instructions, setting in sleeves using the shallow
set-in method.

Belt

Using 4mm (US 6) needles and yarn A,
cast on 11 sts.
Work in rib as given for front opening and hem
trim until belt measures 120 (130: 140: 150: 160)cm,
ending with RS facing for next row.
Cast off in rib.

Chart A

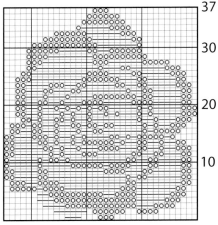

Chart B

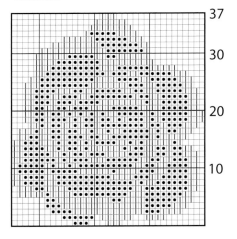

Chart C

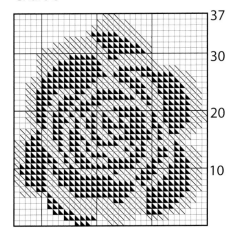

key

☐	A	⊟	E
⊠	B	◲	F
⊡	C	◣	G
Ⅱ	D	◹	H

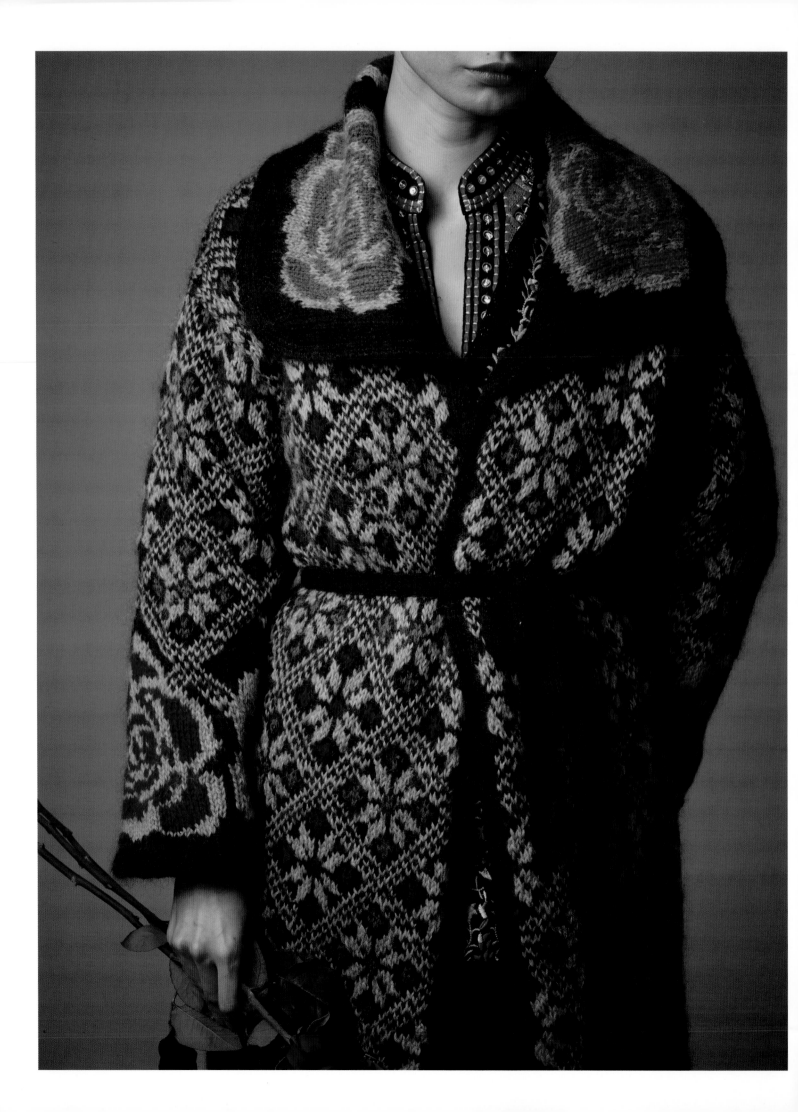

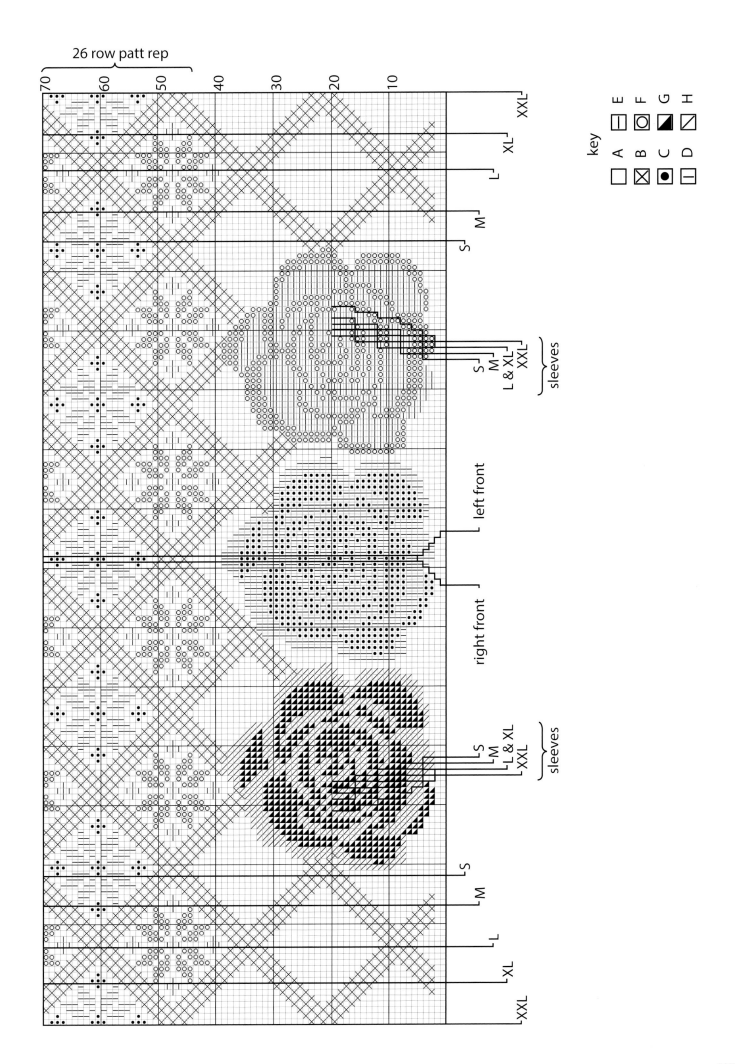

26 row patt rep

70 60 50 40 30 20 10

XXL XL L M S M S L & XL XXL sleeves

left front

right front

S M L & XL XXL sleeves

S M L XL XXL

key

A E
B F
C G
D H

WENTWORTH

Kaffe Fassett

● ●

SIZE

S (M: L: XL: XXL)
To fit bust
81-86 (91-97: 102-107: 112-117: 22-127)cm
32-34 (36-38: 40-42: 44-46: 48-50)in

YARN

Rowan Kidsilk Haze

1 (2: 2: 2: 2) x 25g balls of Rowan Kidsilk Haze in Blushes 583 (A)
1 (1: 1: 1: 1) x 25g ball of Rowan Kidsilk Haze in Candy Girl 606 (B)
1(1: 1: 1: 1) x 25g ball of Rowan Kidsilk Haze in Splendour 579 (C)
1(1: 1: 1: 1) x 25g ball of Rowan Kidsilk Haze in Liqueur 595 (D)
1 (1: 2: 2:2) x 25g balls of Rowan Kidsilk Haze in Anthracite 639 (E)
1 (1: 2: 2:2) x 25g balls of Rowan Kidsilk Haze in Drab 611 (F)
1 (1: 2: 2:2) x 25g balls of Rowan Kidsilk Haze in Dewberry 600 (G)
1 (1: 1: 1: 1) x 25g ball of Rowan Kidsilk Haze in Smoke 605 (H)
1 (1: 1: 1: 2) x 25g balls of Rowan Kidsilk Haze in Trance 582 (I)
1 (1: 1: 1: 1) x 25g ball of Rowan Kidsilk Haze in Meadow 581 (J)
1 (1: 1: 1: 1) x 25g ball of Rowan Kidsilk Haze in Fern 629 (K)
1 (1: 1: 1: 1) x 25g ball of Rowan Kidsilk Haze in Blackcurrant 641 (L)

1 (1: 1: 1: 1) x 25g ball of Rowan Kidsilk Haze in Heavenly 592 (M)
1 (1: 1: 1: 1) x 25g ball of Rowan Kidsilk Haze in Hurricane 632 (N)
1 (1: 1: 1: 1) x 25g ball of Rowan Kidsilk Haze in Blood 627 (O)
1 (1: 1: 1: 1) x 25g ball of Rowan Kidsilk Haze in Brick 649 (P)

NEEDLES

1 pair 3mm (no 11) (US 2/3) needles
1 pair 3¼mm (no 10) (US 3) needles

BUTTONS

5 x BN1367 (15mm) from Bedecked.
Please see information page for contact details.

TENSION

25 sts and 34 rows to 10cm (4in) measured over striped stocking stitch using 3¼mm (US 3) needles.

STRIPE SEQUENCE

Beg with a K row, work in st st in stripe sequence as follows:
Row 1: Using yarn B.
Row 2: Using yarn C.
Rows 3 and 4: Using yarn D.
Rows 5 and 6: Using yarn E.
Row 7: Using yarn F.
Row 8: Using yarn G.
Rows 9 and 10: Using yarn H.
Row 11: Using yarn I.
Row 12: Using yarn J.
Rows 13 to 15: Using yarn F.
Row 16: Using yarn K.
Row 17: Using yarn L.
Row 18: Using yarn D.
Rows 19 and 20: Using yarn E.
Rows 21 and 22: Using yarn I.
Row 23: Using yarn G.
Row 24: Using yarn A.
Row 25: Using yarn M.
Row 26: Using yarn N.
Row 27: Using yarn F.
Row 28: Using yarn C.
Rows 29 and 30: Using yarn G.
Row 31: Using yarn M.
Rows 32 and 33: Using yarn E.

Row 34: Using yarn I.
Rows 35 and 36: Using yarn K.
Row 37: Using yarn O.
Row 38: Using yarn A.
Rows 39 and 40: Using yarn G.
Row 41: Using yarn H.
Rows 42 and 43: Using yarn P.
Row 44: Using yarn A.
These 44 rows form stripe sequence.

Pattern note: To avoid distorting the garment, ensure all cast-on and cast-off edges are worked loosely. If necessary, use a larger size needle.

BACK

Using 3mm (US 2/3) needles and yarn A, cast on 113 (125: 141: 155: 173) sts.
Row 1 (RS): K1, *P1, K1, rep from * to end.
Row 2: As row 1.
These 2 rows form moss st.
Work in moss st for a further 2 rows, ending with RS facing for next row.
Change to 3¼mm (US 3) needles.
Beg with stripe row 1, now work in stripe sequence throughout (see above) as follows:
Dec 1 st at each end of 5th and 3 foll 8th rows.
105 (117: 133: 147: 165) sts.
Work 13 rows, ending with RS facing for next row.
Inc 1 st at each end of next and 3 foll 12th rows.
113 (125: 141: 155: 173) sts.
Cont straight until back measures 30 (31: 32: 33: 34)cm, ending with RS facing for next row.
Shape armholes
Keeping stripes correct, cast off 6 (7: 8: 9: 10) sts at beg of next 2 rows.
101 (111: 125: 137: 153) sts.
Dec 1 st at each end of next 3 (5: 7: 9: 11) rows, then on foll 4 (4: 6: 6: 8) alt rows.
87 (93: 99: 107: 115) sts.
Cont straight until armhole measures 20 (21: 22: 23: 24)cm, ending with RS facing for next row.
Shape back neck
Next row (RS): K31 (34: 36: 40: 43) and turn, leaving rem sts on a holder.
Work each side of neck separately.
Cast off 3 sts at beg of next and foll alt row, ending with RS facing for next row.

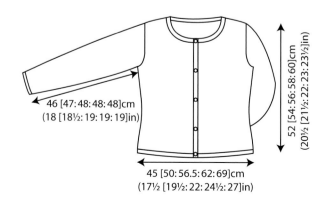

46 [47: 48: 48: 48]cm
(18 [18½: 19: 19: 19]in)

45 [50: 56.5: 62: 69]cm
(17½ [19½: 22: 24½: 27]in)

52 [54: 56: 58: 60]cm
(20½ [21½: 22: 23: 23½]in)

Shape shoulder

Cast off 11 (12: 13: 15: 17) sts at beg of next row, and 3 sts at beg of foll row.

Cast off rem 11 (13: 14: 16: 17) sts.

With RS facing, rejoin yarns to rem sts, cast off centre 25 (25: 27: 27: 29) sts, K to end.

Complete to match first side, reversing shapings.

LEFT FRONT

Using 3mm (US 2/3) needles and yarn A, cast on 55 (61: 69: 77: 85) sts.

Work in moss st as given for back for 4 rows, dec 0 (0: 0: 1: 0) st at end of last row, ending with RS facing for next row. 55 (61: 69: 76: 85) sts.

Change to 3¼mm (US 3) needles.

Beg with stripe row 1, now work in stripe sequence throughout (see above) as follows:

Dec 1 st at beg of 5th and 3 foll 8th rows. 51 (57: 65: 72: 81) sts.

Work 13 rows, ending with RS facing for next row.

Inc 1 st at beg of next and 3 foll 12th rows. 55 (61: 69: 76: 85) sts.

Cont straight until left front matches back to beg of armhole shaping, ending with RS facing for next row.

Shape armhole

Keeping stripes correct, cast off 6 (7: 8: 9: 10) sts at beg of next row.

49 (54: 61: 67: 75) sts.

Work 1 row.

Dec 1 st at armhole edge of next 3 (5: 7: 9: 11) rows, then on foll 4 (4: 6: 6: 8) alt rows. 42 (45: 48: 52: 56) sts.

Cont straight until 35 (35: 37: 37: 39) rows less have been worked than on back to beg of back neck shaping, ending with WS facing for next row.

Shape neck

Keeping stripes correct, cast off 10 sts at beg of next row.

32 (35: 38: 42: 46) sts.

Dec 1 st at neck edge of next 5 rows, then on 2 (2: 3: 3: 4) alt rows, then on 3 foll 4th rows. 22 (25: 27: 31: 34) sts.

Work 17 rows, ending with RS facing for next row.

Shape shoulder

Cast off 11 (12: 13: 15: 17) sts at beg of next row.

Work 1 row.

Cast off rem 11 (13: 14: 16: 17) sts.

RIGHT FRONT

Using 3mm (US 2/3) needles and yarn A, cast on 55 (61: 69: 77: 85) sts.

Work in moss st as given for back for 4 rows, dec 0 (0: 0: 1: 0) st at beg of last row and ending with RS facing for next row.

55 (61: 69: 76: 85) sts.

Change to 3¼mm (US 3) needles.

Beg with stripe row 1, now work in stripe sequence throughout (see above) as follows:

Dec 1 st at end of 5th and 3 foll 8th rows. 51 (57: 65: 72: 81) sts.

Complete to match left front, reversing shapings.

SLEEVES (both alike)

Using 3mm (US 2/3) needles and yarn A, cast on 51 (53: 57: 57: 59) sts.

Work in moss st as given for back for 4 rows, ending with RS facing for next row.

Change to 3¼mm (US 3) needles.

Beg with stripe row 1, now work in stripe sequence throughout (see above) as follows:

Inc 1 st at each end of 3rd and every foll 6th (4th: 6th: 4th: 4th) row to 97 (59: 105: 71: 79) sts, then on every foll – (6th: -: 6th: 6th) row until there are – (101: -: 109: 113) sts.

Cont straight until sleeve measures 46 (47: 48: 48: 48)cm, ending with RS facing for next row.

Shape top

Keeping stripes correct, cast off 6 (7: 8: 9: 10) sts at beg of next 2 rows. 85 (87: 89: 91: 93) sts.

Dec 1 st at each end of next 3 rows, then on every foll alt row until 61 sts rem, then on foll 7 rows, ending with RS facing for next row. 47 sts.

Cast off 7 sts at beg of next 2 rows.

Cast off rem 33 sts.

MAKING UP

Press as described on the information page.

Join both shoulder seams using back stitch, or mattress stitch if preferred.

Button band

With RS facing, using 3mm (US 2/3) needles and yarn A, pick up and knit 117 (121: 125: 129: 133) sts evenly down left front opening edge, from neck shaping to cast-on edge.

Work in moss st as given for back for 4 rows, ending with **WS** facing for next row.

Cast off in moss st (on **WS**).

Buttonhole band

With RS facing, using 3mm (US 2/3) needles and yarn A, pick up and knit 117 (121: 125: 129: 133) sts evenly up right front opening edge, from cast-on edge to neck shaping.

Work in moss st as given for back for 1 row, ending with RS facing for next row.

Row 2 (RS): Moss st 5 sts, ★cast off 2 sts (to make a buttonhole – cast on 2 sts over these cast-off sts on next row), moss st until there are 26 (27: 28: 29: 30) sts on right needle after cast-off, rep from ★ 3 times more.

Work in moss st for a further 2 rows, ending with WS facing for next row.

Cast off in moss st (on WS).

Neckband

With RS facing, using 3mm (US 2/3) needles and yarn A, beg and ending at cast-off edges of front bands, pick up and knit 45 (45: 47: 47: 49) sts up right side of neck, 51 (51: 53: 53: 55) sts from back, then 45 (45: 47: 47: 49) sts down left side of neck. 141 (141: 147: 147: 153) sts.

Work in moss st as given for back for 1 row, ending with RS facing for next row.

Row 2 (RS): Moss st 3 sts, cast off 2 sts (to make 5th buttonhole – cast on 2 sts over these cast-off sts on next row), moss st to end.

Work in moss st for a further 2 rows, ending with **WS** facing for next row.

Cast off in moss st (on **WS**).

See information page for finishing instructions, setting in sleeves using the set-in method.

WINTER FLOWER
Kim Hargreaves

● ● ●

SIZE

XS	S	M	L	XL	
To fit bust					
81	86	91	97	102	cm
32	34	36	38	40	in

YARN

Rowan Felted Tweed and DK Soft

A	Tweed	Cocoa	143				
8	8	9	9	9	x 50gm		
B	DK Soft	Flushed	172				
1	1	1	1	1	x 50gm		
C	DK Soft	Paisley	165				
1	1	1	1	1	x 50gm		
D	DK Soft	Frolic	164				
1	1	1	1	1	x 50gm		
E	DK Soft	Minty	166				
1	1	1	1	1	x 50gm		
F	DK Soft	Glacier	174				
1	1	1	1	1	x 50gm		
G	DK Soft	Sage	175				
1	1	1	1	1	x 50gm		

NEEDLES

1 pair 3¼mm (no 10) (US 3) needles
1 pair 3¾mm (no 9) (US 5) needles

BUTTONS - 7

TENSION

23 sts and 32 rows to 10cm (4in) measured over patterned stocking stitch using 3¾mm (US 5) needles.

BACK

Cast on 105 (111: 117: 123: 129) sts using 3¼mm (US 3) needles and yarn A. Work in garter st for 3 rows.

Row 4 (WS): K0 (1: 0: 1: 0), ★P1, K1, rep from ★ to last 1 (0: 1: 0: 1) st, P1 (0: 1: 0: 1).

Row 5: As row 4.

Last 2 rows form moss st.

Work in moss st for a further 3 rows.

Change to 3¾mm (US 5) needles.

Using the **intarsia** technique described on the information page, starting and ending rows as indicated, joining and breaking off colours as required and beg with a K row, work in patt foll body chart, which is worked entirely in st st, as folls:

Work 2 (2: 4: 4: 6) rows.

Dec 1 st at each end of next and every foll 6th row until 91 (97: 103: 109: 115) sts rem.

Work 7 rows, ending with chart row 46 (46: 48: 48: 50).

Inc 1 st at each end of next and every foll 8th row until there are 105 (111: 117: 123: 129) sts.

Work 9 (11: 11: 13: 13) rows, ending with chart row 104 (106: 108: 110: 112).

Shape armholes

Keeping chart correct, cast off 4 (4: 5: 5: 6) sts at beg of next 2 rows. 97 (103: 107: 113: 117) sts.

Dec 1 st at each end of next 5 (7: 7: 9: 9) rows, then on foll 4 (4: 5: 5: 6) alt rows.

79 (81: 83: 85: 87) sts.

Cont straight until chart row 172 (174: 178: 180: 184) has been completed, ending with a **WS** row.

Shape shoulders and back neck

Cast off 7 (7: 8: 8: 8) sts at beg of next 2 rows. 65 (67: 67: 69: 71) sts.

Next row (RS): Cast off 7 (7: 8: 8: 8) sts, patt until there are 12 (12: 11: 11: 12) sts on right needle and turn, leaving rem sts on a holder.

Work each side of neck separately.

Cast off 4 sts at beg of next row.

Cast off rem 8 (8: 7: 7: 8) sts.

With RS facing, rejoin yarn to rem sts, cast off centre 27 (29: 29: 31: 31) sts, patt to end.

Work to match first side, reversing shapings.

LEFT FRONT

Cast on 58 (61: 64: 67: 70) sts using 3¼mm (US 3) needles and yarn A.

Work in garter st for 3 rows.

Row 4 (WS): ★K1, P1, rep from ★ to last 0 (1: 0: 1: 0) st, K0 (1: 0: 1: 0).

Row 5: K0 (1: 0: 1: 0), ★P1, K1,

rep from ★ to end.

Last 2 rows form moss st.

Work in moss st for a further 2 rows.

Row 8 (WS): Moss st 5 and slip these sts onto a holder for button band, moss st to end. 53 (56: 59: 62: 65) sts.

Change to 3¾mm (US 5) needles and work in patt foll body chart as folls:

Work 2 (2: 4: 4: 6) rows.

Dec 1 st at beg of next and every foll 6th row until 46 (49: 52: 55: 58) sts rem.

Work 7 rows, ending with chart row 46 (46: 48: 48: 50).

Inc 1 st at beg of next and every foll 8th row until there are 53 (56: 59: 62: 65) sts.

Work 9 (11: 11: 13: 13) rows, ending with chart row 104 (106: 108: 110: 112).

Shape armhole

Keeping chart correct, cast off 4 (4: 5: 5: 6) sts at beg of next row. 49 (52: 54: 57: 59) sts.

Work 1 row.

Dec 1 st at armhole edge of next 5 (7: 7: 9: 9) rows, then on foll 4 (4: 5: 5: 6) alt rows.

40 (41: 42: 43: 44) sts.

Cont straight until chart row 151 (153: 157: 157: 161) has been completed, ending with a **RS** row.

Shape neck

Keeping chart correct, cast off 8 sts at beg of next row, and 4 sts at beg of foll alt row. 28 (29: 30: 31: 32) sts.

Dec 1 st at neck edge of next 3 rows, then on foll 2 (3: 3: 4: 4) alt rows, then on foll 4th row. 22 (22: 23: 23: 24) sts.

Cont straight until chart row 172 (174: 178: 180: 184) has been completed, ending with a **WS** row.

Shape shoulder

Cast off 7 (7: 8: 8: 8) sts at beg of next and foll alt row.

Work 1 row. Cast off rem 8 (8: 7: 7: 8) sts.

RIGHT FRONT

Cast on 58 (61: 64: 67: 70) sts using 3¼mm (US 3) needles and yarn A.

Work in garter st for 3 rows.

Row 4 (WS): K0 (1: 0: 1: 0), ★P1, K1, rep from ★ to end.

Row 5: K1, P2tog, yrn (to make a buttonhole), P1, ★K1, P1, rep from ★ to last 0 (1: 0: 1: 0) st, K0 (1: 0: 1: 0).

Work in moss st as set for a further 2 rows.

Row 8 (WS): Moss st to last 5 sts and turn, leaving last 5 sts on a holder for buttonhole band. 53 (56: 59: 62: 65) sts.

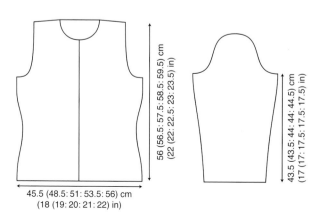

56 (56.5: 57.5: 58.5: 59.5) cm
(22 (22: 22.5: 23: 23.5) in)

45.5 (48.5: 51: 53.5: 56) cm
(18 (19: 20: 21: 22) in)

43.5 (43.5: 44: 44: 44.5) cm
(17 (17: 17.5: 17.5: 17.5) in)

Change to 3¾mm (US 5) needles and work in patt foll
body chart as folls:
Work 2 (2: 4: 4: 6) rows. Dec 1 st at end of next and
every foll 6th row until 46 (49: 52: 55: 58) sts rem.
Work to match left front, reversing shapings.

SLEEVES (both alike)
Cast on 49 (49: 53: 53: 53) sts using 3¼mm (US 3)
needles and yarn A.
Work in garter st for 3 rows.
Work in moss st as given for back for 5 rows, ending
with a **WS** row.
Change to 3¾mm (US 5) needles and work in patt foll
sleeve chart as folls:
Work 2 rows.
Inc 1 st at each end of next and every foll 8th row until
there are 79 (79: 83: 83: 87) sts.
Cont straight until chart row 132 (132: 134: 134: 136)
has been completed, ending with a **WS** row.
Shape top
Keeping chart correct, cast off 4 (4: 5: 5: 6) sts at beg of
next 2 rows. 71 (71: 73: 73: 75) sts.
Dec 1 st at each end of next 3 rows, then on foll 3 alt rows,
then on every foll 4th row until
47 (47: 49: 49: 51) sts rem.
Work 1 row, ending with a **WS** row.
Dec 1 st at each end of next and foll 1 (1: 2: 2: 3) alt rows,
then on foll 7 rows. 29 sts.
Cast off 4 sts at beg of next 2 rows.
Cast off rem 21 sts.

MAKING UP
PRESS all pieces as described on the info page.
Join both shoulder seams using back stitch.
Button band
Slip 5 sts left on holder for button band onto 3¼mm
(US 3) needles and rejoin yarn A with RS facing.
Cont in moss st as set until band, when slightly stretched,
fits up left front opening edge to neck shaping, ending
with a **WS** row. Cast off.
Slip stitch band in place.
Mark positions for 7 buttons on this band – lowest
button level with buttonhole already made in right front,
top button 1 cm below neck shaping and rem 5 buttons
evenly spaced between.
Buttonhole band
Work as given for button band, rejoining yarn with
WS facing and with the addition of a further 6
buttonholes to correspond with positions marked for
buttons worked as folls:
Buttonhole row (RS): K1, P2tog, yrn (to make a
buttonhole), P1, K1.
Slip stitch band in place.
Neckband
With RS facing, 3¼mm (US 3) needles and yarn A,
starting and ending halfway across top of front bands,
pick up and knit 36 (37: 37: 39: 39) sts up right side of
neck, 35 (37: 37: 39: 39) sts from back, and
36 (37: 37: 39: 39) sts down left side of neck.
107 (111: 111: 117: 117) sts.
Row 1 (WS): K1, *P1, K1, rep from * to end.
Rep last row 4 times more.
Knit 3 rows.
Cast off knitwise (on **WS**).
See information page for finishing instructions, setting in
sleeves using the set-in method.

Key

□ A
− B
⊠ C
± D
☑ E
· F
○ G

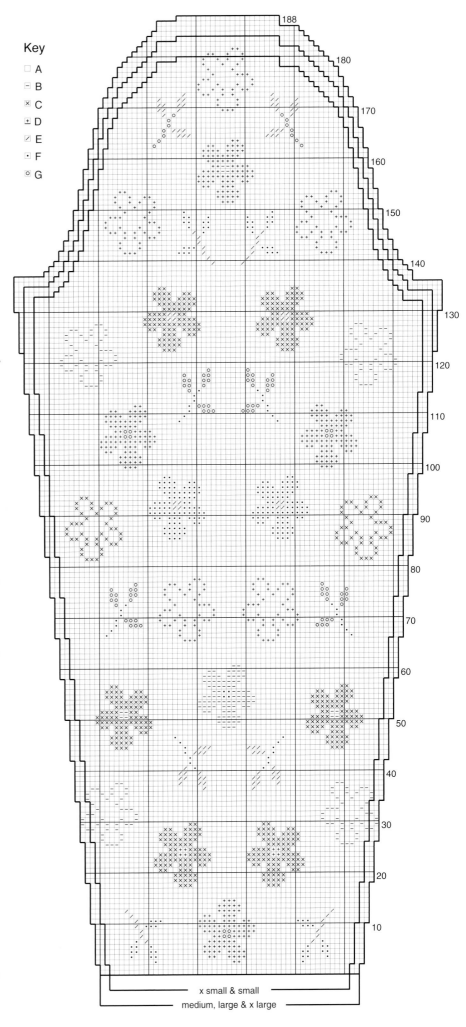

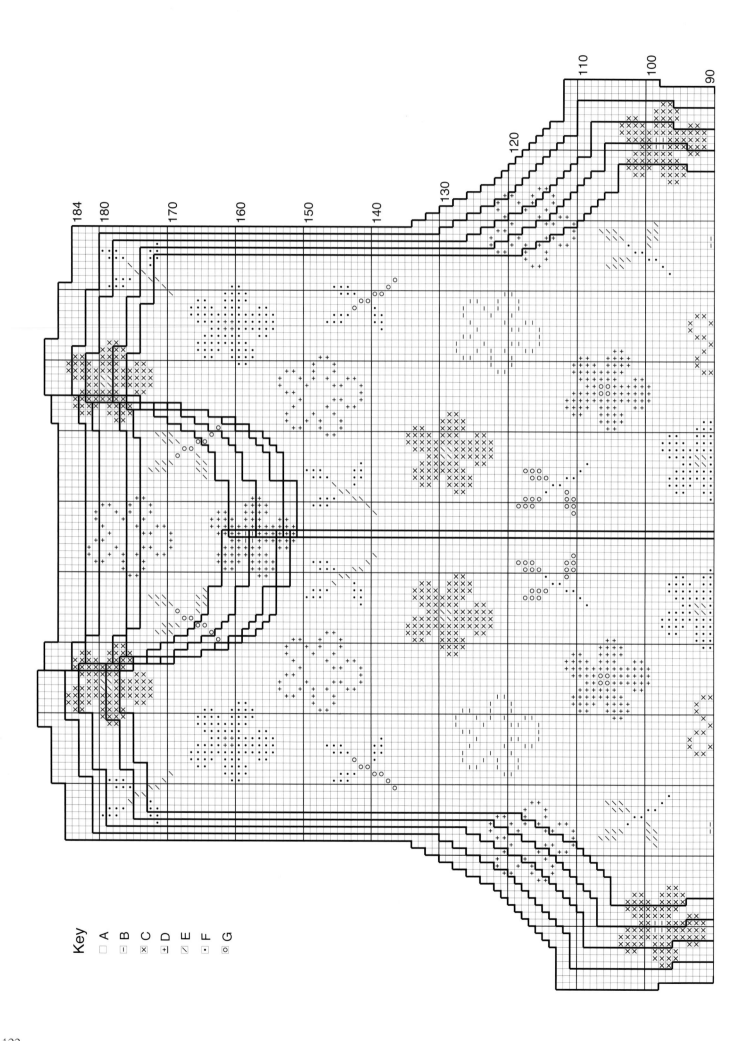

Key

A □
B │
C ⊠
D +
E ╲
F ·
G ○

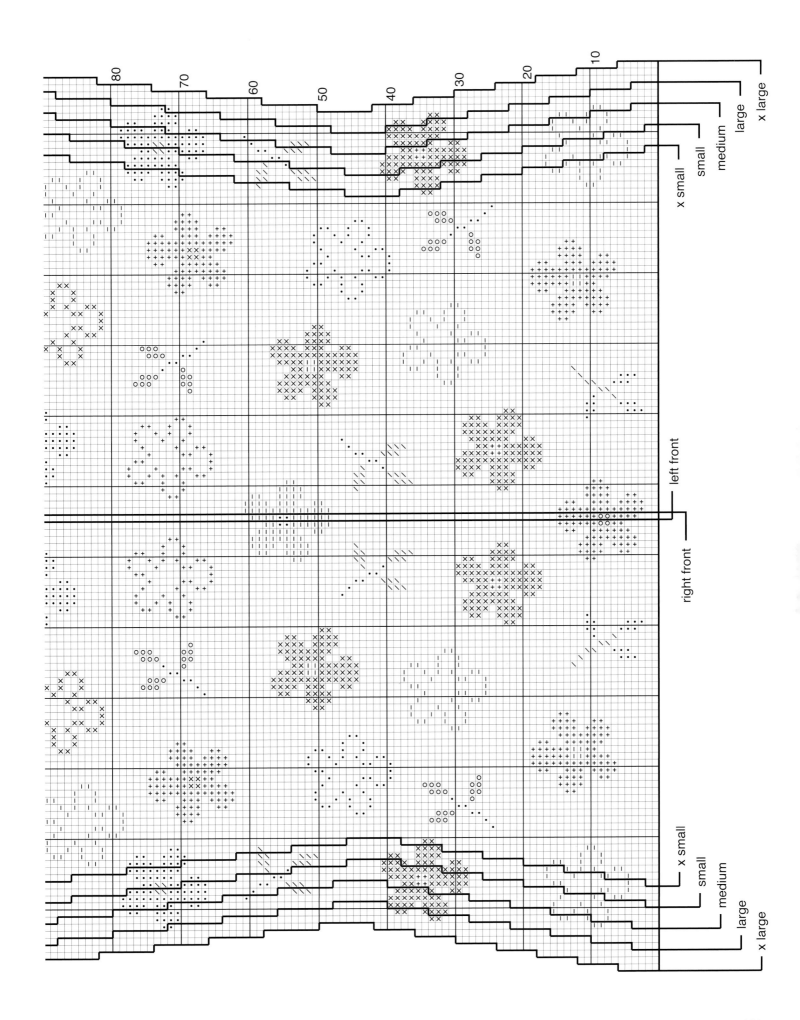

RE-PHOTOGRAPHED
& RESTYLED

ROWAN

Fashions come and go, but Rowan's timeless designs will always be the epitome of style.
In this section we've taken 20 of our classic patterns from the past 40 years and knitted them in new yarns
and refreshed colour palettes. The stunning results, photographed in a picturesque Cotswold village, prove
that you can make any of these pieces your own. Restyled and re-shot, but unmistakably Rowan.

Designs featured:

Agnes (Magazine 35)   Monty (Magazine 28)
Bressay Hap Shawl (Magazine 42)   Olive (Magazine 26)
Brocade (Magazine 38)   Onza (Magazine 28)
Burghley (Magazine 46)   Orkney (Magazine 52)
Celtic (Magazine 40)   Plaid Coat (Magazine 10)
Dhurrie (Magazine 54)   Plain Cellini (Magazine 44)
Flora MacDonald (Magazine 30)   Powder Puff (Magazine 34)
Gameboard Jacket (Magazine 28)   Robinia (Magazine 50)
Kirkwall Wrap (Magazine 52)   Soumak Wrap (Magazine 54)
Martha (Magazine 28)   Wayfarer (Magazine 48)

RESTYLED PHOTOGRAPHY
Photographer Jesse Wild
Art Direction & Styling Georgina Brant
Hair & Make-up Lauren Palmer
Models Lanna Alder & Kate Waldron (Boss Models)

ARCHIVE
GALLERY

ROWAN

AGNES	BRESSAY HAP SHAWL	BROCADE	BURGHLEY	CELTIC

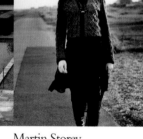

Kim Hargreaves	Sharon Miller	Kaffe Fassett	Marie Wallin	Martin Storey
Magazine 35	Magazine 42	Magazine 38	Magazine 46	Magazine 40
Page 168	*Page 172*	*Page 174*	*Page 176*	*Page 178*

DHURRIE	FLORA MacDONALD	GAMEBOARD JACKET	KIRKWALL WRAP	MARTHA

Lisa Richardson	Sarah Dallas	Brandon Mably	Julia Frank	Kim Hargreaves
Magazine 54	Magazine 30	Magazine 28	Magazine 52	Magazine 28
Page 180	*Page 182*	*Page 184*	*Page 188*	*Page 190*

MONTY   OLIVE   ONZA   ORKNEY   PLAID COAT

Kim Hargreaves
Magazine 28
Page 192

Kim Hargreaves
Magazine 26
Page 194

Kim Hargreaves
Magazine 28
Page 196

Marie Wallin
Magazine 52
Page 198

Kim Hargreaves
Magazine 10
Page 202

PLAIN
CELLINI   POWDER
PUFF   ROBINIA   SOUMAK
WRAP   WAYFARER

Marie Wallin
Magazine 44
Page 206

Kaffe Fassett
Magazine 34
Page 208

Marie Wallin
Magazine 50
Page 210

Lisa Richardson
Magazine 54
Page 214

Lisa Richardson
Magazine 48
Page 216

AGNES
Kim Hargreaves
Magazine 35
Page 168

BRESSAY HAP SHAWL

Sharon Miller

Magazine 42

Page 172

BROCADE

Kaffe Fassett
Magazine 38
Page 174

CELTIC

Martin Storey
Magazine 40
Page 178

DHURRIE
Lisa Richardson
Magazine 54
Page 180

FLORA MacDONALD

Sarah Dallas

Magazine 30

Page 182

GAMEBOARD JACKET

Brandon Mably

Magazine 28

Page 184

KIRKWALL WRAP

Julia Frank
Magazine 52
Page 188

MARTHA

Kim Hargreaves
Magazine 28
Page 190

MONTY

Kim Hargreaves
Magazine 28
Page 192

MONTY
Kim Hargreaves
Magazine 28

ONZA
Kim Hargreaves
Magazine 28
Page 196

ORKNEY

Marie Wallin
Magazine 52
Page 198

PLAID COAT

Kim Hargreaves
Magazine 10
Page 202

PLAIN CELLINI

Marie Wallin
Magazine 44
Page 206

POWDER PUFF

Kaffe Fassett
Magazine 34
Page 208

ROBINIA

Marie Wallin
Magazine 50
Page 210

SOUMAK WRAP

Lisa Richardson

Magazine 54

Page 214

WAYFARER

Lisa Richardson
Magazine 48
Page 216

AGNES
Kim Hargreaves

●●

SIZE

To fit bust

81	86	91	97	102	cm
32	34	36	38	40	in

Actual bust measurement of garment

86	91	96.5	101.5	107	cm
34	36	38	40	42	in

YARN

Rowan Cotton Glace

A Oyster 730

10	11	11	12	12	x 50gm

B Nightshade 746

1	1	1	1	1	x 50gm

NEEDLES

1 pair 2¾mm (no 12) (US 2) needles
1 pair 3mm (no 11) (US 2/3) needles
1 pair 3¼mm (no 10) (US 3) needles

BUTTONS

7 x BN 1510/20 from Bedecked. Please see information page for contact details.

TENSION

23 sts and 39 rows to 10cm (4in) measured over moss stitch, 23 sts and 32 rows to 10cm (4in) measured over st st using 3¼mm (US 3) needles.

BACK

Lower section

Using 3mm (US 2/3) needles and yarn A, cast on 99 [105: 111: 117: 123] sts.
Row 1 (RS): K1, *P1, K1, rep from * to end.
Row 2: As row 1.
These 2 rows form moss st.
Work in moss st for a further 4 rows, ending with RS facing for next row.
Change to 3¼mm (US 3) needles.
Work a further 14 rows, ending with RS facing for next row.
Place markers on 26th [28th: 30th: 32nd: 34th] st in from both ends of last row.
Next row (RS): Work 2tog, moss st to within 1 st of first marker, work 3tog (marked st is centre st of this group), moss st to within 1 st of 2nd marker, work 3tog (marked st is centre st of this group), moss st to last 2 sts, work 2tog.
Work 15 rows.
Rep last 16 rows once more, then first of these rows (the dec row) again. 81 [87: 93: 99: 105] sts.
Work a further 9 rows, ending with RS facing.
Cast off in moss st.

Upper section

With WS facing (so that ridge is formed on RS of work), using 3¼mm (US 3) needles and yarn A, pick up and knit 81 [87: 93: 99: 105] sts across cast-off edge of lower section.
Beg with a K row, work in st st for 8 rows, ending with RS facing for next row.
Cont in patt as follows:
Row 1 (RS): K2, M1, K6 [1: 4: 7: 2],
*P1, K7, rep from * to last 9 [4: 7: 10: 5] sts, P1, K6 [1: 4: 7: 2], M1, K2.
Working all side seam increases as set by last row and beg with a P row, work in st st for 9 rows, inc 1 st at each end of 6th of these rows.
85 [91: 97: 103: 109] sts.
Row 11 (RS): K6 [9: 4: 7: 2], *P1, K7, rep from * to last 7 [10: 5: 8: 3] sts, P1, K6 [9: 4: 7: 2].
Beg with a P row, work in st st for 9 rows, inc 1 st at each end of 2nd and foll 6th row.
89 [95: 101: 107: 113] sts.
Last 20 rows form patt and start side seam shaping.
Cont in patt, shaping side seams by inc 1 st at each end of 5th and every foll 6th row to 95 [101: 107: 113: 119] sts, then on every foll 4th row until there are
99 [105: 111: 117: 123] sts, taking inc sts into patt.

Cont straight until back measures 35 [36: 36: 37: 37]cm **from cast-on edge of lower section**, ending with RS facing for next row.

Shape armholes

Keeping patt correct, cast off 3 [4: 4: 5: 5] sts at beg of next 2 rows. 93 [97: 103: 107: 113] sts.
Dec 1 st at each end of next 5 [5: 7: 7: 9] rows, then on foll 2 [3: 3: 4: 4] alt rows, then on foll 4th row. 77 [79: 81: 83: 85] sts.
Cont straight until armhole measures 20 [20: 21: 21: 22]cm, ending with RS facing for next row.

Shape shoulders and back neck

Cast off 8 sts at beg of next 2 rows.
61 [63: 65: 67: 69] sts.
Next row (RS): Cast off 8 sts, patt until there are 11 [11: 12: 12: 13] sts on right needle and turn, leaving rem sts on a holder.
Work each side of neck separately.
Cast off 4 sts at beg of next row.
Cast off rem 7 [7: 8: 8: 9] sts.
With RS facing, rejoin yarn to rem sts, cast off centre 23 [25: 25: 27: 27] sts, patt to end.
Complete to match first side, reversing shapings.

LEFT FRONT

Lower section

Using 3mm (US 2/3) needles and yarn A, cast on 53 [56: 59: 62: 65] sts.
Row 1 (RS): *K1, P1, rep from * to last 1 [0: 1: 0: 1] st, K1 [0: 1: 0: 1].
Row 2: K1 [0: 1: 0: 1], *P1, K1, rep from * to end.
These 2 rows form moss st.
Work in moss st for a further 4 rows, ending with RS facing for next row.
Change to 3¼mm (US 3) needles.
Work a further 14 rows, ending with RS facing for next row.
Place marker on 26th [28th: 30th: 32nd: 34th] st in from end of last row.
Next row (RS): Work 2tog, moss st to within 1 st of marker, work 3tog (marked st is centre st of this group), moss st to end.
Work 15 rows.
Rep last 16 rows once more, then first of these rows (the dec row) again. 44 [47: 50: 53: 56] sts.
Work a further 9 rows, ending with RS facing for next row.
Next row (RS): Cast off first 39 [42: 45: 48: 51] sts, moss st to end.

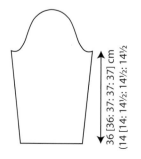

36 [36: 37: 37: 37] cm
(14 [14: 14½: 14½: 14½] in)

55 [56: 57: 58: 59] cm
(21½ [22: 22½: 23: 23] in)

43 [45.5: 48.5: 51: 53.5] cm
(17 [18: 19: 20: 21] in)

Do NOT break yarn.

Upper section

Using 3¼mm (US 3) needles and yarn A, moss st 5 sts on needle, then with WS facing (so that ridge is formed on RS of work), pick up and knit 39 [42: 45: 48: 51] sts across cast-off edge of lower section. 44 [47: 50: 53: 56] sts.

Next row (RS): K to last 5 sts, moss st 5 sts.

Next row: Moss st 5 sts, P to end.

These 2 rows set the sts – front opening edge 5 sts still in moss st with all other sts in st st. Work a further 6 rows as set, ending with RS facing for next row.

Cont in patt as follows:

Row 1 (RS): K2, M1, K6 [1: 4: 7: 2], *P1, K7, rep from * to last 12 sts, P1, K6, moss st 5 sts.

Working all side seam increases as set by last row, keeping moss st border correct and working all other sts in st st, beg with a P row, work 9 rows, inc 1 st at beg of 6th of these rows. 46 [49: 52: 55: 58] sts.

Row 11 (RS): K6 [9: 4: 7: 2], *P1, K7, rep from * to last 8 sts, P1, K2, moss st 5 sts.

Work 9 rows, inc 1 st at beg of 2nd and foll 6th row. 48 [51: 54: 57: 60] sts.

Last 20 rows form patt and start side seam shaping.

Cont in patt, shaping side seam by inc 1 st at beg of 5th and every foll 6th row to 51 [54: 57: 60: 63] sts, then on every foll 4th row until there are 53 [56: 59: 62: 65] sts, taking inc sts into patt.

Cont straight until left front matches back to beg of armhole shaping, ending with RS facing for next row.

Shape armhole

Keeping patt correct, cast off 3 [4: 4: 5: 5] sts at beg of next row. 50 [52: 55: 57: 60] sts.

Work 1 row.

Dec 1 st at armhole edge of next 5 [5: 7: 7: 9] rows, then on foll 2 [3: 3: 4: 4] alt rows, then on foll 4th row. 42 [43: 44: 45: 46] sts.

Cont straight until 22 [22: 22: 24: 24] rows less have been worked to start of shoulder shaping, ending with RS facing for next row.

Shape lapel

Next row (RS): Patt to last 5 sts, moss st 5 sts.

Next row: Moss st 6 sts, P to end.

Next row: Patt to last 7 sts, moss st 7 sts.

Next row: Moss st 8 sts, P to end.

Work 8 [9: 9: 10: 10] rows, working one extra st in moss st on every row as set by last 4 rows (16 [17: 17: 18: 18] sts now in moss st).

Work a further 10 [9: 9: 10: 10] rows but now working one extra st in moss st on 3rd and every foll 3rd row, ending with RS facing for next row – 19 [20: 20: 21: 21] sts now in moss st.

Shape shoulder

Cast off 8 sts at beg of next and foll alt row, then 7 [7: 8: 8: 9] sts at beg of foll alt row.

Work 1 row, ending with RS facing for next row.

Break yarn and leave rem 19 [20: 20: 21: 21] sts on a holder.

Mark positions for 7 buttons along opening edge of upper section, first to come in row 5,

last to come 6 rows below lapel shaping and rem 5 buttons evenly spaced between.

RIGHT FRONT

Lower section

Using 3mm (US 2/3) needles and yarn A, cast on 53 [56: 59: 62: 65] sts.

Row 1 (RS): K1 [0: 1: 0: 1], *P1, K1, rep from * to end.

Row 2: *K1, P1, rep from * to last 1 [0: 1: 0: 1] st, K1 [0: 1: 0: 1].

These 2 rows form moss st.

Work in moss st for a further 4 rows, ending with RS facing for next row.

Change to 3¼mm (US 3) needles.

Work a further 14 rows, ending with RS facing for next row.

Place marker on 26th [28th: 30th: 32nd: 34th] st in from beg of last row.

Next row (RS): Moss st to within 1 st of marker, work 3tog (marked st is centre st of this group), moss st to last 2 sts, work 2tog.

Work 15 rows.

Rep last 16 rows once more, then first of these rows (the dec row) again. 44 [47: 50: 53: 56] sts.

Work a further 3 rows, ending with RS facing for next row.

Next row (RS): Moss st 2 sts, work 2tog, yrn (to make first buttonhole), moss st to end.

Work a further 5 rows, ending with RS facing for next row.

Next row (RS): Moss st 5 sts, cast off rem 39 [42: 45: 48: 51] sts.

Upper section

With WS facing (so that ridge is formed on RS of work), using 3¼mm (US 3) needles and yarn A, pick up and knit 39 [42: 45: 48: 51] sts across cast-off edge of lower section, then moss st rem 5 sts. 44 [47: 50: 53: 56] sts.

Next row (RS): Moss st 5 sts, K to end.

Next row: P to last 5 sts, moss st 5 sts.

These 2 rows set the sts – front opening edge 5 sts still in moss st with all other sts in st st. Work a further 2 rows as set, ending with a WS row.

Next row (RS): Moss st 2 sts, work 2tog, yrn (to make a buttonhole), patt to end.

Working a further 6 buttonholes in this way to correspond with positions marked for buttons on left front and noting that no further reference will be made to buttonholes, cont as follows:

Work a further 3 rows as set, ending with a WS row.

Cont in patt as follows:

Row 1 (RS): Moss st 5 sts, K6, *P1, K7, rep from * to last 9 [4: 7: 10: 5] sts, P1, K6 [1: 4: 7: 2], M1, K2.

Working all side seam increases as set by last row, keeping moss st border correct and working all other sts in st st, beg with a P row, work 9 rows, inc 1 st at end of 6th of these rows. 46 [49: 52: 55: 58] sts.

Row 11 (RS): Moss st 5 sts, K2, *P1, K7, rep from * to last 7 [10: 5: 8: 3] sts, P1, K6 [9: 4: 7: 2].

Work 9 rows, inc 1 st at end of 2nd and foll 6th row. 48 [51: 54: 57: 60] sts.

Last 20 rows form patt and start side seam shaping.

Cont in patt, shaping side seam by inc 1 st at end of 5th and every foll 6th row to 51 [54: 57: 60: 63] sts, then on every foll 4th row until there are 53 [56: 59: 62: 65] sts, taking inc sts into patt.

Cont straight until right front matches back to beg of armhole shaping, ending with WS facing for next row.

Shape armhole

Keeping patt correct, cast off 3 [4: 4: 5: 5] sts at beg of next row. 50 [52: 55: 57: 60] sts.

Dec 1 st at armhole edge of next 5 [5: 7: 7: 9] rows, then on foll 2 [3: 3: 4: 4] alt rows, then on foll 4th row. 42 [43: 44: 45: 46] sts.

Cont straight until 22 [22: 22: 24: 24] rows less have been worked to start of shoulder shaping, ending with RS facing for next row.

Shape lapel

Next row (RS): Moss st 5 sts, patt to end.

Next row: Patt to last 6 sts, moss st 6 sts.

Next row: Moss st 7 sts, patt to end.

Next row: Patt to last 8 sts, moss st 8 sts.

Work 8 [9: 9: 10: 10] rows, working one extra st in moss st on every row as set by last 4 rows – 16 [17: 17: 18: 18] sts now in moss st.

Work a further 11 [10: 10: 11: 11] rows but now working one extra st in moss st on 3rd and every foll 3rd row, ending with WS facing for next row. – 19 [20: 20: 21: 21] sts now in moss st.

Shape shoulder

Cast off 8 sts at beg of next and foll alt row, then 7 [7: 8: 8: 9] sts at beg of foll alt row, ending with RS facing for next row. **Do NOT break yarn** but leave rem 19 [20: 20: 21: 21] sts on a holder and set aside this ball of yarn.

SLEEVES (both alike)

Using 3¼mm (US 3) needles and yarn A, cast on 59 [59: 61: 63: 63] sts.

Beg with a K row, work in st st for 10 rows, ending with RS facing for next row.

Cont in patt as follows:

Row 1 (RS): K5 [5: 6: 7: 7], *P1, K7, rep from * to last 6 [6: 7: 8: 8] sts, P1, K5 [5: 6: 7: 7].

Working all increases in same way as for back and fronts and beg with a P row, work in st st for 9 rows, inc 1 st at each end of 4th of these rows. 61 [61: 63: 65: 65] sts.

Row 11 (RS): K2 [2: 3: 4: 4], *P1, K7, rep from * to last 3 [3: 4: 5: 5] sts, P1, K2 [2: 3: 4: 4].

Beg with a P row, work in st st for 9 rows, inc 1 st at each end of 0 [8th: 8th: 8th: 6th] of these rows. 61 [63: 65: 67: 67] sts.

Last 20 rows form patt and start sleeve shaping.

Cont in patt, shaping sides by inc 1 st at each end of next [11th: 13th: 13th: 9th] and every foll 14th [12th: 12th: 12th: 12th] row to 73 [75: 77: 79: 73] sts, then on every foll - [-: -: -: 10th] row until there are - [-: -: -: 81] sts, taking inc sts into patt.

Cont straight until sleeve measures 36 [36: 37: 37: 37]cm, ending with a WS row.

Shape top

Keeping patt correct, cast off 3 [4: 4: 5: 5] sts at
beg of next 2 rows. 67 [67: 69: 69: 71] sts.
Dec 1 st at each end of next 5 rows, then on foll
2 alt rows, then on every foll 4th row until
41 [41: 43: 43: 45] sts rem.
Work 1 row, ending with a WS row.
Dec 1 st at each end of next and every foll alt
row to 35 sts, then on foll row, ending with RS
facing for next row. 33 sts.
Cast off 4 sts at beg of next 2 rows.
Cast off rem 25 sts.

MAKING UP

Press as described on the information page.
Join both shoulder seams using back stitch, or
mattress stitch if preferred.

Collar

With RS facing, using 3mm (US 2/3) needles
and ball of yarn A set to one side with right front,
moss st across 19 [20: 20: 21: 21] sts of right front,
pick up and knit 31 [33: 33: 35: 35] sts from back,
then moss st across 19 [20: 20: 21: 21] sts of left
front. 69 [73: 73: 77: 77] sts.
Work in moss st as set by fronts for 3cm.
Cast off in moss st.

Cuffs (both alike)

Using 2¾mm (US 2) needles and yarn A, cast on
63 [63: 65: 67: 67] sts.
Work in moss st as given for back for 7.5cm.
Cast off in moss st.
See information page for finishing instructions,
setting in sleeves using the set-in method. Join
row-end edges of cuffs for 3cm from cast-off
edge. Positioning cuff seam directly opposite
sleeve seam, sew cast-off edge of cuffs to lower
edges of sleeves. Fold cuffs to RS. Using yarn B,
embroider a French knot onto each P st
of pattern on upper sections of back, fronts
and sleeves.

BRESSAY HAP SHAWL

Sharon Miller

FINISHED SIZE

Completed shawl measures approx 134cm (53in) square when pressed

YARN

Rowan Felted Tweed

A Watery 152	4	x 50gm
B Pine 158	1	x 50gm
C Treacle 145	1	x 50gm
D Rage 150	1	x 50gm
E Ginger 154	1	x 50gm
F Peony 183	1	x 50gm
G Camel 157	1	x 50gm

NEEDLES

1 pair 6mm (no 4) (US 10) needles

TENSION

10 sts and 24 rows to 10cm (4in) measured over border pattern when pressed using 6mm (US 10) needles.

SHAWL

Edging

Using 6mm (US 10) needles and yarn A, cast on 11 sts.
Knit 1 row.
Now work edging patt as follows:
Row 1 (WS): Yfwd, K2tog, K7, yfwd, K2. 12 sts.
Row 2: K1, K2tog, yfwd, K2tog, K6, K1 tbl. 11 sts.
Row 3: Yfwd, K2tog, K4, K2tog, yfwd, K2tog, K1. 10 sts.
Row 4: K1, K2tog, yfwd, K2tog, K4, K1 tbl. 9 sts.

Row 5: Yfwd, K2tog, K2, K2tog, yfwd, K2tog, K1. 8 sts.
Row 6: K1, K2tog, yfwd, K2tog, K2, K1 tbl. 7 sts.
Row 7: Yfwd, K2tog, K2, K2tog, K1. 6 sts.
Row 8: K1, K2tog, K2, K1 tbl. 5 sts.
Row 9: Yfwd, K2tog, K3.
Row 10: K4, K1 tbl.
Row 11: Yfwd, K2tog, K1, yfwd, K2. 6 sts.
Row 12: K2, yfwd, K3, K1 tbl. 7 sts.
Row 13: Yfwd, K2tog, K3, yfwd, K2. 8 sts.
Row 14: K2, yfwd, K5, K1 tbl. 9 sts.
Row 15: Yfwd, K2tog, K5, yfwd, K2. 10 sts.
Row 16: K2, yfwd, K7, K1 tbl. 11 sts.
These 16 rows form edging patt.
Rep last 16 rows 14 times more.
Cast off.

Work border

With WS facing, using 6mm (US 10) needles and yarn A, pick up and knit 120 sts evenly along straight row-end edge of edging, picking up 8 sts for each edging patt rep and working through the "yfwd" along side of edging.
Rows 1 and 2: Inc in first st, K to last st, inc in last st. 124 sts.
Rows 3 and 4: Knit.
Break off yarn A and join in yarn B.
Rows 5 to 8: Knit.
Row 9 (RS): K5, *K1, (K2tog) 3 times, (yfwd, K1) 5 times, yfwd, (sl 1, K1, psso) 3 times, K1, rep from * to last 5 sts, K5.
Row 10: Knit.
Rows 5 to 10 form border patt.
Joining in and breaking off colours as required and keeping border patt correct, work in stripes as follows:
Rows 11 to 16: Using yarn C.
Rows 17 to 20: Using yarn D.
Rows 21 to 26: Using yarn E.
Rows 27 and 28: Using yarn F.
Rows 29 and 30: Using yarn G.
Rows 31 to 34: Using yarn F.
Rows 35 to 40: Using yarn G.
Rows 41 to 44: Using yarn F.
Rows 45 and 46: Using yarn G.
Rows 47 and 48: Using yarn F.
Rows 49 to 54: Using yarn E.
Rows 55 and 56: Using yarn D.
Now shape corners as follows:
Place markers 24 sts in from both ends of last row.
Row 57 (RS): Using yarn D, K3, (K2tog) 5 times, (yfwd, K1) 4 times, yfwd, (sl 1, K1, psso) 3 times, K1, slip marker onto right needle, patt to next marker, slip marker onto right needle, K1, (K2tog) 3 times, (yfwd, K1) 4 times, yfwd, (sl 1, K1, psso) 5 times, K3. 118 sts.
Row 58: Using yarn D, knit.
Rows 59 to 62: Using yarn C, knit.
Row 63: Using yarn C, K3, (K2tog) 4 times, (yfwd, K1) 3 times, yfwd, (sl 1, K1, psso) 3 times, K1, slip marker onto right needle, patt to next marker, slip marker onto right needle, K1, (K2tog) 3 times, (yfwd, K1) 3 times, yfwd, (sl 1, K1, psso) 4 times, K3. 112 sts.
Row 64: Using yarn C, knit.
Rows 65 to 68: Using yarn B, knit.
Row 69: Using yarn B, K3, (K2tog) 3 times,

(yfwd, K1) twice, yfwd, (sl 1, K1, psso) 3 times, K1, slip marker onto right needle, patt to next marker, slip marker onto right needle, K1, (K2tog) 3 times, (yfwd, K1) twice, yfwd, (sl 1, K1, psso) 3 times, K3. 106 sts.
Row 70: Using yarn B, K to last 2 sts, K2tog. 105 sts.
Break off contrasts and cont using yarn A only.
Work in g st for 6 rows, dec 1 st at each end of every row and ending with RS facing for next row. 93 sts.
Cast off loosely.
Make a further edging and border in this way. These 2 sections form side borders of centre section.
Now make a further 2 edging and border sections in exactly the same way but do NOT cast off at ends of these sections.
Slip sts of one of these sections onto a holder – this forms top border.

Centre section

Working on 93 sts still on needles after 4th edging and border section is complete, cont as follows:
Row 1 (RS): K1, *yfwd, K2tog, rep from * to end. 93 sts.
Row 2: As row 1.
Work in g st for 8 rows, ending with RS facing for next row.
Now work in centre lace patt as follows:
Row 1 (RS): K4, *K2tog, yfwd, K1, yfwd, sl 1, K1, psso, K3, rep from * to last st, K1.
Row 2 and every foll alt row: Knit.
Row 3: K3, *K2tog, yfwd, K3, yfwd, sl 1, K1, psso, K1, rep from * to last 2 sts, K2.
Row 5: K2, K2tog, yfwd, *K5, yfwd, sl 1, K2tog, psso, yfwd, rep from * to last 9 sts, K5, yfwd, sl 1, K1, psso, K2.
Row 7: K3, *yfwd, sl 1, K1, psso, K3, K2tog, yfwd, K1, rep from * to last 2 sts, K2.
Row 9: K4, *yfwd, sl 1, K1, psso, K1, K2tog, yfwd, K3, rep from * to last st, K1.
Row 11: K5, *yfwd, sl 1, K2tog, psso, yfwd, K5, rep from * to end.
Row 12: As row 2.
These 12 rows form centre lace patt.
Rep last 12 rows 13 times more.
Work in g st for 6 rows, ending with RS facing for next row.
Join sts of this section to sts of top border by grafting sts together.

MAKING UP

Sew side border sections to row-end edges of centre section, then join corners of border and edging sections.
Pin out to measurement given, cover with damp cloths and leave to dry naturally.

BROCADE
Kaffe Fassett

● ● ●

SIZE
To fit bust

81	86	91	97	102	cm
32	34	36	38	40	in

Actual bust measurement of garment

84	89	94	100	105	cm
33	35	37	39½	41½	in

YARN
Rowan Felted Tweed and Kidsilk Haze

A Felted Tweed Watery 152

5	5	5	6	6	x 50gm

B Kidsilk Haze Peacock 671

4	4	4	4	4	x 25gm

C Felted Tweed Avocado 161

4	4	5	5	5	x 50gm

D Kidsilk Haze Jelly 597

3	3	4	4	4	x 25gm

NEEDLES
1 pair 4mm (no 8) (US 6) needles
1 pair 4½mm (no 7) (US 7) needles

TENSION
22 sts and 28 rows to 10cm (4in) measured over patterned st st using 4½mm (US 7) needles.

Note: Yarns A and B are used together throughout and Yarns C and D are used together throughout.

BACK
Using 4mm (US 6) needles and yarns A and B together, cast on 90 [98: 102: 110: 114] sts. Break off yarns A and B and join in yarns C and D.
Row 1 (RS): K2, *P2, K2, rep from * to end.
Row 2: P2, *K2, P2, rep from * to end.
These 2 rows form rib.
Work in rib for a further 14 rows, inc 1 [0: 1: 0: 1] st at each end of last row and ending with RS facing for next row.
92 [98: 104: 110: 116] sts.
Change to 4½mm (US 7) needles.
Beg and ending rows as indicated and using the intarsia technique as described on the information page, cont in patt from chart, which is worked entirely in st st beg with a K row, as follows:
Cont straight until chart row 92 [94: 96: 98: 98] has been completed, ending with RS facing for next row. Back should measure 37 [37: 39: 40: 40]cm.
Shape armholes
Place markers at both ends of last row to denote base of armholes.
Keeping chart correct, dec 1 st at each end of next 6 rows. 80 [86: 92: 98: 104] sts.
Cont straight until chart row 140 [142: 146: 148: 152] has been completed, ending with RS facing for next row. Armhole should measure 17 [17: 18: 18: 19]cm.
Shape shoulders and back neck
Next row (RS): Cast off 12 [13: 14: 15: 17] sts, patt until there are 16 [17: 19: 20: 21] sts on right needle and turn, leaving rem sts on a holder.
Work each side of neck separately.
Cast off 4 sts at beg of next row.
Cast off rem 12 [13: 15: 16: 17] sts.
With RS facing, rejoin yarns to rem sts, cast off centre 24 [26: 26: 28: 28] sts, patt to end.
Complete to match first side, reversing shapings.

FRONT
Work as given for back until 16 [16: 16: 18: 18] rows less have been worked than on back to beg of shoulder shaping, ending with RS facing for next row.
Shape neck
Next row (RS): Patt 32 [34: 37: 40: 43] sts and turn, leaving rem sts on a holder.
Work each side of neck separately.
Keeping patt correct, dec 1 st at neck edge of next 4 rows, then on foll 4 [4: 4: 5: 5] alt rows.
24 [26: 29: 31: 34] sts.

Work 3 rows, ending with RS facing for next row.
Shape shoulder
Cast off 12 [13: 14: 15: 17] sts at beg of next row.
Work 1 row.
Cast off rem 12 [13: 15: 16: 17] sts.
With RS facing, rejoin yarns to rem sts, cast off centre 16 [18: 18: 18: 18] sts, patt to end.
Complete to match first side, reversing shapings.

SLEEVES (both alike)
Using 4mm (US 6) needles and yarns A and B together, cast on 42 [42: 46: 46: 46] sts. Break off yarns A and B and join in yarns C and D.
Work in rib as given for back for 12 rows, ending with RS facing for next row.
Change to 4½mm (US 7) needles.
Beg and ending rows as indicated, cont in patt from chart as follows:
Inc 1 st at each end of 3rd and every foll 6th [6th: 6th: 6th: 4th] row to 76 [76: 78: 78: 58] sts, then on every foll – [–: 8th: 8th: 6th] row until there are – [–: 80: 80: 84] sts, taking inc sts into patt.
Cont straight until chart row 112 [112: 114: 114: 114] has been completed, ending with RS facing for next row. Sleeve should measure 44 [44: 45: 45: 45]cm.
Shape top
Place markers at both ends of last row to denote base of armholes.
Keeping patt correct, dec 1 st at each end of next 6 rows, ending with RS facing for next row.
Cast off rem 64 [64: 68: 68: 72] sts.

MAKING UP
Press as described on the information page.
Join right shoulder seam using back stitch, or mattress stitch if preferred.
Collar
With RS facing, using 4½mm (US 7) needles and yarns C and D, pick up and knit 17 [17: 17: 18: 20] sts down left side of neck, 16 [18: 18: 18: 18] sts from front, and 17 [17: 17: 18: 20] sts up right side of neck, then 32 [34: 34: 36: 36] sts from back.
82 [86: 86: 90: 94] sts.
Work in rib as given for back for 20cm.
Break off yarns C and D and join in yarns A and B.
Using yarns A and B, cast off in rib.
See information page for finishing instructions, setting in sleeves using the shallow set-in method and reversing collar seam for turn-back.

42 [44.5: 47: 50: 52.5] cm
16½ [17½: 18½: 19½: 20½] in

55 [55: 58: 59: 60] cm
21½ [21½: 23: 23: 23½] in

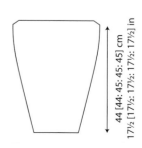

44 [44: 45: 45: 45] cm
17½ [17½: 17½: 17½: 17½] in

■ A & B used together
■ C & D used together

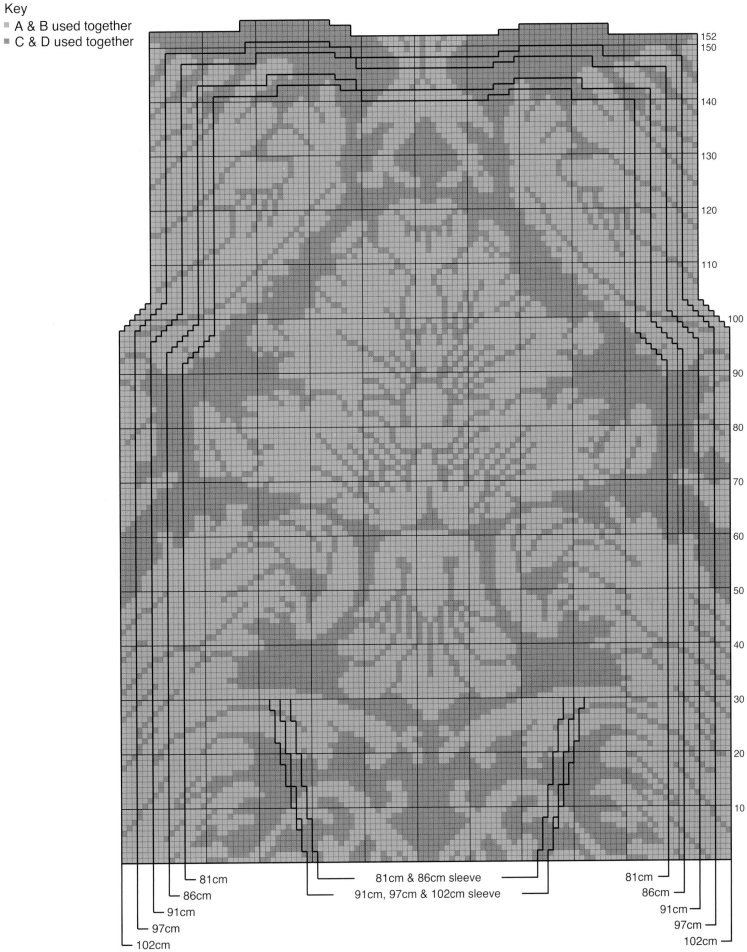

81cm
86cm
91cm
97cm
102cm

81cm & 86cm sleeve
91cm, 97cm & 102cm sleeve

81cm
86cm
91cm
97cm
102cm

152
150
140
130
120
110
100
90
80
70
60
50
40
30
20
10

BURGHLEY
Marie Wallin

● ● ●

SIZE

To fit bust

81-86	91-97	102-107	112-117	122-127	cm
32-34	36-38	40-42	44-46	48-50	in

Actual bust measurement of garment

94.5	104	116	128.5	142.5	cm
37¼	41	45½	50½	56	in

YARN

Rowan Felted Tweed

A Treacle 145

8	8	9	10	11	x 50gm

B Tawny 186

5	5	6	6	6	x 50gm

C Ancient 172

2	3	3	3	3	x 50gm

NEEDLES

1 pair 3¾mm (no 9) (US 5) needles
3¾mm (no 9) (US 5) circular needle at least
140cm long

TENSION

26 sts and 40 rows to 10cm (4in) measured over main
and sleeve patterns, 26 sts and 50 rows to 10cm (4in)
measured over border pattern, both using 3¾mm
(US 5) needles.

Pattern note: When working patt, work all slipped sts
purlwise with yarn at WS (back on RS rows, front on
WS rows) of work.

BACK

Using 3¾mm (US 5) needles and yarn A, cast on
135 [147: 163: 179: 197] sts.
Row 1 (RS): Using yarn A, K3 [1: 1: 1: 2],
*sl 1, K3, rep from * to last 4 [2: 2: 2: 3] sts, sl 1,
K3 [1: 1: 1: 2].
Row 2: As row 1.
Join in yarn C.
Rows 3 and 4: Using yarn C, K1 [3: 3: 3: 4],
*sl 1, K3, rep from * to last 2 [4: 4: 4: 5] sts, sl 1,
K1 [3: 3: 3: 4].
These 4 rows form border patt.
Cont in border patt until back measures 12cm,
ending with WS facing for next row.
Break off yarn C.
Now work in main patt as follows:
Row 1 (WS): Using yarn A, purl.
Join in yarn B.
Row 2: Using yarn B, K3 [1: 1: 1: 2], *sl 1, K3,
rep from * to last 4 [2: 2: 2: 3] sts, sl 1, K3 [1: 1: 1: 2].
Row 3: As row 2.
Row 4: Using yarn A, K1 [3: 3: 3: 4], *sl 1, K3,
rep from * to last 2 [4: 4: 4: 5] sts, sl 1,
K1 [3: 3: 3: 4].
Row 5: As row 4.
Row 6: As row 2.
Row 7: Using yarn B, purl.
Row 8: As row 4.
These 8 rows form main patt.
Cont in main patt, shaping side seams by dec
1 st at each end of 2nd and 5 foll 12th rows.
123 [135: 151: 167: 185] sts.
Cont straight until back measures
51 [52: 53: 54: 55]cm, ending with RS facing for
next row.

Shape armholes

Keeping patt correct, cast off 6 [7: 8: 9: 10] sts at
beg of next 2 rows. 111 [121: 135: 149: 165] sts.
Dec 1 st at each end of next 3 [5: 7: 9: 11] rows,
then on foll 4 [4: 6: 7: 8] alt rows.
97 [103: 109: 117: 127] sts.
Cont straight until armhole measures
20 [21: 22: 23: 24]cm, ending with RS facing for
next row.

Shape back neck

Next row (RS): Patt 33 [36: 38: 42: 46] sts and
turn, leaving rem sts on a holder.
Work each side of neck separately.

Cast off 2 sts at beg of next and foll 2 alt rows,
ending with RS facing for next row.
27 [30: 32: 36: 40] sts.

Shape shoulder

Cast off 12 [14: 15: 17: 19] sts at beg of next row,
then 2 sts at beg of foll row.
Cast off rem 13 [14: 15: 17: 19] sts.
With RS facing, rejoin yarns to rem sts, cast off
centre 31 [31: 33: 33: 35] sts, patt to end.
Complete to match first side, reversing shapings.

LEFT FRONT

Using 3¾mm (US 5) needles and yarn A, cast on
83 [89: 97: 105: 114] sts.
Row 1 (RS): Using yarn A, K3 [1: 1: 1: 2], *sl
1, K3, rep from * to end.
Row 2: Using yarn A, K3, *sl 1, K3, rep from *
to last 4 [2: 2: 2: 3] sts, sl 1, K3 [1: 1: 1: 2].
Join in yarn C.
Row 3: Using yarn C, K1 [3: 3: 3: 4], *sl 1, K3,
rep from * to last 2 sts, sl 1, K1.
Rows 4: Using yarn C, K1, *sl 1, K3, rep from
* to last 2 [4: 4: 4: 5] sts, sl 1, K1 [3: 3: 3: 4].
These 4 rows form border patt.
Cont in border patt until left front measures
12cm, ending with WS facing for next row.
Break off yarn C.
Now work in main patt as follows:
Row 1 (WS): Using yarn A, cast off 16 sts,
P to end. 67 [73: 81: 89: 98] sts.
Join in yarn B.
Row 2: Using yarn B, K3 [1: 1: 1: 2], *sl 1, K3,
rep from * to end.
Row 3: Using yarn B, K3, *sl 1, K3, rep from
* to last 4 [2: 2: 2: 3] sts, sl 1, K3 [1: 1: 1: 2].
Row 4: Using yarn A, K1 [3: 3: 3: 4], *sl 1, K3,
rep from * to last 2 sts, sl 1, K1.
Row 5: Using yarn A, K1, *sl 1, K3, rep from
* to last 2 [4: 4: 4: 5] sts, sl 1, K1 [3: 3: 3: 4].
Row 6: As row 2.
Row 7: Using yarn B, purl.
Row 8: As row 4.
Last 8 rows set position of main patt as given
for back.
Cont in main patt, shaping side seam by
dec 1 st at beg of 2nd and 5 foll 12th rows.
61 [67: 75: 83: 92] sts.
Cont straight until left front matches back to

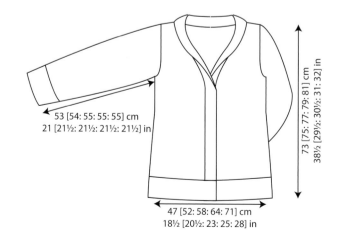

53 [54: 55: 55: 55] cm
21 [21½: 21½: 21½: 21½] in

47 [52: 58: 64: 71] cm
18½ [20½: 23: 25: 28] in

73 [75: 77: 79: 81] cm
38½ [29½: 30½: 31: 32] in

beg of armhole shaping, ending with RS facing for next row.

Shape armhole

Keeping patt correct, cast off 6 [7: 8: 9: 10] sts at beg of next row. 55 [60: 67: 74: 82] sts.

Work 1 row.

Dec 1 st at armhole edge of next 3 [5: 7: 9: 11] rows, then on foll 4 [3: 2: 1: 0] alt rows. 48 [52: 58: 64: 71] sts.

Work 1 row, ending with RS facing for next row.

Shape front slope

Keeping patt correct, dec 1 st at end of next and foll 14 [12: 12: 10: 10] alt rows, then on 8 [10: 11: 13: 14] foll 4th rows **and at same time** dec 1 st at armhole edge on 0 [next: next: next: next] and foll 0 [0: 3: 5: 7] alt rows. 25 [28: 30: 34: 38] sts.

Cont straight until left front matches back to beg of shoulder shaping, ending with RS facing for next row.

Shape shoulder

Cast off 12 [14: 15: 17: 19] sts at beg of next row. Work 1 row.

Cast off rem 13 [14: 15: 17: 19] sts.

RIGHT FRONT

Using 3¾mm (US 5) needles and yarn A, cast on 83 [89: 97: 105: 114] sts.

Row 1 (RS): Using yarn A, K3, *sl 1, K3, rep from * to last 4 [2: 2: 2: 3] sts, sl 1, K3 [1: 1: 1: 2].

Row 2: Using yarn A, K3 [1: 1: 1: 2], *sl 1, K3, rep from * to end.

Join in yarn C.

Row 3: Using yarn C, K1, *sl 1, K3, rep from * to last 2 [4: 4: 4: 5] sts, sl 1, K1 [3: 3: 3: 4].

Row 4: Using yarn C, K1 [3: 3: 3: 4], *sl 1, K3, rep from * to last 2 sts, sl 1, K1.

These 4 rows form border patt.

Cont in border patt until right front measures 12cm, ending with WS facing for next row.

Break off yarn C.

Now work in main patt as follows:

Row 1 (WS): Using yarn A, P to last 16 sts, cast off rem 16 sts. 67 [73: 81: 89: 98] sts.

Join in yarn B.

Row 2: Using yarn B, K3, *sl 1, K3, rep from * to last 4 [2: 2: 2: 3] sts, sl 1, K3 [1: 1: 1: 2].

Row 3: Using yarn B, K3 [1: 1: 1: 2], *sl 1, K3, rep from * to end.

Rejoin yarn A.

Row 4: Using yarn A, K1, *sl 1, K3, rep from * to last 2 [4: 4: 4: 5] sts, sl 1, K1 [3: 3: 3: 4].

Row 5: Using yarn A, K1 [3: 3: 3: 4], *sl 1, K3, rep from * to last 2 sts, sl 1, K1.

Row 6: As row 2.

Row 7: Using yarn B, purl.

Row 8: As row 4.

Last 8 rows set position of main patt as given for back.

Cont in main patt, shaping side seam by dec 1 st at end of 2nd and 5 foll 12th rows. 61 [67: 75: 83: 92] sts.

Complete to match left front, reversing shapings.

SLEEVES (both alike)

Using 3¾mm (US 5) needles and yarn A, cast on 75 [79: 79: 79: 83] sts.

Row 1 (RS): Using yarn A, K3, *sl 1, K3, rep from * to end.

Row 2: As row 1.

Join in yarn C.

Rows 3 and 4: Using yarn C, K1, *sl 1, K3, rep from * to last 2 sts, sl 1, K1.

These 4 rows form border patt.

Cont in border patt until sleeve measures 8cm, ending with WS facing for next row.

Break off yarn C.

Now work in sleeve patt as follows:

Row 1 (WS of cuff, RS of main section):

Using yarn A, K2, *sl 1, K into loop lying between needles, sl 1, K1, lift 4th st on right needle over first, 2nd and 3rd sts and off right needle, K1, rep from * to last st, K1.

Row 2: Using yarn A, purl.

Join in yarn B.

Row 3: Using yarn B, K4, *sl 1, K into loop lying between needles, sl 1, K1, lift 4th st on right needle over first, 2nd and 3rd sts and off right needle, K1, rep from * to last 3 sts, K3.

Row 4: Using yarn B, purl.

These 4 rows form sleeve patt.

Cont in patt for a further 28 rows, ending with RS facing for next row.

Inc 1 st at each end of next and every foll 8th [10th: 8th: 8th: 8th] row to 79 [105: 95: 115: 119] sts, then on every foll 10th [12th: 10th: –: –] row until there are 103 [107: 111: –: –] sts, taking inc sts into patt.

Cont straight until sleeve measures 53 [54: 55: 55: 55]cm from cast-on edge, ending with RS facing for next row.

Shape top

Keeping patt correct, cast off 6 [7: 8: 9: 10] sts at beg of next 2 rows.

91 [93: 95: 97: 99] sts.

Dec 1 st at each end of next 3 rows, then on every foll alt row until 65 sts rem, then on foll 11 rows, ending with RS facing for next row. 43 sts.

Cast off 5 sts at beg of next 4 rows.

Cast off rem 23 sts.

MAKING UP

Press as described on the information page.

Join both shoulder seams using back stitch, or mattress stitch if preferred.

Front band and collar

With RS facing, using 3¾mm (US 5) circular needle and yarn A, beg and ending at inner edge of 16 cast-off sts at top of border patt, pick up and knit 112 [114: 116: 120: 122] sts up right front opening edge to beg of front slope shaping, 50 [52: 55: 57: 60] sts up right front slope, 47 [47: 49: 49: 51] sts from back, 50 [52: 55: 57: 60] sts down left front slope to beg of front slope shaping, then 112 [114: 116: 120: 122] sts down left front opening edge. 371 [379: 391: 403: 415] sts.

Beg with row 2, work in border patt as given for sleeves for 15 rows, ending with RS facing for next row.

Keeping patt correct, cont as follows:

Row 16 (RS): Patt 258 [264: 274: 282: 292] sts, wrap next st (by slipping next st from left needle onto right needle, taking yarn to opposite side of work between needles and then slipping same st back onto left needle – when working back across wrapped sts, work the wrapping loop and the wrapped st tog as one st) and turn.

Row 17: Patt 145 [149: 157: 161: 169] sts, wrap next st and turn.

Row 18: Patt 141 [145: 153: 157: 165] sts, wrap next st and turn.

Row 19: Patt 137 [141: 149: 153: 161] sts, wrap next st and turn.

Row 20: Patt 133 [137: 145: 149: 157] sts, wrap next st and turn.

Row 21: Patt 129 [133: 141: 145: 153] sts, wrap next st and turn.

Cont in this way, working 4 less sts on every row before wrapping next st and turning, until the foll row has been worked:

Next row (WS): Patt 41 [45: 53: 41: 49] sts, wrap next st and turn.

Next row: Patt to end.

Work in patt across all sts for a further 15 rows, ending with RS facing for next row.

Cast off.

Neatly slip stitch row-end edges of front band to cast-off sts at top of front border patt.

See information page for finishing instructions, setting in sleeves using the set-in method.

Belt

Using 3¾mm (US 5) circular needle and yarn A, cast on 391 [403: 415: 427: 439] sts.

Work in border patt as given for sleeves for 6cm, ending with RS facing for next row.

Cast off.

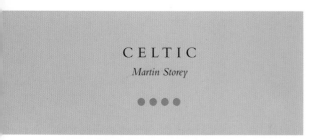

CELTIC

Martin Storey

● ● ● ●

SIZE

To fit bust

82	87	92	97	102	107	112	117cm
32	34	36	38	40	42	44	46 in

Actual measurement of garment

85	89	92	95	104	111	117	122cm
33	35	36	39	41	44	46	48 in

YARN

Rowan Felted Tweed and Kid Classic

A Felted Tweed Carbon 159

7	7	7	8	8	8	9	9 x 50gm

B Kid Classic Smoke 831

2	2	2	2	2	2	2	2 x 50gm

NEEDLES

1 pair 3¼mm (no 10) (US 3) needles
1 pair 33/4mm (no 9) (US 5) needles Cable needle

ZIP – Open-ended zip to fit

TENSION

23 sts and 32 rows to 10cm (4in) measured over st st using 3¾mm (US 5) needles and yarn A.

Pattern note: The number of sts varies whilst working the chart. All st counts given assume there are 44 sts in chart at all times. When working shaping through chart sts, ensure extra sts are decreased (or cast off) to balance the extra sts that have been increased.

SPECIAL ABBREVIATIONS

C4B = slip next 2 sts onto cable needle and leave at back of work, K2, then K2 from cable needle; **C4F** = slip next 2 sts onto cable needle and leave at front of work, K2, then K2 from cable needle; **C6B** = slip next 3 sts onto cable needle and leave at back of work, K3, then K3 from cable needle; **C6F** = slip next 3 sts onto cable needle and leave at front of work, K3, then K3 from cable needle; **Cr5R** = slip next 2 sts onto cable needle and leave at back of work, K3, then P2 from cable needle; **Cr5L** = slip next 3 sts onto cable needle and leave at front of work, P2, then K3 from cable needle; **dec7** = with yarn at front of work slip next 4 sts onto right needle, ★lift 2nd st on right needle over first st and off right needle, slip first st on right needle back onto left needle, lift 2nd st on left needle over first st and off left needle, slip first st on left needle back onto right needle, rep from ★ twice more, slip first st on right needle back onto left needle and K this st; **inc2** = (K1 tbl, K1) into next st, insert left needle point behind vertical strand that runs downwards from between 2 sts just made and K1 tbl into this loop.

BACK

Using 3¼mm (US 3) needles and yarn B cast on 84 [88: 92: 100: 106: 114: 120: 126] sts.
Work in g st for 7 rows, ending with WS facing for next row.
Row 8 (WS): K6 [8: 10: 14: 17: 21: 24: 27], M1, K2, M1, K1, M1, K13, M1, K2, M1, K1, M1, K13, M1, K2, M1, K1, M1, K2, M1, K2, M1, K1, M1, K13, M1, K2, M1, K1, M1, K13, M1, K2, M1, K1, M1, K to end.
102 [106: 110: 118: 124: 132: 138: 144] sts.
Break off yarn B and join in yarn A.
Change to 3¾mm (US 5) needles.
Place charts
Row 1 (RS): P6 [8: 10: 14: 17: 21: 24: 27], work next 44 sts as row 1 of chart, P2, work next 44 sts as row 1 of chart, P to end.
Row 2: K6 [8: 10: 14: 17: 21: 24: 27], work next 44 sts as row 2 of chart, K2, work next 44 sts as row 2 of chart, K to end.
These 2 rows set the sts – 2 charts with rev st st between and at sides.
Cont as set, shaping side seams by inc 1 st at each end of 9th and every foll 10th row until there are 116 [120: 124: 132: 138: 146: 152: 158] sts, taking inc sts into rev st st.
Cont straight until back meas
28 [28: 27: 30: 29: 31: 30: 32] cm, ending with RS facing for next row.
Shape armholes
Keeping patt correct, cast off
5 [6: 6: 7: 7: 8: 8: 9] sts at beg of next 2 rows.
106 [108: 112: 118: 124: 130: 136: 140] sts.
Dec 1 st at each end of next
3 [3: 5: 5: 7: 7: 9: 9] rows, then on foll
3 [3: 2: 3: 2: 4: 3: 3] alt rows, then on foll 4th row.
92 [94: 96: 100: 104: 106: 110: 114] sts.
Cont straight until armhole meas
19 [19: 20: 20: 21: 21: 22: 22] cm, ending with RS facing for next row.

Shape shoulders and back neck

Cast off 9 [9: 9: 10: 10: 11: 11: 12] sts at beg of next 2 rows. 74 [76: 78: 80: 84: 84: 88: 90] sts.
Next row (RS): Cast off
9 [9: 9: 10: 10: 11: 11: 12] sts, patt until there are 12 [13: 14: 14: 15: 14: 16: 16] sts on right needle and turn, leaving rem sts on a holder.
Work each side of neck separately. Cast off 4 sts at beg of next row.
Cast off rem 8 [9: 10: 10: 11: 10: 12: 12] sts.
With RS facing, rejoin yarn to rem sts, cast off centre 32 [32: 32: 32: 34: 34: 34: 34] sts dec 6 sts evenly, patt to end.
Complete to match first side, reversing shapings.

LEFT FRONT

Using 3¼ mm (US 3) needles and yarn B cast on 43 [45: 47: 51: 54: 58: 61: 64] sts.
Work in g st for 7 rows, ending with WS facing for next row.
Row 8 (WS): K2, M1, K2, M1, K1, M1, K13, M1, K2, M1, K1, M1, K13, M1, K2, M1, K1, M1, K to end. 52 [54: 56: 60: 63: 67: 70: 73] sts.
Break off yarn B and join in yarn A.
Change to 3¾ mm (US 5) needles.
Place chart
Row 1 (RS): P6 [8: 10: 14: 17: 21: 24: 27], work next 44 sts as row 1 of chart, P2.
Row 2: K2, work next 44 sts as row 2 of chart, K to end. These 2 rows set the sts – chart with rev st st at both sides.
Cont as set, shaping side seam by inc 1 st at beg of 9th and every foll 10th row until there are 59 [61: 63: 67: 70: 74: 77: 80] sts, taking inc sts into rev st st.
Cont straight until left front matches back to beg of armhole shaping, ending with RS facing for next row.
Shape armhole
Keeping patt correct, cast off
5 [6: 6: 7: 7: 8: 8: 9] sts at beg of next row.
54 [55: 57: 60: 63: 66: 69: 71] sts.
Work 1 row.
Dec 1 st at armhole edge of next
3 [3: 5: 5: 7: 7: 9: 9] rows, then
on foll 3 [3: 2: 3: 2: 4: 3: 3] alt rows, then on foll 4th row. 47 [48: 49: 51: 53: 54: 56: 58] sts.
Cont straight until
17 [17: 17: 19: 19: 19: 21: 21] rows less have been worked than on back to beg of shoulder shaping, ending with WS facing for next row.
Shape neck
Keeping patt correct, cast off
10 [10: 10: 9: 10: 10: 9: 9] sts at beg of next row. 37 [38: 39: 42: 43: 44: 47: 49] sts.
Dec 1 st at neck edge of next 7 rows, then on foll 4 [4: 4: 5: 5: 5: 6: 6] alt rows.
26 [27: 28: 30: 31: 32: 34: 36] sts.
Work 1 row, ending with RS facing for next row.
Shape shoulder
Cast off 9 [9: 9: 10: 10: 11: 11: 12] sts at beg of next and foll alt row.
Work 1 row.
Cast off rem 8 [9: 10: 10: 11: 10: 12: 12] sts.

RIGHT FRONT

Using 3¼mm (US 3) needles and yarn B cast on 43 [45: 47: 51: 54: 58: 61: 64] sts.

Work in g st for 7 rows, ending with WS facing for next row.

Row 8 (WS): K6 [8: 10: 14: 17: 21: 24: 27], M1, K2, M1, K1, M1, K13, M1, K2, M1, K1, M1, K13, M1, K2, M1, K1, M1, K2.

52 [54: 56: 60: 63: 67: 70: 73] sts.

Break off yarn B and join in yarn A.

Change to 3¾ mm (US 5) needles.

Place chart

Row 1 (RS): P2, work next 44 sts as row 1 of chart, P to end.

Row 2: K6 [8: 10: 14: 17: 21: 24: 27], work next 44 sts as row 2 of chart, K2.

These 2 rows set the sts – chart with rev st st at both sides.

Cont as set, shaping side seam by inc 1 st at end of 9th and every foll 10th row until there are 59 [61: 63: 67: 70: 74: 77: 80] sts, taking inc sts into rev st st.

Complete to match left front, reversing shapings.

SLEEVES

Using 3¼mm (US 3) needles and yarn B cast on 57 [57: 59: 59: 61: 61: 63: 63] sts.

Work in g st for 7 rows, ending with WS facing for next row.

Row 8 (WS): K11 [11: 12: 12: 13: 13: 14: 14], M1, K2, M1, K1, M1, K13, M1, K2, M1, K1, M1, K13, M1, K2, M1, K1, M1, K to end.

66 [66: 68: 68: 70: 70: 72: 72] sts.

Break off yarn B and join in yarn A.

Change to 3¾mm (US 5) needles.

Place chart

Row 1 (RS): P11 [11: 12: 12: 13: 13: 14: 14], work next 44 sts as row 1 of chart, P to end.

Row 2: K11 [11: 12: 12: 13: 13: 14: 14], work next 44 sts as row 2 of chart, K to end.

These 2 rows set the sts – chart with rev st st at both sides.

Cont as set, shaping sides by inc 1 st at each end of 11th [9th: 9th: 9th: 9th: 7th: 7th: 7th] and every foll 14th [12th: 14th: 12th: 12th: 10th: 10th: 10th] row to 74 [72: 86: 84: 84: 76: 80: 92] sts, then on every foll 16th [14th: –: 14th: 14th: 12th: 12th: 12th] row until there are 82 [84: –: 88: 90: 92: 94: 96] sts, taking inc sts into rev st st.

Cont straight until sleeve meas 45 [45: 46: 46: 47: 47: 46: 46] cm, ending with RS facing for next row.

Shape top

Keeping patt correct, cast off 5 [6: 6: 7: 7: 8: 8: 9] sts at beg of next 2 rows. 72 [72: 74: 74: 76: 76: 78: 78] sts.

Dec 1 st at each end of next 3 rows, then on foll 3 alt rows, then on every foll 4th row until 50 [50: 52: 52: 54: 54: 56: 56] sts rem.

Work 1 row.

Dec 1 st at each end of next and every foll alt row to 42 sts, then on foll 9 rows, ending with RS facing for next row.

Cast off rem 24 sts dec 3 sts evenly.

MAKING UP

Press.

Join shoulder seams using back stitch, or mattress stitch if preferred.

Front bands (both alike)

With RS facing, using 3¼ mm (US 3) needles and yarn B, pick up and knit 100 [100: 100: 105: 105: 110: 108: 113] sts evenly along front opening edge, between cast-on edge and neck shaping.

Work in g st for 2 rows, ending with WS facing for next row.

Cast off knitwise (on WS).

Collar

With RS facing, using 3¼ mm (US 3) needles and yarn B, beg and ending at cast-off edges of front bands, pick up and knit 34 [34: 34: 35: 36: 36: 37: 37] sts up right side of neck, 37 [37: 37: 37: 39: 39: 39: 39] sts from back, then 34 [34: 34: 35: 36: 36: 37: 37] sts down left side of neck. 105 [105: 105: 107: 111: 111: 113: 113] sts.

Work in g st for 10 cm, ending with WS of collar (RS of body) facing for next row.

Cast off knitwise (on WS).

Set in sleeves using the set-in method and inserting zip into front opening.

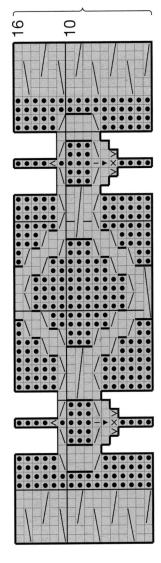

16 row patt rep

16

10

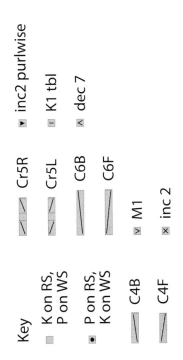

Key

■ K on RS, P on WS

• P on RS, K on WS

◢ C4B

◣ C4F

◢ Cr5R

◣ Cr5L

◢ C6B

◣ C6F

▶ inc2 purlwise

– K1 tbl

◁ dec 7

◹ M1

☒ inc 2

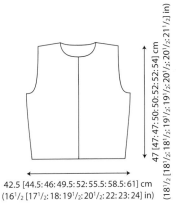

42.5 [44.5: 46: 49.5: 52: 55.5: 58.5: 61] cm
(16½ [17½: 18: 19½: 20½: 22: 23: 24] in)

47 [47: 47: 50: 50: 52: 52: 54] cm
(18½ [18½: 18½: 19½: 19½: 20½: 20½: 21½] in)

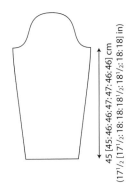

45 [45: 46: 46: 47: 47: 46: 46] cm
(17½ [17½: 18: 18: 18½: 18½: 18: 18] in)

DHURRIE
Lisa Richardson

● ● ●

SIZE
To fit bust

81-86	91-97	102-107	112-117	122-127	cm
32-34	36-38	40-42	44-46	48-50	in

Actual bust measurement of garment

72	78	84	90	96	cm
28½	30½	33	35½	38	in

YARN
Rowan Felted Tweed Aran

A Carbon 759

9	9	10	12	13	x 50g

B Clay 777

7	7	8	9	10	x 50g

NEEDLES
1 pair 4½mm (no 7) (US 7) needles
4½mm (no 7) (US 7) circular needle, at least 100cm long
5mm (no 6) (US 8) circular needle, at least 100cm long

TENSION
16½ sts and 17 rows to 10cm (4in) measured over pattern using 5mm (US 8) needles.

SPECIAL ABBREVIATIONS
sl 5 = slip 5 sts – take care not to pull yarn tightly across back (WS) of work; **wyab** = with yarn held at back of work (this is WS of work on RS rows, or RS of work on WS rows); **wyaf** = with yarn held at front of work (this is RS of work on RS rows, or WS of work on WS rows).

Pattern note: Each row is worked twice – once in each colour. Pattern is formed by first working the sts in one colour, and then sliding the sts back to the other end of the needle. The row is then worked again using the other colour. Once the row has been worked in **both** colours, turn the work ready to start the next double row.

Rows given in tension refer to actual number of **completed** rows – you will actually work 34 rows in total to achieve these 17 **completed** rows. Similarly, all rows stated in pattern instructions refer to **completed** rows.

CAPE (worked in one piece to shoulders)
Using 4½mm (US 7) circular needle and yarn A, cast on 237 [257: 277: 297: 317] sts.
Row 1 (RS): Purl.
Row 2: As row 1.
Rep last 2 rows once more, ending with RS facing for next row.
Change to 5mm (US 8) circular needle.
Join in yarn B and now work in patt as follows:
Row 1 (RS): Using yarn B, K1, *(sl 1 wyaf, sl 1 wyab) twice, sl 1 wyaf, K5, rep from * to last 6 sts, (sl 1 wyaf, sl 1 wyab) twice, sl 1 wyaf, K1, **slip sts back to other end of needle** (see pattern note), using yarn A, K1, **K5, sl 5 wyab, rep from ** to last 6 sts, K6.
Row 2: Using yarn B, K1, *(sl 1 wyaf, sl 1 wyab) twice, sl 1 wyaf, P5, rep from * to last 6 sts, (sl 1 wyaf, sl 1 wyab) twice, sl 1 wyaf, K1, **slip sts back to other end of needle**, using yarn A, K1, **P5, sl 5 wyaf, rep from ** to last 6 sts, P5, K1.
Rows 3 and 4: As rows 1 and 2.
Row 5: Using yarn B, K1, *(sl 1 wyaf, sl 1 wyab) twice, sl 1 wyaf, K5, rep from * to last 6 sts, (sl 1 wyaf, sl 1 wyab) twice, sl 1 wyaf, K1, **slip sts back to other end of needle**, using yarn A, K1, **K5, (sl 1 wyaf, sl 1 wyab) twice, sl 1 wyaf, rep from ** to last 6 sts, K6.
Row 6: Using yarn B, K1, *sl 5 wyaf, P5, rep from * to last 6 sts, sl 5 wyaf, K1, **slip sts back to other end of needle**, using yarn A, K1, **P5, (sl 1 wyaf, sl 1 wyab) twice, sl 1 wyaf, rep from ** to last 6 sts, P5, K1.
Row 7: Using yarn B, K1, *sl 5 wyab, K5, rep from * to last 6 sts, sl 5 wyab, K1, **slip sts back to other end of needle**, using yarn A, K1, **K5, (sl 1 wyaf, sl 1 wyab) twice, sl 1 wyaf, rep from ** to last 6 sts, K6.
Rows 8 and 9: As rows 6 and 7.
Row 10: Using yarn B, K1, *(sl 1 wyab, sl 1 wyaf) twice, sl 1 wyab, P5, rep from * to last 6 sts, (sl 1 wyab, sl 1 wyaf) twice, sl 1 wyab, K1, **slip sts back to other end of needle**, using yarn A, K1, **P5, sl 5 wyaf, rep from ** to last 6 sts, P5, K1.
Row 11: Using yarn B, K1, *(sl 1 wyab, sl 1 wyaf) twice, sl 1 wyab, K5, rep from * to last 6 sts, (sl 1 wyaf, sl 1 wyab) twice, sl 1 wyab, K1, **slip sts back to other end of needle**, using yarn A, K1, **K5, sl 5 wyab, rep from ** to last 6 sts, K6.
Rows 12 and 13: As rows 10 and 11.
Row 14: Using yarn B, K1, *(sl 1 wyab, sl 1 wyaf) twice, sl 1 wyab, P5, rep from * to last 6 sts, (sl 1 wyab, sl 1 wyaf) twice, sl 1 wyab, K1, **slip sts back to other end of needle**, using yarn A, K1, **P5, (sl 1 wyab, sl 1 wyaf) twice, sl 1 wyab, rep from * to last 6 sts, P5, K1.
Row 15: Using yarn B, K1, *sl 5 wyab, K5, rep from * to last 6 sts, sl 5 wyab, K1, **slip sts back to other end of needle**, using yarn A, K1, **K5, (sl 1 wyab, sl 1 wyaf) twice, sl 1 wyab, rep from ** to last 6 sts, K6.
Row 16: Using yarn B, K1, *sl 5 wyaf, P5, rep from * to last 6 sts, sl 5 wyaf, K1, **slip sts back to other end of needle**, using yarn A, K1, **P5, (sl 1 wyab, sl 1 wyaf) twice, sl 1 wyab, rep from ** to last 6 sts, P5, K1.
Rows 17 and 18: As rows 15 and 16.
These 18 rows form patt. **(Note: You are actually working 36 rows as each row is worked twice – once in each colour.)**
Work in patt for a further 2 rows, ending with RS facing for next row.
Counting in from both ends of last row, place markers after 59th [65th: 70th: 75th: 79th] sts in from both ends of row – there should be 119 [127: 137: 147: 159] sts between markers.
Keeping patt correct, now shape side seam darts as follows:
Row 21 (RS): *Patt to within 2 sts of marker, sl 1, K1, psso, slip marker onto right needle, K2tog, rep from * once more, patt to end. 233 [253: 273: 293: 313] sts.
(**Note:** When working decreases, work them on the sts that are actually knitted in this row – this may be a section using yarn A or yarn B.)
Work 3 rows.
Rep last 4 rows 2 [2: 2: 3: 3] times more.
225 [245: 265: 281: 301] sts.
Next row (RS): As row 21.
Work 1 row.
Rep last 2 rows 10 [10: 11: 10: 11] times more.
181 [201: 217: 237: 253] sts.
Next row (RS): *Patt to within 2 sts of marker, sl 1, K1, psso, slip marker onto right needle, K2tog, rep from * once more, patt to end.
Next row: *Patt to within 2 sts of marker, P2tog, slip marker onto right needle, P2tog tbl, rep from * once more, patt to end.
Rep last 2 rows 2 [3: 3: 4: 4] times more, ending with RS facing for next row.
157 [169: 185: 197: 213] sts.
Shape front neck
Still decreasing 1 st at each side of both markers on every row as now set, cast off 9 [11: 11: 11: 9] sts at beg of next 2 rows.
131 [139: 155: 167: 187] sts.
Dec 1 st at each end of next 1 [1: 3: 3: 5] rows, ending with WS facing for next row, **and at same time** still dec 1 st at each side of both markers on every row as now set.
125 [133: 137: 149: 157] sts.
Divide for shoulders
Next row (WS): (P2tog) 1 [1: 1: 1: 0] times, patt to within 2 sts of marker, P2tog and turn.
Work on this set of 24 [26: 26: 29: 31] sts only for left front as follows:
Keeping patt correct, cast off 3 sts at beg of next and foll alt row, then 4 [5: 5: 6: 7] sts at beg of foll alt row, then 5 [5: 6: 7: 7] sts at beg of foll alt row **and at same time** dec 1 st at neck edge of

next and foll 2 [2: 0: 0: 0] rows, then on foll
1 [1: 2: 2: 2] alt rows.
Work 1 row, ending with RS facing for next
row. Cast off rem 5 [6: 6: 7: 8] sts.

Shape back
With WS facing, rejoin yarn to sts left on holder,
P2tog tbl, patt to within 2 sts of next marker,
P2tog and turn.
Work on this set of 71 [75: 79: 85: 91] sts **only**
for back.
Keeping patt correct, cast off 3 sts at beg of next
4 rows, ending with RS facing for next row.
59 [63: 67: 73: 79] sts.

Shape back neck
Next row (RS): Cast off 4 [5: 5: 6: 7] sts, patt
until there are 16 [17: 18: 20: 21] sts
on right needle and turn, leaving rem sts on
a holder.
Work each side of neck separately.
Cast off 3 sts at beg of next row, 5 [5: 6: 7: 7] sts
at beg of foll row, and 3 sts at beg of next row.
Cast off rem 5 [6: 6: 7: 8] sts.
With RS facing, rejoin yarns and cast off centre
19 [19: 21: 21: 23] sts, patt to end.
Complete to match first side, reversing shapings.

Shape right front
With WS facing, rejoin yarn to sts left on holder,
P2tog tbl, patt to last 2 [2: 2: 2: 0] sts,
(P2tog) 1 [1: 1: 1: 0] times. 24 [26: 26: 29: 31] sts.
Complete to match left front, reversing shapings.

MAKING UP
Press as described on the information page.
Join both shoulder seams using back stitch,
or mattress stitch if preferred.

Front borders (both alike)
With RS facing, using 4½mm (US 7) needles
and yarn A, pick up and knit
58 [60: 62: 66: 68] sts evenly along front opening
edge, between cast-on edge and neck shaping.
Work in g st for 2 rows, ending with WS facing
for next row.
Cast off knitwise (on WS).

Scarf
Using 5mm (US 8) circular needle and yarn A,
cast on 37 sts.
(**Note:** As there are far fewer sts on scarf than
main body, you may prefer to work on double-
pointed needles.)
Row 1 (WS): Purl.
Join in yarn B and now work in patt as given
for main body until scarf strip measures approx
250cm, ending after patt row 18.
Cast off.
Mark centre point of one long edge of scarf
section. Matching this point to centre back neck
and using photograph as a guide, sew scarf strip
to neck edges.
See information page for finishing instructions.

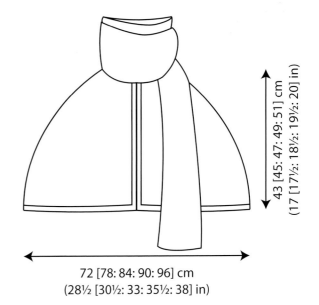

43 [45: 47: 49: 51] cm
(17 [17½: 18½: 19½: 20] in)

72 [78: 84: 90: 96] cm
(28½ [30½: 33: 35½: 38] in)

SIZE

To fit bust

81	86	91	97	102	cm
32	34	36	38	40	in

Actual bust measurement of garment

88	92	98	102	108	cm
35	36	39	40	43	in

YARN

Rowan Kidsilk Haze

A ★ Hurricane 632
2	2	3	3	3	x 25gm

B ★ Jelly 597
2	2	2	2	2	x 25gm

C ★ Shadow 653
2	2	2	2	2	x 25gm

D ★ Candy Girl 606
2	2	2	2	2	x 25gm

E ★ Liqueur 595
2	2	2	2	2	x 25gm

F ★ Romance 681
1	2	2	2	2	x 25gm

G ★ Mulberry 679
2	2	2	2	2	x 25gm

H ★ Vanilla 670
2	2	2	2	2	x 25gm

★Use Kidsilk Haze **DOUBLE** throughout.

NEEDLES

1 pair 3mm (no 11) (US 2/3) needles 1 pair 3¼mm
(no 10) (US 3) needles

BUTTONS - 6 x 15mm Shell Buttons from Groves
and Banks. See information page for contact details.

TENSION

28 sts and 36 rows to 10cm (4in) measured over
stocking stitch using 3¼mm (US 3) needles and
yarn **DOUBLE**.

WIDE STRIPE SEQUENCE

Work in 64 row stripe sequence as folls:
Rows 1 to 12: Using yarn D.
Rows 13 to 16: Using yarn F.
Rows 17 to 28: Using yarn C.
Rows 29 to 32: Using yarn B.
Rows 33 to 44: Using yarn E.
Rows 45 to 48: Using yarn G.
Rows 49 to 60: Using yarn H.
Rows 61 to 64: Using yarn A.
Rep these 64 rows.

NARROW STRIPE SEQUENCE

Work in 32 row stripe sequence as folls:
Rows 1 to 4: Using yarn D.
Rows 5 to 8: Using yarn F.
Rows 9 to 12: Using yarn C.
Rows 13 to 16: Using yarn B.
Rows 17 to 20: Using yarn E.
Rows 21 to 24: Using yarn G.
Rows 25 to 28: Using yarn H.
Rows 29 to 32: Using yarn A.
Rep these 32 rows.

BACK

Using 3mm (US 2/3) needles and yarn B
DOUBLE cast on 243 [259: 275: 283: 299] sts.
★★Break off yarn B and join in yarn A.
Row 1 (RS): P3, ★K5, P3, rep from ★ to end.
Row 2: K3, ★P5, K3, rep from ★ to end.
Rows 3 and 4: As rows 1 and 2.
Row 5: P3, ★K1, sl 1, K2tog, psso, K1, P3, rep
from ★ to end. 183 [195: 207: 213: 225] sts.
Row 6: K3, ★P3, K3, rep from ★ to end.
Row 7: P3, ★K3, P3, rep from ★ to end.
Row 8: As row 6.
Row 9: P3, ★sl 1, K2tog, psso, P3, rep from
★ to end. 123 [131: 139: 143: 151] sts.
Row 10: K3, ★P1, K3, rep from ★ to end.★★
Work in g st for 4 rows, dec 0 [1: 1: 0: 0] sts at
each end of first of these rows.
123 [129: 137: 143: 151] sts.
Change to 3¼mm (US 3) needles.
Using the **intarsia** technique as described on
the information page and starting and ending
rows as indicated, work 24 rows in patt from
chart, which is worked entirely in st st.
(**Note:** if desired, vertical lines of chart worked
using yarn B and spots in yarn D can be swiss
darned onto work afterwards and chart simply
knitted in stripes.)
Beg with a K row, cont in st st in wide stripe
sequence (as detailed above) as folls:
Cont straight until back measures
23 [24: 24: 25: 25] cm from cast-on edge, ending
with RS facing for next row.
Shape armholes
Keeping stripe sequence correct, cast off 4 sts at
beg of next 2 rows. 115 [121:129: 135: 143] sts.
Dec 1 st at each end of next and foll 6 alt rows.
101 [107: 115: 121: 129] sts.
Cont straight until armhole measures

21 [21: 22: 22: 23] cm, ending with RS facing
for next row.
Shape shoulders and back neck
Keeping stripe sequence correct, cast off
9 [10: 11: 12: 13] sts at beg of next 2 rows.
83 [87: 93: 97: 103] sts.
Next row (RS): Cast off 9 [10: 11: 12: 13] sts,
K until there are 14 [14: 16: 16: 18] sts on right
needle and turn, leaving rem sts on a holder.
Work each side of neck separately.
Cast off 4 sts at beg of next row.
Cast off rem 10 [10: 12: 12: 14] sts.
With RS facing, rejoin yarn to rem sts, cast off
centre 37 [39: 39: 41: 41] sts, K to end.
Complete to match first side, reversing shapings.

LEFT FRONT

Using 3mm (US 2/3) needles and yarn B
DOUBLE cast on 123 [131: 139: 147: 155] sts.
Work as given for back from ★★ to ★★.
63 67: 71: 75: 79) sts.
Work in g st for 4 rows, dec 1 [2: 2: 3: 3] sts
evenly across first of these rows.
62 [65: 69: 72: 76] sts.
Change to 3¼mm (US 3) needles.
Starting and ending rows as indicated, work
24 rows in patt from chart.
Beg with a K row, cont in st st in wide stripe
sequence (as detailed above) as folls:
Cont straight until left front matches back to
beg of armhole shaping, ending with RS facing
for next row.
Shape armhole
Keeping stripe sequence correct, cast off 4 sts at
beg of next row. 58 [61: 65: 68: 72] sts.
Work 1 row.
Dec 1 st at armhole edge of next and foll 6 alt
rows. 51 [54: 58: 61: 65] sts.
Cont straight until 19 [19: 19: 21: 21] rows
less have been worked than on back to start of
shoulder shaping, ending with WS facing for
next row.
Shape neck
Cast off 9 [10: 10: 10: 10] sts at beg of next row,
and 5 sts at beg of foll alt row.
37 [39: 43: 46: 50] sts.
Dec 1 st at neck edge on next 7 rows, then on
foll 1 [1: 1: 2: 2] alt rows, then on foll 4th row.
28 (30: 34: 36: 40) sts.
Work 3 rows, ending with RS facing for next
row.
Shape shoulder
Keeping stripe sequence correct, cast off
9 [10: 11: 12: 13] sts at beg of next and foll
alt row.
Work 1 row.
Cast off rem 10 [10: 12: 12: 14] sts.

RIGHT FRONT

Work to match left front, reversing shapings.

SLEEVES

Using 3mm (US 2/3) needles and yarn B
DOUBLE cast on 63 [63: 65: 67: 67] sts.
Work in g st for 2 rows.
Break off yarn B and join in yarn A.
Work in g st for 6 rows.
Change to 3¼mm (US 3) needles.

Beg with a K row, cont in st st in narrow stripe sequence (as detailed above) as folls:
Inc 1 st at each end of 3rd and every foll 6th row to 111 [111: 109: 115: 103] sts, then on every foll 4th row until there are 113 [113: 119: 119: 125] sts.
Cont straight until sleeve measures 46 [46: 47: 47: 47] cm, ending with RS facing for next row.

Shape top
Keeping stripe sequence correct, cast off 4 sts at beg of next 2 rows. 105 [105: 111: 111: 117] sts.
Dec 1 st at each end of next and foll 5 alt rows.
Work 1 row.
Cast off rem 93 [93: 99: 99: 105] sts.

MAKING UP
Press as described on the information page.
Join shoulder seams using back stitch, or mattress stitch if preferred.

Buttonhole border
With RS facing, using 3mm (US 2/3) needles and yarn A **DOUBLE**, pick up and knit 102 [102: 102: 107: 107] sts evenly along right front opening edge between top of bell edging and beg of front neck shaping.
Work in g st for 3 rows.
Row 4 (RS): K3, yfwd, K2tog,
*K17 [17: 17: 18: 18], yfwd, K2tog, rep from * 4 times more, K2.
Work in g st for a further 2 rows.
Cast off (on **WS**).

Button border
Work to match buttonhole border, picking up sts along left front opening edge and omitting buttonholes.

Neckband
With RS facing, using 3mm (US 2/3) needles and yarn A **DOUBLE**, pick up and knit 38 [39: 39: 42: 42] sts up right side of front neck, 45 [47: 47: 49: 49] sts from back, then 38 [39: 39: 42: 42] sts down left side of front neck. 121 [125: 125: 133: 133] sts.
Work in g st for 6 rows.
Cast off (on **WS**).
See information page for finishing instructions, setting in sleeves using the shallow set-in method.

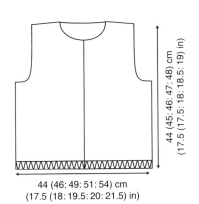

44 (46: 49: 51: 54) cm
(17.5 (18: 19.5: 20: 21.5) in)

44 (45: 46: 47: 48) cm
(17.5 (17.5: 18: 18.5: 19) in)

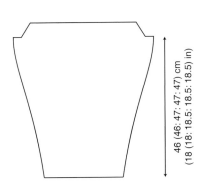

46 (46: 47: 47: 47) cm
(18 (18: 18.5: 18.5: 18.5) in)

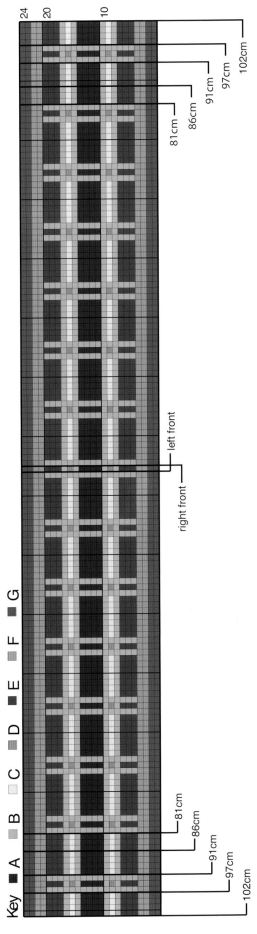

Key ■A ▨B ▫C ▨D ▨E ▨F ■G

GAMEBOARD JACKET

Brandon Mably

SIZE

To fit bust

81-86	91-97	97-107	cm
32-34	36	38-40	in

Actual bust measurement of garment

182.5	191	200	cm
72	75	78½	in

YARN

Rowan Alpaca Classic and Felted Tweed

A Alpaca Classic Noir 103

4	4	5	x 25gm

B Alpaca Classic Charcoal Melange 102

2	2	2	x 25gm

C Felted Tweed Boulder 195

1	1	2	x 50gm

D Felted Tweed Delft 194

3	3	3	x 50gm

E Alpaca Classic Purple Rain 123

2	2	2	x 25gm

F Alpaca Classic Deep Teal 109

3	3	3	x 25gm

G Felted Tweed Stone 190

2	2	2	x 50gm

H Alpaca Classic Green Moss 111

3	3	3	x 25gm

J Felted Tweed Cumin 193

2	2	2	x 50gm

L Felted Tweed Camel 157

2	2	2	x 50gm

NEEDLES

1 pair 3¼mm (no 10) (US 3) needles
1 pair 3¾mm (no 9) (US 5) needles

BUTTONS

BUTTONS - 7 x A2384 from Groves and Banks. Please see information page for contact details.

TENSION

23 sts and 32 rows to 10cm (4in) measured over patterned stocking stitch using 3¾mm (US 5) needles.

BACK

Using 3¼mm (US 3) needles and yarn D, cast on 210 [220: 230] sts. Work 10 rows in garter st. Change to 3¾mm (US 5) needles.
Beg and ending rows as indicated and using the **intarsia** technique as described on the information page, cont in patt from chart, which is worked entirely in st st beg with a K row as folls:
Cont straight until chart row 196 [200: 204] has been completed, ending with a RS facing for next row.

Shape shoulders and back neck

Cast off 17 [18: 19] sts at beg of next 6 rows. 108 [112: 116] sts.
Next row (RS): Cast off 17 [18: 19] sts, patt until there are 21 [22: 23] sts on right needle and turn, leaving rem sts on a holder.
Work each side of neck separately. Cast off 4 sts at beg of next row. Cast off rem 17 [18: 19] sts. With RS facing, rejoin yarn to rem sts, cast off centre 32 sts, patt to end. Work to match first side, reversing shapings.

LEFT FRONT

Using 3¼mm (US 3) needles and yarn D, cast on 110 [115: 120] sts. Work 10 rows in garter st. Change to 3¾mm (US 5) needles.
Beg and ending rows as indicated, cont in patt from chart as folls:
Cont straight until chart row 175 [179: 183] has been completed, ending with WS facing for next row.

Shape neck

Cast off 15 sts at beg of next row.
95 [100: 105] sts. Dec 1 st at neck edge on next 5 rows, then on foll 4 alt rows, then on foll 4th row. 85 [90: 95] sts.
Work 3 rows, ending with chart row 196 [200: 204].

Shape shoulder

Cast off 17 [18: 19] sts at beg of next and foll 3 alt rows. Work 1 row. Cast off rem 17 [18: 19] sts.

RIGHT FRONT

Work to match left front, reversing shaping and making buttonholes in chart row 17 [21: 25] and every foll 26th row as folls:
Buttonhole row (RS): K4, cast off 2 sts (for buttonhole - cast on 2 sts over these sts on next row), K to end.

SLEEVES (both alike)

Using 3¼mm (US 3) needles and yarn D, cast on 70 sts. Work 10 rows in garter st.
Change to 3¾mm (US 5) needles.

Beg and ending rows as indicated, cont in patt from chart as folls:
Work 2 rows.
Inc 1 st at each end of next and every foll 6th row until there are 86 sts, then on every foll 4th row until there are 104 sts, taking inc sts into patt.
Cont straight until chart row 90 has been completed, ending with RS facing.
Cast off.

MAKING UP

PRESS all pieces as described on the information page.
Join shoulder seams using back stitch, or mattress stitch if preferred.

Left front facing

With RS facing, using 3¼mm (US 3) needles and yarn D, pick up and knit 136 [139: 142] sts evenly along left front opening edge.
Row 1 (WS): Knit (to form foldline).
Beg with a K row, work in st st for 14 rows.
Cast off.

Right front facing

With RS facing, using 3¼mm (US 3) needles and yarn D, pick up and knit 136 [139: 142] sts evenly along right front opening edge.
Row 1 (WS): Knit (to form foldline).
Beg with a K row, work in st st for 4 rows.
Row 6 (RS): K18 [21: 24] and turn.
Purl 1 row on these 18 [21: 24] sts.
Break yarn.
★★Return to rem sts, rejoin yarn with RS facing, K2tog, K17 and turn.
Purl 1 row on these 18 sts.
Break yarn.
Rep from **★★** 5 times more.
Return to rem 4 sts, rejoin yarn with RS facing, K2tog, K2.
Purl 1 row on these 3 sts.
Break yarn.
With RS facing, join all sections as folls:
Row 8 (RS): K first 17 [20: 23] sts, inc in next st, *K next 17 sts, inc in next st, rep from * 5 times more, K rem 3 sts.
Beg with a P row, work a further 6 rows in st st. Cast off.
Fold facing to inside along foldline and slip stitch in position. Oversew layers tog around buttonholes.

Neckband

With RS facing, using 3¼mm (US 3) needles and yarn D, pick up and knit 38 sts up right side of neck, 40 sts from back, and 38 sts down left side of neck. 116 sts.
Work in garter st for 6 rows.
Cast off knitwise (on WS).
See information page for finishing instructions, setting in sleeves using the straight cast-off method.

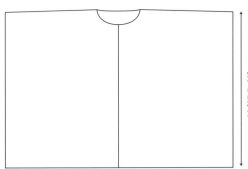

66 [67.5: 69] cm
26 [26½: 27] in

91 [95.5: 100] cm
36 [37½: 39½] in

30.5 cm
12 in

Key A ■ B ⊡ C ☑ D ⊟ E ▲ F ☒ G ◉ H ⊡ J ☑ L ◩

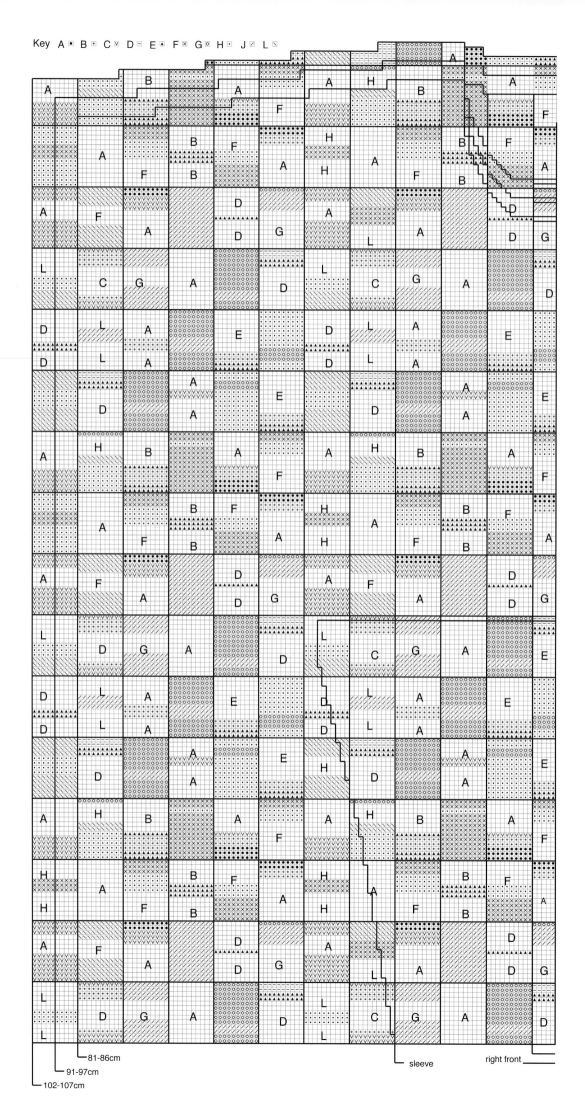

81-86cm
91-97cm
102-107cm
sleeve
right front

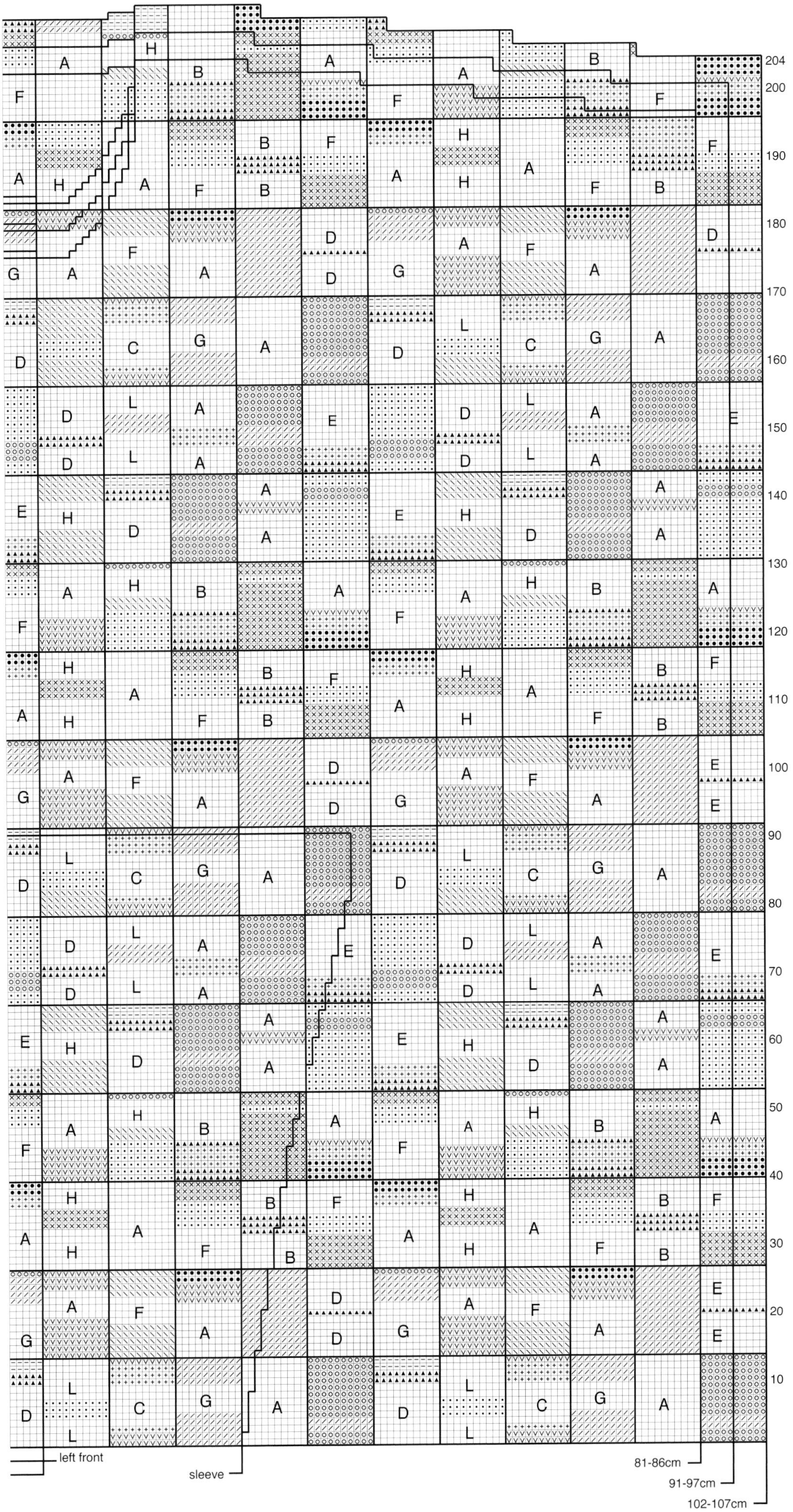

204
200
190
180
170
160
150
140
130
120
110
100
90
80
70
60
50
40
30
20
10

left front

sleeve

81-86cm

91-97cm

102-107cm

KIRKWALL WRAP
Julia Frank

FINISHED SIZE
Completed wrap measures approx 40cm (16in) wide and 180cm (71in) long

YARN
Rowan Felted Tweed

A Seafarer 170	4	x 50g
B Rage 150	4	x 50g

NEEDLES
1 pair 3¼mm (no 10) (US 3) needles
1 pair 3¾mm (no 9) (US 5) needles
3¼mm (no 10) (US 3) circular needle, 120cm long

TENSION
23 sts and 29 rows to 10cm (4in) measured over patt using 3¾mm (US 5) needles.

Pattern note: When working patt, all slipped sts should be worked purlwise with yarn at WS of work - this is back of work on RS rows and front of work on WS rows.

MAIN SECTION
Using 3¾mm (US 5) needles and yarn A, cast on 80 sts. Joining in colours as required, work in patt as follows:
Row 1 (RS): Using yarn A, knit.
Row 2: Using yarn A, *(P2, P1 winding yarn 3 times round needle) twice, P2, rep from * to end.
Row 3: Using yarn B, *(K2, sl 1 dropping extra loops - see pattern note) twice, K2, rep from * to end.
Row 4: Using yarn B, *(P2, sl 1) twice, P2, rep from * to end.

Row 5: Using yarn B, *(K2, sl 1) twice, K2, rep from * to end.
Rows 6 and 7: As rows 4 and 5.
Row 8: As row 4.
Row 9: Using yarn A, knit.
Row 10: Using yarn A, *(P2, P1 winding yarn twice round needle) twice, P2, rep from * to end.
Row 11: Using one strand each of yarns A and B held together, *(K2, sl 1 dropping extra loop) twice, K2, rep from * to end.
Row 12: Using one strand each of yarns A and B held together, *(P2, sl 1) twice, P2, rep from * to end.
Row 13: Using one strand each of yarns A and B held together, *(K2, sl 1) twice, K2, rep from * to end.
Row 14: As row 12.
Row 15: Using yarn A, knit.
Row 16: Using yarn A, *(P2, P1 winding yarn 4 times round needle) twice, P2, rep from * to end.
Row 17: As row 3.
Rows 18 to 23: As rows 4 and 5, 3 times.
Row 24: As row 4.
Rows 25 to 30: As rows 9 to 14.
These 30 rows form patt.
Cont in patt until work measures approx 175cm, ending after patt row 1, 9, 15 or 25 and with WS facing for next row.
Next row (WS): Using yarn A, purl.
Cast off.

MAKING UP
Press as described on the information page.
Side borders (both alike)
With RS facing, using 3¼mm (US 3) circular needle and yarn A, pick up and knit 424 sts evenly along one entire row-end edge.
Row 1 (WS): K1, P2, *K2, P2, rep from * to last st, K1.
Row 2: K3, *P2, K2, rep from * to last st, K1.
These 2 rows form rib.
Work in rib for a further 5 rows, ending with RS facing for next row.
Cast off in rib.
End borders (both alike)
With RS facing, using 3¼mm (US 3) needles and yarn A, pick up and knit 96 sts evenly along one end of wrap between cast-off edges of side borders.
Beg with row 1, work in rib as given for side borders for 7 rows, ending with RS facing for next row.
Cast off in rib.
See information page for finishing instructions.

M A R T H A

Kim Hargreaves

• •

SIZE

To fit bust

81	86	91	97	102	cm
32	34	36	38	40	in

Actual bust measurement of finished garment

91	96	101	106	111	cm
36	38	40	42	44	in

YARN

Rowan Felted Tweed

7	7	8	8	8	x 50gm

(photographed in Maritime 167)

NEEDLES

1 pair 3mm (no 11) (US 2/3) needles 1 pair 3¾mm (no 9) (US 5) needles

BUTTONS – 7 x A0502 from Groves and Banks. See information page for contact details.

TENSION

24 sts and 42 rows to 10cm (4in) measured over patt using 3¾mm (US 5) needles.

Pattern note: The pattern is worked over a multiple of 8 sts plus 1 as folls:

Row 1 (RS): K2, ★slip next 5 sts purlwise with yarn at front of work, K3, rep from ★, ending with slip 5, K2.

Rows 2 and 4: K2, ★P5, K3, rep from ★, ending P5, K2.

Row 4: K4, ★insert right needle point under loose strand laying across front of work and knit this loop tog with next st, K7, rep from ★, ending last rep K4.

Where part patt reps occur resulting in slipped sts being worked at side edges, strand yarn loosely to and from row ends before working next st.

BACK

Using 3mm (US 2/3) needles cast on 109 [115: 121: 127: 133] sts .

Work 11 rows in g st, ending with WS facing for next row.

Change to 3¾mm (US 5) needles.

Next row (WS): P0 [0: 3: 0: 1], K0 [3: 3: 1: 3], ★P5, K3, rep from ★ to last 5 [0: 3: 6: 1] sts, P5 [0: 3: 5: 1], K0 [0: 0: 1: 0].

Cont in patt setting sts as folls:

Row 1 (RS): Slip next 5 [0: 3: 0: 0] sts purlwise with yarn at front of work, K3 [3: 3: 1: 4], ★slip next 5 sts purlwise with yarn at front of work, K3, rep from ★ to last 5 [0: 3: 6: 1] sts, slip next 5 [0: 3: 5: 0] sts purlwise with yarn at front of work, K0 [0: 0: 1: 1].

Row 2: P0 [0: 3: 0: 1], K0 [3: 3: 1: 3], ★P5, K3, rep from ★ to last 5 [0: 3: 6: 1] sts, P5 [0: 3: 5: 1], K0 [0: 0: 1: 0].

Row 3: K2 [0: 0: 0: 0], (insert right needle point under loose strand laying across front of work and knit this loop tog with next st) 1 [0: 1: 0: 0] times, K5 [3: 5: 1: 4], ★K2, insert right needle point under loose strand laying across front of work and knit this loop tog with next st, K5, rep from ★ to last 5 [0: 3: 6: 1] sts, K2 [0: 2: 2: 0], (insert right needle point under loose strand laying across front of work and knit this loop tog with next st) 1 [0: 1: 1: 0] times, K2 [0: 0: 3: 1].

Row 4: As row 2.

These 4 rows form patt and are repeated throughout. Patt a further 4 [6: 6: 8: 8] rows, ending with RS facing for next row.

Keeping patt correct, dec 1 st at each end of next and every foll 6th row until 91 [97: 103: 109: 115] sts rem.

Patt 13 rows, ending with RS facing for next row.

Keeping patt correct, inc 1 st at each end of next and every foll 8th row until there are 109 [115: 121: 127: 133] sts, taking inc sts into patt.

Cont straight until back measures 37 [38: 38: 39: 39] cm from cast-on edge, ending with RS facing for next row.

Shape armholes

Keeping patt correct, cast off 4 sts at beg of next 2 rows. 101 [107: 113: 119: 125] sts.

Dec 1 st at each end of next 3 [5: 7: 9: 11] rows, then on every foll alt row until 77 [79: 81: 83: 85] sts rem.

Cont straight until armhole measures 20 [20: 21: 21: 22] cm, ending with RS facing for next row.

Shape shoulders and back neck

Cast off 7 [7: 8: 8: 8] sts at beg of next 2 rows. 63 [65: 65: 67: 69] sts.

Next row (RS): Cast off 7 [7: 8: 8: 8] sts, patt until there are 12 [12: 11: 11: 12] sts on right needle and turn, leaving rem sts on a holder.

Work each side of neck separately.

Cast off 4 sts at beg of next row.

Cast off rem 8 [8: 7: 7: 8] sts.

With RS facing, rejoin yarn to rem sts, cast off centre 25 [27: 27: 29: 29] sts, patt to end.

Work to match first side, reversing shapings.

LEFT FRONT

Note: As row end edges of fronts form actual finished edges of garment, it is important these edges are kept neat. Therefore, all new balls of yarn should be joined in at side seam or armhole edges of rows.

Using 3mm (US 2/3) needles cast on 59 [62: 65: 68: 71] sts.

Work 11 rows in g st, ending with WS facing for next row.

Change to 3¾mm (US 5) needles.

Next row (WS): K6, ★P5, K3, rep from ★ to last 5 [0: 3: 6: 1] sts, P5 [0: 3: 5: 1], K0 [0: 0: 1: 0].

Cont in patt as folls:

Row 1 (RS): Slip next 5 [0: 3: 0: 0] sts purlwise with yarn at front of work, K3 [3: 3: 1: 4], ★slip next 5 sts purlwise with yarn at front of work, K3, rep from ★ to last 3 sts, K3.

Row 2: K6, ★P5, K3, rep from ★ to last 5 [0: 3: 6: 1] sts, P5 [0: 3: 5: 1], K0 [0: 0: 1: 0].

Row 3: K2 [0: 0: 0: 0], (insert right needle point under loose strand laying across front of work and knit this loop tog with next st) 1 [0: 1: 0: 0] times, K5 [3: 5: 1: 4], ★K2, insert right needle point under loose strand laying

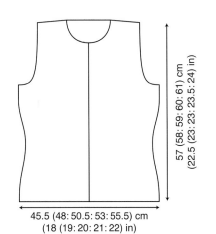

45.5 (48: 50.5: 53: 55.5) cm
(18 (19: 20: 21: 22) in)

57 (58: 59: 60: 61) cm
(22.5 (23: 23: 23.5: 24) in)

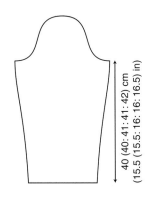

40 (40: 41: 41: 42) cm
(15.5 (15.5: 16: 16: 16.5) in)

across front of work and knit this loop tog with next st, K5, rep from ★ to last 3 sts, K3.

Row 4: As row 2.

These 4 rows form patt and are repeated throughout.

Patt a further 4 [6: 6: 8: 8] rows, ending with RS facing for next row.

Keeping patt correct, dec 1 st at beg of next and every foll 6th row until 50 [53: 56: 59: 62] sts rem.

Patt 13 rows, ending with RS facing for next row.

Keeping patt correct, inc 1 st at beg of next and every foll 8th row until there are 59 [62: 65: 68: 71] sts, taking inc sts into patt.

Cont straight until left front matches back to beg of armhole shaping, ending with RS facing for next row.

Shape armholes

Keeping patt correct, cast off 4 sts at beg of next row. 55 [58: 61: 64: 67] sts.

Work 1 row.

Dec 1 st at armhole edge of next 3 [5: 7: 9: 11] rows, then on every foll alt row until 43 [44: 45: 46: 47] sts rem.

Cont straight until 29 [29: 29: 31: 31] rows less have been worked than on back to start of shoulder shaping, ending with a RS row.

Shape neck

Keeping patt correct, cast off 7 [8: 8: 8: 8] sts at beg of next row and 5 sts at beg of foll alt row. 31 [31: 32: 33: 34] sts.

Dec 1 st at neck edge on next 3 rows, then on foll 4 [4: 4: 5: 5] alt rows, then on every foll 4th row until 22 [22: 23: 23: 24] sts rem.

Work 7 rows, ending with RS facing for next row.

Shape shoulder

Cast off 7 [7: 8: 8: 8] sts at beg of next and foll alt row.

Work 1 row.

Cast off rem 8 [8: 7: 7: 8] sts.

Mark positions for 7 buttons along left front opening edge – lowest button to be 5 cm up from cast-on edge, last button 2 cm below neck shaping and rem 5 buttons evenly spaced between.

RIGHT FRONT

Cast on 59 [62: 65: 68: 71] sts using 3mm (US 2/3) needles.

Work 11 rows in g st, ending with **WS** facing for next row.

Change to 3¾mm (US 5) needles.

Next row (WS): P0 [0: 3: 0: 1], K0 [3: 3: 1: 3], ★P5, K3, rep from ★ to last 3 sts, K3.

Cont in patt as folls:

Row 1 (RS): K6, ★slip next 5 sts purlwise with yarn at front of work, K3, rep from ★ to last 5 [0: 3: 6: 1] sts, slip next 5 [0: 3: 5: 0] sts purlwise with yarn at front of work, K0 [0: 0: 1: 1].

Row 2: P0 [0: 3: 0: 1], K0 [3: 3: 1: 3], ★P5, K3, rep from ★ to last 3 sts, K3.

Row 3: K6, ★K2, insert right needle point under loose strand laying across front of work and knit this loop tog with next st, K5, rep from ★ to last 5 [0: 3: 6: 1] sts, K2 [0: 2: 2: 0], (insert right needle point under loose strand laying

across front of work and knit this loop tog with next st] 1 [0: 1: 1: 0] times, K2 [0: 0: 3: 1].

Row 4: As row 2.

These 4 rows form patt and are repeated throughout.

Complete to match left front, reversing shapings and working buttonholes to correspond with positions marked for buttons on left front as folls:

Buttonhole row (RS): K2, K2tog, yfwd, patt to end.

SLEEVES

Using 3mm (US 2/3) needles cast on 51 [51: 55: 55: 59] sts.

Work 11 rows in g st, inc 1 st at each end of last row and ending with **WS** facing for next row. 53 [53: 57: 57: 61] sts.

Change to 3¾mm (US 5) needles.

Next row (WS): P1 [1: 3: 3: 5], K3, ★P5, K3, rep from ★ to last 1 [1: 3: 3: 5] sts, P1 [1: 3: 3: 5].

Cont in patt as folls:

Row 1 (RS): Slip next 0 [0: 3: 3: 5] sts purlwise with yarn at front of work, K4 [4: 3: 3: 3], ★slip next 5 sts purlwise with yarn at front of work, K3, rep from ★ to last 1 [1: 3: 3: 5] sts, slip next 0 [0: 3: 3: 5] sts purlwise with yarn at front of work, K1 [1: 0: 0: 0].

Row 2: P1 [1: 3: 3: 5], K3, ★P5, K3, rep from ★ to last 1 [1: 3: 3: 5] sts, P1 [1: 3: 3: 5].

Row 3: K0 [0: 0: 0: 2], (insert right needle point under loose strand laying across front of work and knit this loop tog with next st) 0 [0: 0: 1: 1: 1] times, K4 [4: 5: 5: 5], ★K2, insert right needle point under loose strand laying across front of work and knit this loop tog with next st, K5, rep from ★ to last 1 [1: 3: 3: 5] sts, K1 [1: 2: 2: 2], (insert right needle point under loose strand laying across front of work and knit this loop tog with next st) 0 [0: 1: 1: 1] times, K0 [0: 0: 0: 2].

Row 4: As row 2.

These 4 rows form patt and are repeated throughout.

Keeping patt correct, inc 1 st at each end of 7th and every foll 12th row until there are 79 [79: 83: 83: 87] sts, taking inc sts into patt.

Cont straight until sleeve measures 40 [40: 41: 41: 42] cm from cast-on edge, ending with RS facing for next row.

Shape top

Keeping patt correct, cast off 4 sts at beg of next 2 rows.

71 [71: 75: 75: 79] sts.

Dec 1 st at each end of next 3 rows, then on foll 3 [3: 4: 4: 5] alt rows, then on every foll 4th row until 55 [55: 53: 53: 55] sts rem.

Work 5 rows, ending with RS facing for next row.

Dec 1 st at each end of next and every foll 6th row until 49 [49: 49: 49: 51] sts rem, then on every foll 4th row until 45 [45: 45: 45: 47] sts rem, then on every foll alt row until 39 sts rem.

Dec 1 st at each end of next 5 rows, ending with RS facing for next row. 29 sts.

Cast off 4 sts at beg of next 2 rows.

Cast off rem 21 sts.

MAKING UP

Press as described on the information page.

Join both shoulder seams using back stitch, or mattress stitch if preferred.

Collar

With RS facing, using 3mm (US 2/3) needles, starting and ending 3 sts in from front opening edges, pick up and knit 29 [29: 29: 31: 31] sts up right side of neck, 35 [37: 37: 39: 39] sts from back, and 29 [29: 29: 31: 31] sts down left side of neck. 93 [95: 95: 101: 101] sts.

Work 8 cm in g st, ending with RS of collar (**WS** of body) facing for next row.

Cast off.

See information page for finishing instructions, setting in sleeves using the set-in method.

MONTY

Kim Hargreaves

• •

SIZE

To fit bust

81	86	91	97	102	cm
32	34	36	38	40	in

Actual bust measurement of garment

117	23	129	135	141.5	cm
46	48½	51	53	55½	in

YARN

Rowan Brushed Fleece

20	21	22	23	24	x 100gm

(photographed in Heath 256)

NEEDLES

1 pair 5½mm (no 5) (US 9) needles
1 pair 6½mm (no 3) (US 10½) needles

BUTTONS – 7 x BN 1368 from Bedecked. Please see information page for contact details.

TENSION

13 sts and 22 rows to 10cm (4in) measured over moss stitch using 6½mm (US 10½) needles.

POCKET LININGS (make 2)
Using 6½mm (US 10½) needles, cast on 19 sts
Row 1 (RS): K1, ★P1, K1, rep from ★ to end.
Row 2: As row 1.
These 2 rows form moss st.
Work a further 22 rows in moss st.
Break yarn and leave sts on a holder.

LEFT FRONT

Note: As row end edges of fronts form actual finished edges of garment, it is important these edges are kept neat. Therefore, all new balls of yarn should be joined in at side seam or armhole edges of rows.

Lower left front
Using 5½ mm (US 9) needles, cast on 43 [45: 47: 49: 51] sts.
Knit 3 rows, ending with WS facing for next row.
Change to 6½mm (US 10½) needles.
Cont in moss st as given for pocket linings until work measures 70 cm from cast-on edge, ending with RS facing for next row.
(**Note:** if you wish to alter finished length of coat, alter length to this point accordingly.)

Place pocket
Next row (RS): Moss st 12 [12: 14: 14: 16], slip next 31 [33: 33: 35: 35] sts onto a holder and in their place moss st across 19 sts of first pocket lining.
Work 39 rows on these 31 [31: 33: 33: 35] sts, ending with RS facing.
Break yarn and leave sts on a second holder.

Work pocket front
With RS facing, rejoin yarn to sts from first holder and work 40 rows in moss st.
Break yarn.

Join sections
Next row (RS): Moss st first 12 [12: 14: 14: 16] sts from second holder, then holding WS of pocket front against RS of pocket lining, work tog first st of pocket front with next st of pocket lining, work tog rem 18 sts of pocket lining with next 18 sts of pocket front, then moss st rem 12 [14: 14: 16: 16] sts.
Cont straight until lower left front measures 104 cm from cast-on edge, ending with RS facing.
(**Note:** if length to pocket has been adjusted, remember to adjust this length by same amount.)
Cast off in moss st.

Upper left front
Using 6½mm (US 10½). cast on 43 [45: 47: 49: 51] sts.
Work in moss st as given for pocket linings until work measures 11 cm from cast-on edge, ending with RS facing for next row.

Shape armhole

Cast off 4 sts at beg of next row.
39 [41: 43: 45: 47] sts.
Work 1 row.
Dec 1 st at armhole edge of next 6 rows.
33 [35: 37: 39: 41] sts.
Cont straight until armhole measures 21 [21: 22: 21: 22] cm, ending with WS facing for next row.

Shape neck

Cast off 9 [10: 10: 11: 11] sts at beg of next row.
24 [25: 27: 28: 30] sts.
Dec 1 st at neck edge on next and every foll alt row until 19 [20: 22: 23: 25] sts rem.
Cont straight until armhole measures 28 [28: 29: 29: 30] cm, ending with RS facing for next row.

Shape shoulder

Cast off 6 [7: 7: 8: 8] sts at beg of next and foll alt row.
Work 1 row.
Cast off rem 7 [6: 8: 7: 9] sts.
Holding pieces with WS tog, join left fronts using back stitch.
Mark positions for 7 buttons on left front – lowest button to be 55 cm up from lower edge, top button to be 3 cm below neck shaping and rem 5 buttons evenly spaced between.

RIGHT FRONT

Lower right front
Work as given for lower left front until work measures 55 cm from cast-on edge, ending with RS facing for next row.
Next row (RS) (buttonhole row): Moss st 5, cast off 2 sts (for buttonhole - cast on 2 sts over these sts on next row), moss st to end.
Making a further 6 buttonholes to correspond with positions marked for buttons on left front, cont as folls:
Cont straight until lower right front matches lower left front to start of pocket, ending with RS facing for next row.

Place pocket
Next row (RS): Moss st 31 [33: 33: 35: 35] and turn, leaving rem 12 [12: 14: 14: 16] sts on a holder.
Work 39 rows on these 31 [31: 33: 33: 35] sts for pocket front, ending with RS facing.

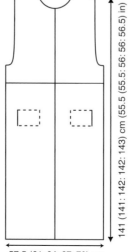

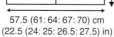

57.5 (61: 64: 67: 70) cm
(22.5 (24: 25: 26.5: 27.5) in)

141 (141: 142: 142: 143) cm (55.5 (55.5: 56: 56: 56.5) in)

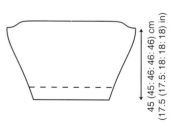

45 (45: 46: 46: 46) cm
(17.5 (17.5: 18: 18: 18) in)

Leave these sts on a second holder and set aside this ball of yarn.

Work pocket back

With RS facing and using new ball of yarn, rejoin yarn to 19 sts of second pocket lining and moss st to end, then moss st across 12 [12: 14: 14: 16] sts from first holder.
Work 39 rows on these 31 [33: 33: 35: 35] sts.
Break yarn.

Join sections

Next row (RS): Using ball of yarn set to one side, moss st first 12 [14: 14: 16: 16] sts of pocket front, then holding WS of pocket front against RS of pocket lining, work tog next st of pocket front with first st of pocket lining, work tog rem 18 sts of pocket front with next 18 sts of pocket lining, then moss st rem 12 [12: 14: 14: 16] sts.
Cont straight until lower right front matches lower left front to cast-off edge, ending with RS facing.
Cast off in moss st.

Upper right front

Using 6½ mm (US 10½) needles, cast on 43 [45: 47: 49: 51] sts.
Remembering to make buttonholes at positions required, work in moss st as given for pocket linings until upper right front measures 11 cm from cast-on edge, ending with rows facing for next row.

Shape armhole

Cast off 4 sts at beg of next row.
39 [41: 43: 45: 47] sts.
Complete to match upper left front, reversing shapings.
Holding pieces with WS tog, join right fronts using back stitch.

RIGHT BACK

Note: As row end edges of backs form actual finished edges of vent for first 56 cm, it is important these edges are kept neat. Therefore, all new balls of yarn should be joined in at side seam edges of rows.
Using 5½ mm (US 9) needles, cast on 39 [41: 43: 45: 47] sts.
Knit 3 rows, ending with WS facing for next row.
Change to 6½mm (US 10½) needles and cont in moss st as given for pocket linings until right back matches fronts to beg of armhole shaping, ending with RS facing for next row..

Shape armhole

Cast off 4 sts at beg of next row.
35 [37: 39: 41: 43] sts.
Work 1 row.
Dec 1 st at armhole edge of next 6 rows.
29 [31: 33: 35: 37] sts.
Cont straight until right back matches fronts to start of shoulder shaping, ending with RS facing for next row.

Shape shoulder and back neck

Cast off 6 [7: 7: 8: 8] sts at beg of next row, 6 [7: 7: 8: 8] sts at beg of foll row, 6 [7: 7: 8: 8] sts at beg of next row, and 4 sts at beg of foll row.
Cast off rem 7 [6: 8: 7: 9] sts.

LEFT BACK

Using 5½mm (US 9) needles, cast on 47 [49: 51: 53: 55] sts.
Knit 3 rows, ending with WS facing for next row.
Change to 6½mm (US 10½) needles and cont in moss st as given for pocket linings until left back measures 56 cm from cast-on edge, ending with RS facing for next row.

Shape back vent

Dec 1 st at beg of next row and at same edge on foll 7 rows. 39 [41: 43: 45: 47] sts.
Cont straight until left back matches fronts to beg of armhole shaping, ending with WS facing for next row.

Shape armhole

Cast off 4 sts at beg of next row.
35 [37: 39: 41: 43] sts.
Complete to match right back, reversing shapings and ending with a RS row before shaping shoulder and back neck.
Holding pieces with WS tog, join centre back seam above vent using back stitch. Lay right back over left back so first 56 cm overlap by 8 sts and sew through all layers along shaped edge at top of vent.

SLEEVES (both alike)

Using 6½mm (US 10½), cast on 43 [43: 45: 47: 47] sts.
Purl 2 rows, ending with RS facing for next row.
Work in moss st as given for pocket linings for 18 rows, dec 1 st at each end of 9th and foll 8th row. 39 [39: 41: 43: 43] sts.
Change to 5½mm (US 9) needles and cont in moss st for a further 16 rows, inc 1 st at each end of 7th and foll 6th row. 43 [43: 45: 47: 47] sts.
Change to 6½mm (US 10½) needles and cont in moss st, inc 1 st at each end of 3rd and every foll 6th row until there are 63 [63: 65: 71: 67] sts, then on every foll 4th row until there are 73 [73: 75: 75: 77] sts.
Cont straight until sleeve measures 55 [55: 56: 56: 56] cm from cast-on edge, ending with RS facing for next row.

Shape top

Cast off 4 sts at beg of next 2 rows.
65 [65: 67: 67: 69] sts.
Dec 1 st at each end of next and foll 6 alt rows.
Work 1 row, ending with RS facing.
Cast off rem 51 [51: 53: 53: 55] sts.

MAKING UP

PRESS all pieces as described on the information page.
Join both shoulder seams using back stitch.

Collar

Using 5½ mm (US 9) needles, cast on 57 [61: 61: 65: 65] sts.
Work in moss st as given for pocket linings for 20 cm.
Cast off in moss st.
Fold collar in half lengthways with WS tog and sew ends closed. Sew open edges to neck edge, placing ends of collar halfway across top of front neck cast-off sts.
See information page for finishing instructions, setting in sleeves using the shallow set-in

method and reversing sleeve seam for first 13 cm for turnback cuff. Fold first 10 cm to RS to form cuff. To help support weight of coat and stop neck and shoulders stretching, lay coat flat and cut a length of tape to fit across entire shoulder and back neck edge. On inside of coat, lay tape over seams and slip stitch in place along both edges.

O L I V E
Kim Hargreaves

● ●

SIZE
To fit bust

81	86	91	97	102	cm
32	34	36	38	40	in

Actual bust measurement of garment

97	102	107	112	117	cm
38	40	42	44	46	in

YARN
Rowan Felted Tweed

6	6	7	7	8	x 50gm

(photographed in Boulder 195 and for the embroidered version only 1 x 25gm ball of Alpaca Classic Snowflake White 115)

NEEDLES
1 pair 3mm (no 11) (US 2/3) needles
1 pair 3¾mm (no 9) (US 5) needles
Plain version only: 3.25mm (no 10) (US D/3) crochet hook

BUTTONS – 7 x G427224100 (metal shank) from Groves and Banks. Please see information page for contact details.

TENSION
23 sts and 32 rows to 10cm (4in) measured over st st using 3¾mm (US 5) needles.

CROCHET ABBREVIATIONS
dc = double crochet; **ch** = chain.

BACK
Using 3mm (US 2/3) needles, cast on 101 [107: 113: 119: 125] sts.
Work in g st for 5 rows, ending with WS facing for next row.
Row 6: P1 [0: 1: 0: 1], ★K1, P1, rep from ★ to last 0 [1: 0: 1: 0] st, K0 [1: 0: 1: 0].
Last row forms moss st.
Work a further 4 rows in moss st, ending with RS facing for next row.
Change to 3¾mm (US 5) needles.
Marker row: K10 [3:6:9:2], ★ P1, K9, rep from ★ to last 1 [4:7:10:3] sts, P0[1: 1: 1: 1], K1 [3: 6: 9: 2].
Beg with a P row, work in st st, shaping side seams by inc 1 st at each end of 8th row and every foll 16th row until there are 111 [117: 123: 129: 135] sts.
Cont straight until back measures 29 [30: 30: 31: 31] cm, ending with RS facing for next row.
Shape armholes
Cast off 4 [4: 5: 5: 6] sts at beg of next 2 rows. 103 [109: 113: 119: 123] sts.
Dec 1 st at each end on next 5 [7: 7: 9: 9] rows, then on foll 6 [6: 7: 7: 8] alt rows. 81 [83: 85: 87: 89] sts.
Cont without further shaping until armhole measures 20 [20: 21: 21: 22] cm, ending with RS facing for next row.
Shape shoulders and back neck
Cast off 8 [8: 8: 8: 9] sts at beg of next 2 rows. 65 [67: 69: 71: 71] sts.
Next row (RS): Cast off 8 [8: 8: 8: 9] sts, K until there are 12 [12: 13: 13:12] sts on right needle and turn, leaving rem sts on a holder.
Work each side of neck separately.
Cast off 4 sts at beg of next row. Cast off rem 8 [8: 9: 9: 8] sts.
With RS facing, rejoin yarn to rem sts, cast off centre 25 [27: 27: 29: 29] sts, K to end.
Work to match first side, reversing shapings.

LEFT FRONT
Using 3mm (US 2/3) needles, cast on 58 [61: 64: 67: 70] sts.
Work in g st for 5 rows, ending with WS facing for next row.
Row 6: ★K1, P1, rep from ★ to last 0 [1: 0: 1: 0] st, K0 [1: 0: 1: 0].

Last row sets position of moss st as given for back.
Work a further 3 rows in moss st, ending with WS facing for next row.
Row 10: Patt 8 sts and slip these 8 sts onto a safety pin, M1, patt to end. 51 [54: 57: 60: 63] sts.
Change to 3¾mm (US 5) needles.
Marker row: K10 [3: 6: 9: 2], ★ P1, K9, rep from ★ to last st, K1.
Beg with a P row, work in st st, shaping side seam by inc 1 st at beg of 8th row and every foll 16th row until there are 56 [59: 62: 65: 68] sts.
Cont straight until left front matches back to start of armhole shaping, ending with RS facing for next row.
Shape armhole
Cast off 4 [4: 5: 5: 6] sts at beg of next row. 52 [55: 57: 60: 62] sts.
Work 1 row.
Dec 1 st at armhole edge on next 5 [7: 7: 9: 9] rows, then on foll 6 [6: 7: 7: 8] alt rows. 41 [42: 43: 44: 45] sts.
Cont without further shaping until 25 rows less have been worked than on back to start of shoulder and back neck shaping, thus ending with WS facing for next row.
Shape neck
Cast off 5 [6: 6: 7: 7] sts at beg of next row and 4 sts at beg of foll alt row. 32 [32: 33: 33: 34] sts.
Dec 1 st at neck edge on next 3 rows, then on foll 3 alt rows. 26 [26: 27: 27: 28] sts.
Work 3 rows.
Dec 1 st at neck edge on next and foll 4th row. 24 [24: 25: 25: 26] sts.
Work 5 rows, thus ending at armhole edge.
Shape shoulder
Cast off 8 [8: 8: 8: 9] sts at beg of next and foll alt row.
Work 1 row. Cast off rem 8 [8: 9: 9: 8] sts.

RIGHT FRONT
Using 3mm (US 2/3) needles, cast on 58 [61: 64: 67: 70] sts.
Work in g st for 5 rows, ending with WS facing for next row.
Row 6: K0 [1: 0: 1: 0], ★P1, K1, rep from ★ to end.
Last row sets position of moss st as given for back.

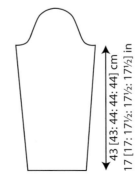

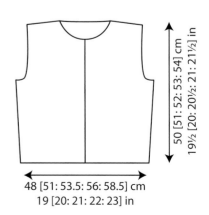

43 [43: 44: 44: 44] cm
17 [17: 17½: 17½: 17½] in

50 [51: 52: 53: 54] cm
19½ [20: 20½: 21: 21½] in

48 [51: 53.5: 56: 58.5] cm
19 [20: 21: 22: 23] in

Row 7 (RS) (buttonhole row): K1, P1, K1, yfwd, K2tog, patt to end. Work a further 2 rows in moss st, ending with WS facing for next row.

Row 10: Patt to last 8 sts, M1 and turn, leaving last 8 sts on a safety pin. 51 [54: 57: 60: 63] sts. Change to 3¾mm (US 5) needles.

Marker row: K10, ★ P1, K9, rep from ★ to last 1[4: 7: 10: 3] sts, P0 [1: 1: 1: 1], K1 [3: 6: 9: 2]. Complete to match left front, reversing shapings.

SLEEVES (both alike)
Using 3mm (US 2/3) needles, cast on 45 [45: 49: 49: 53] sts.
Work in g st for 5 rows, ending with WS facing for next row.

Row 6: P1, ★K1, P1, rep from ★ to end.
Last row sets position of moss st as given for back.
Work a further 4 rows in moss st, end with ending with RS facing for next row.
Change to 3¾mm (US 5) needles.

Marker row: K2 [2: 4: 4: 6], ★ P1, K9, rep from ★ to last 3 [3: 5: 5: 7] sts, P1, K2 [2: 4: 4: 6].
Beg with a P row, work in st st, shaping sleeve seam by inc 1 st at each end of every 8th [6th: 8th: 6th: 8th] row until there are 73 [53: 77: 55: 81] sts.

2nd & 4th sizes only
Inc 1 st at each end of every foll 8th row until there are [75: 79] sts.

All sizes
Cont without further shaping until sleeve measures 43 [43: 44: 44: 44] cm, ending with RS facing for next row.

Shape top
Cast off 4 [4: 5: 5: 6] sts at beg of next 2 rows. 65 [67: 67: 69: 69] sts.
Dec 1 st at each end of next 5 rows, then on foll 1 [2: 1: 2: 1] alt rows. 53 [53: 55: 55: 57] sts.
Work 3 rows, thus ending with RS facing for next row.
Dec 1 st at each end of next and every foll 4th row until 41 [43: 41: 43: 41] sts rem, then on every foll alt row until 37 sts rem.
Dec 1 st at each end on next 5 rows, thus ending with RS facing. 27 sts.
Cast off 4 sts at beg of next 2 rows.
Cast off rem 19 sts.

MAKING UP
PRESS all pieces as described on the info page. Join shoulder seams using back stitch, or mattress stitch if preferred.

Button border
Slip 8 sts from left front safety pin onto 3mm (US 2/3) needles and rejoin yarn with RS facing.
Cont in moss st as set until border, when slightly stretched, fits up left front opening edge to neck, ending with RS facing.
Cast off. Slip stitch border in place.
Mark positions for 7 buttons on this border – lowest button level with buttonhole already worked in right front, top button 1 cm below neck shaping and rem 5 buttons evenly spaced between.

Buttonhole border
Work as given for button border, rejoining yarn with WS facing and with the addition of a further 6 buttonholes to correspond with positions marked for buttons worked as follows:
Buttonhole row (RS): K1, P1, K1, yfwd, K2tog, P1, K1, P1. Slip stitch border in place.

Embroidered version only Collar
Using 3mm (US 2/3) needles, cast on 105 [109: 109: 113: 113] sts.
Work in g st for 3 rows, ending with WS facing for next row.
Row 4: K1, ★P1, K1, rep from ★ to end.
Rep last row twice more.
Row 7 (Marker row): (K1, P1) twice, K3 [5: 5: 7: 7], ★ P1, K9, rep from ★ to last 8 [10: 10: 12: 12] sts, P1, K3 [5: 5: 7: 7], (P1, K1) twice.
Row 8: K1, P1, K1, P to last 3 sts, K1, P1, K1.
Keeping 4 sts at each edge in moss st, cont in st st until work measures 7.5 cm.
Cast off.
Sew cast-off edge of collar to neck edge, positioning ends of collar midway across top of borders.

Embroidery
Using photograph and sketch as a guide and using yarn double, embroider vertical lines of running stitch from each purl stitch on **marker** rows of back, fronts, sleeves and collar.
Work horizontal lines of running stitch in the same way on rows 26 and 41 of body and row 17 of collar.
See information page for finishing instructions.

Plain version only Collar
Using 3mm (US 2/3) needles, cast on 110 sts.
Beg with a K row, work 4 rows in st st.
Row 5 (RS) (inc): (K10, M1) 5 times, K10, (M1, K10) 5 times. 120 sts.
Work 5 rows in st st.
Row 11 (RS) (inc): (K11, M1) 5 times, K10, (M1, K11) 5 times. 130 sts.
Work 5 rows in st st.
Row 17 (RS) (inc): (K12, M1) 5 times, K10, (M1, K12) 5 times. 140 sts.
Work 5 rows in st st.
Cast off.

Collar edging
With WS facing and using 3.25mm (US D/3) crochet hook, rejoin yarn at end of row 1 and work 1 row of dc evenly along first row end edge, along cast-off edge and then along other row end edge to beg of row 1, turn.
Next row (RS): 1 ch (does NOT count as st), 1 dc into first dc, ★3 ch, 1 dc into same place as last dc★★, 1 dc into next dc, rep from ★ to end, ending last rep at ★★. Fasten off.
Sew cast-on edge of collar to neck edge, positioning ends of collar midway across top of borders.

Cuff edging
Work as given for collar edging.
See information page for finishing instructions.

ONZA

Kim Hargreaves

● ●

SIZE

To fit bust

81	86	91	97	102	cm
32	34	36	38	40	in

Actual bust measurement of garment

90	96	102	108	113	cm
35	38	40	43	44	in

YARN

Rowan Kid Classic

9	9	10	10	11	x 50gm

(photographed in Canard 871)

NEEDLES

1 pair 3¾mm (no 9) (US 5) needles
1 pair 4mm (no 8) (US 6) needles

BUTTONS – 5 x BN1365 from Bedecked.

See information page for contact details.

TENSION

21 sts and 40 rows to 10cm (4in) measured over g st
using 4mm (US 6) needles.

BACK

Using 3¾mm (US 5) needles cast on
95 [101: 107: 113: 119] sts. Beg with a RS row, cont in
g st throughout as folls:
Work 10 rows.
Change to 4mm (US 6) needles.
Work 8 [10: 10: 12: 12] rows, ending with RS facing
for next row.

Place markers on 26th [27th: 28th: 29th: 30th] st
in from both ends of last row.
Next row (RS) (dec): K2tog, K to within
1 st of first marked st, K3tog (centre st is marked st),
K to within 1 st of second marked st, K3tog tbl,
K to last 2 sts, K2tog tbl.
89 [95: 101: 107: 113] sts.
Work 19 rows.
Rep last 20 rows once more and then first of
these rows (the dec row) again.
77 [83: 89: 95: 101] sts.
Work 17 rows, ending with RS facing for
next row.
Next row (RS) (inc): Inc in first st, *K to
marked st, M1, K marked st, M1, rep from
* once more, K to last st, inc in last st.
Work 19 rows.
Rep last 20 rows once more and then first of
these rows (the inc row) again.
95 [101: 107: 113: 119] sts.
Cont straight until back measures
34 [35: 35: 36: 36] cm from cast-on edge, ending
with RS facing for next row.
Shape armholes
Cast off 4 [4: 5: 5: 6] sts at beg of next 2 rows.
87 [93: 97: 103: 107] sts.
Dec 1 st at each end of next 3 [5: 5: 7: 7] rows,
then on every foll alt row until
73 [75: 77: 79: 81] sts rem.
Cont straight until armhole measures
21 [21: 22: 22: 23] cm, ending with RS facing
for next row.
Shape shoulders and back neck
Cast off 7 [7: 8: 8: 8] sts at beg of next 2 rows.
59 [61: 61: 63: 65] sts.
Next row (RS): Cast off 7 [7: 8: 8: 8] sts,
K until there are 12 [12: 11: 11:12] sts on right
needle and turn, leaving rem sts on a holder.
Work each side of neck separately.
Cast off 4 sts at beg of next row.
Cast off rem 8 [8: 7: 7: 8] sts.
With RS facing, rejoin yarn to rem sts, cast off
centre 21 [23: 23: 25: 25] sts, K to end.
Work to match first side, reversing shapings.

LEFT FRONT

Using 3¾mm (US 5) needles cast on
51 [54: 57: 60: 63] sts. Beg with a RS row,

cont in g st throughout as folls:
Work 10 rows.
Change to 4mm (US 6) needles.
Work 8 [10: 10: 12: 12] rows, ending with RS
facing for next row.
Place marker on 26th [27th: 28th: 29th: 30th] st
in from end of last row.
Next row (RS) (dec): K2tog, K to within 1 st
of marked st, K3tog,
K to end.
Work 19 rows.
Rep last 20 rows once more and then first of
these rows (the dec row) again.
42 [45: 48: 51: 54] sts.
Work 17 rows, ending with RS facing for
next row.
Next row (RS) (inc): Inc in first st, K to
marked st, M1, K marked st, M1, K to end.
Work 19 rows.
Rep last 20 rows once more and then first of
these rows (the inc row) again
51 [54: 57: 60: 63] sts.
Cont straight until left front matches back to
beg of armhole shaping, ending with RS facing
for next row.
Shape armhole
Cast off 4 [4: 5: 5: 6] sts at beg of next row.
47 [50: 52: 55: 57] sts.
Work 1 row.
Dec 1 st at armhole edge of next
3 [5: 5: 7: 7] rows, then on every foll alt row
until 40 [41: 42: 43: 44] sts rem.
Cont straight until armhole measures
12 [12: 13: 13: 14] cm, ending with WS facing
for next row.
Shape neck
Cast off 10 [11: 11: 12: 12] sts at beg of next row.
30 [30: 31: 31: 32] sts.
Work 2 rows, ending with RS facing for
next row.
Dec 1 st at neck edge of next and every foll
4th row until 22 [22: 23: 23: 24] sts rem.
Cont straight until left front matches back to
start of shoulder shaping, ending with RS facing
for next row.
Shape shoulder
Cast off 7 [7: 8: 8: 8] sts at beg of next and foll
alt row.

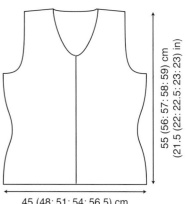

43 (43: 44: 44: 44) cm
(17 (17: 17.5: 17.5: 17.5) in)

55 (56: 57: 58: 59) cm
(21.5 (22: 22.5: 23: 23) in)

45 (48: 51: 54: 56.5) cm
(17.5 (19: 20: 21.5: 22) in)

Work 1 row.

Cast off rem 8 [8: 7: 7: 8] sts.

Mark positions for 5 buttons along left front opening edge – lowest button to be level with 2nd dec row up from cast-on edge, top button level with beg of armhole shaping and rem 3 buttons evenly spaced between.

RIGHT FRONT

Using 3¾mm (US 5) needles cast on 51 [54: 57: 60: 63] sts. Beg with a RS row, cont in g st throughout as folls:

Work 10 rows.

Change to 4mm (US 6) needles.

Work 8 [10: 10: 12: 12] rows, ending with RS facing for next row.

Place marker on 26th [27th: 28th: 29th: 30th] st in from beg of last row.

Next row (RS) (dec): K to within 1 st of marked st, K3tog tbl, K to last 2 sts, K2tog tbl.

Work 19 rows.

Next row (RS) (dec) (buttonhole row): K2, K2tog, yfwd (to make a buttonhole), K to within 1 st of marked st, K3tog tbl, K to last 2 sts, K2tog tbl.

Making a further 4 buttonholes (in same way as 1st buttonhole) to correspond with positions marked for buttons on left front, complete to match left front, reversing shapings.

SLEEVES (both alike)

Using 3¾mm (US 5) needles cast on 47 [47: 49: 49: 51] sts. Beg with a RS row, cont in g st throughout as folls: Work 10 rows.

Change to 4mm (US 6) needles.

Cont in g st, inc 1 st at each end of 3rd and every foll 12th [10th: 12th: 10th: 10th] row until there are 63 [51: 75: 61: 63] sts, then on 4 [11: 0: 8: 8] foll 14th [12th: –: 12th: 12th] rows. 71 [73: 75: 77: 79] sts.

Cont straight until sleeve measures 43 [43: 44: 44: 44] cm from cast-on edge, ending with RS facing for next row.

Shape top

Cast off 4 [4: 5: 5: 6] sts at beg of next 2 rows. 63 [65: 65: 67: 67] sts.

Dec 1 st at each end of next 3 rows, then on foll alt row, then on foll 4th row. 53 [55: 55: 57: 57] sts.

Work 5 rows.

Dec 1 st at each end of next and every foll 6th row until 41 [45: 43: 47: 43] sts rem, then on every foll 4th row until 39 [41: 39: 41: 41] sts rem, then on every foll alt row until 35 sts rem.

Dec 1 st at each end of next 3 rows, ending with RS facing for next row. 29 sts.

Cast off 4 sts at beg of next 2 rows.

Cast off rem 21 sts.

MAKING UP

Press as described on the information page.

Join both shoulder seams using back stitch.

Collar

Using 4mm (US 6) needles cast on 69 [73: 73: 77: 77] sts.

Beg with a RS row, cont in g st throughout as folls:

Work 1 row.

Row 2: K to last 10 sts, wrap next st (by slipping next st and then taking yarn to opposite side of work between needles, slip same st back onto left needle – when working back across wrapped sts, work loop made and st to as 1 st), turn.

Row 3: As row 2.

Rows 4 and 5: K to last 16 sts, wrap next st and turn.

Rows 6 and 7: K to last 22 sts, wrap next st and turn.

Rows 8 and 9: K to last 28 sts, wrap next st and turn.

Row 10: Knit to end.

Cont in g st, inc 1 st at both ends of next and foll 3 [3: 4: 4: 5] alt rows.

77 [81: 83: 87: 89] sts.

Place markers at both ends of last row.

Work 12 [12: 12: 14: 14] rows.

Cast off.

Sew collar to neck edge as folls: positioning collar markers halfway across top of front neck cast-off sts, sew shaped row end edges of collar to front cast-off sts, then sew cast-on edge of collar to front slope and back neck edges.

Shoulder pads (make 2)

Cast on 1 st using 4mm (US 6) needles.

Beg with a RS row, cont in g st throughout as folls:

Inc 1 st at beg of next 24 rows. 25 sts.

Dec 1 st at beg of next 24 rows. 1 st.

Fasten off.

Fold shoulder pad in half along longest row and sew shaped edges tog.

Sew in shoulder pad by attaching ends of longest row to armhole seam and pointed end to shoulder seam.

See information page for finishing instructions, setting in sleeves using the set-in method.

ORKNEY

Marie Wallin

●●

SIZE

To fit bust

81-86	91-97	102-107	112-117	122-127	cm
32-34	36-38	40-42	44-46	48-50	in

Actual bust measurement of garment

89	98.5	109.5	122.5	137	cm
35	39	43	48	54	in

YARN

Rowan Felted Tweed

A Camel 157					
2	2	2	2	3	x 50gm
B Carbon 159					
1	1	1	2	2	x 50gm
C Bilberry 151					
1	1	1	1	2	x 50gm
D Peony 183					
1	1	1	1	1	x 50gm
E Watery 152					
1	1	1	1	1	x 50gm
F Seafarer 170					
1	1	1	1	1	x 50gm
G Pine 158					
1	1	1	1	1	x 50gm
H Ginger 154					
1	1	1	1	1	x 50gm
I Celadon 184					
1	1	1	1	1	x 50gm
J Cinnamon 175					
1	1	1	1	1	x 50gm
K Phantom 153					
1	1	1	1	1	x 50gm
L Cumin 193					
1	1	1	1	1	x 50gm
M Mineral 181					
1	1	1	1	1	x 50gm

NEEDLES

1 pair 2¾mm (no 12) (US 2) needles
1 pair 3¼mm (no 10) (US 3) needles

BUTTONS

9 x 15 mm grey buttons from Groves and Banks. Please see information page for contact details.

TENSION

25 sts and 29 rows to 10cm (4in) measured over patterned stocking st using 3¼mm (US 3) needles.

BACK

Using 2¾mm (US 2) needles and yarn A, cast on 110 [122: 138: 154: 170] sts.
Row 1 (RS): K2, *P2, K2, rep from * to end.
Row 2: P2, *K2, P2, rep from * to end.
Join in yarn B.
Row 3: Using yarn A K2, *using yarn B P2, using yarn A K2, rep from * to end.
Row 4: Using yarn A P2, *using yarn B K2, using yarn A P2, rep from * to end.
Rows 5 to 18: As rows 3 and 4, 7 times.
Break off yarn B.
Rows 19 and 20: As rows 1 and 2, inc [inc: dec: dec: inc] 1 st at end of row 20.
111 [123: 137: 153: 171] sts.
Change to 3¼mm (US 3) needles.
Beg and ending rows as indicated, using the fairisle technique as described on the information page and repeating the 106 row patt rep throughout, cont in patt from chart for body, which is worked entirely in st st beg with a K row, as follows:
Cont in patt until back measures 31 [32: 33: 34: 35]cm, ending with RS facing for next row.
Shape armholes
(Note: Armhole shaping is NOT shown on chart.)
Keeping patt correct, cast off 5 [6: 7: 8: 9] sts at beg of next 2 rows. 101 [111: 123: 137: 153] sts.
Dec 1 st at each end of next 5 [7: 7: 9: 15] rows, then on foll 5 [6: 8: 9: 7] alt rows.
81 [85: 93: 101: 109] sts.
Cont straight until armhole measures 18 [19: 20: 21: 22]cm, ending with RS facing for next row.

Shape shoulders and back neck

Next row (RS): Cast off 6 [7: 8: 9: 10] sts, patt until there are 16 [17: 19: 22: 24] sts on right needle and turn, leaving rem sts on a holder.
Work each side of neck separately.
Dec 1 st at neck edge of next 3 rows, ending with RS facing for next row, **and at same time** cast off 6 [7: 8: 9: 10] sts at beg of 2nd row.
Cast off rem 7 [7: 8: 10: 11] sts.
With RS facing, rejoin yarns to rem sts, cast off centre 37 [37: 39: 39: 41] sts, patt to end.
Complete to match first side, reversing shapings.

LEFT FRONT

Using 2¾mm (US 2) needles and yarn A, cast on 59 [63: 71: 79: 87] sts.
Row 1 (RS): K2, *P2, K2, rep from * to last st, K1.
Row 2: K1, P2, *K2, P2, rep from * to end.
Join in yarn B.
Row 3: Using yarn A K2, *using yarn B P2, using yarn A K2, rep from * to last st, using yarn A K1.
Row 4: Using yarn A K1, P2, *using yarn B K2, using yarn A P2, rep from * to end.
Rows 5 to 18: As rows 3 and 4, 7 times.
Break off yarn B.
Rows 19 and 20: As rows 1 and 2, inc 0 [2: 1: 1: 2] sts evenly across row 20.
59 [65: 72: 80: 89] sts.
Change to 3¼mm (US 3) needles.
Beg and ending rows as indicated, using the fairisle technique as described on the information page and repeating the 106 row patt rep throughout, cont in patt from chart for body, which is worked entirely in st st beg with a K row, as follows:
Cont in patt until left front matches back to beg of armhole shaping, ending with RS facing for next row.
Shape armhole
(Note: Armhole shaping is NOT shown on chart.)
Keeping patt correct, cast off 5 [6: 7: 8: 9] sts at beg of next row. 54 [59: 65: 72: 80] sts.
Work 1 row.
Dec 1 st at armhole edge of next 5 [7: 7: 9: 15] rows, then on foll 5 [6: 8: 9: 7] alt rows.
44 [46: 50: 54: 58] sts.

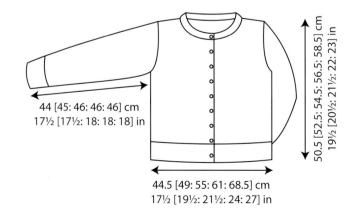

44 [45: 46: 46: 46] cm
17½ [17½: 18: 18: 18] in

44.5 [49: 55: 61: 68.5] cm
17½ [19½: 21½: 24: 27] in

50.5 [52.5: 54.5: 56.5: 58.5] cm
19½ [20½: 21½: 22: 23] in

Cont straight until 24 [24: 26: 26: 28] rows less have been worked than on back to beg of shoulder shaping, ending with RS facing for next row.

Shape front neck

Next row (RS): Patt 31 [33: 37: 41: 45] sts, cast off rem 13 sts.

Rejoin yarns with WS facing and cont as follows:

Dec 1 st at neck edge of next 6 rows, then on foll 5 [5: 6: 6: 7] alt rows, then on foll 4th row. 19 [21: 24: 28: 31] sts.

Work 3 rows, ending with RS facing for next row.

Shape shoulder

Cast off 6 [7: 8: 9: 10] sts at beg of next and foll alt row.

Work 1 row.

Cast off rem 7 [7: 8: 10: 11] sts.

Mark positions for 9 buttons along left front opening edge – first button to come level with row 5, last button to come just above neck shaping, and rem 7 buttons evenly spaced between.

RIGHT FRONT

Using 2¾mm (US 2) needles and yarn A, cast on 59 [63: 71: 79: 87] sts.

Row 1 (RS): K3, *P2, K2, rep from * to end.

Row 2: P2, *K2, P2, rep from * to last st, K1.

Join in yarn B.

Row 3: Using yarn A K3, *using yarn B P2, using yarn A K2, rep from * to end.

Row 4: Using yarn A P2, *using yarn B K2, using yarn A P2, rep from * to last st, using yarn A K1.

Row 5: Using yarn A K3, using yarn B yfrn, P2tog (to make first buttonhole), using yarn A K2, *using yarn B P2, using yarn A K2, rep from * to end.

Row 6: As row 4.

Rows 7 to 18: As rows 3 and 4, 6 times.

Break off yarn B.

Rows 19 and 20: As rows 1 and 2, inc 0 [2: 1: 1: 2] sts evenly across row 20. 59 [65: 72: 80: 89] sts.

Change to 3¼mm (US 3) needles.

Beg and ending rows as indicated, using the fairisle technique as described on the information page and repeating the 106 row patt rep throughout, cont in patt from chart for body, which is worked entirely in st st beg with a K row, as follows:

Cont straight until right front measures same as left front **to point marked on left front for 2nd button,** ending with RS facing for next row.

Next row (buttonhole row) (RS): Patt 3 sts, yfwd, K2tog (to make a buttonhole), patt to end.

Making a further 6 buttonholes in this way to correspond with positions marked for buttons on left front, complete to match left front, reversing shapings and working first row of neck shaping as follows:

Shape front neck

Next row (RS): Cast off 13 sts, patt to end. 31 [33: 37: 41: 45] sts.

SLEEVES (both alike)

Using 2¾mm (US 2) needles and yarn A, cast on 46 [46: 50: 50: 54] sts.

Work rows 1 to 20 as given for back, dec [inc: dec: inc: dec] 1 st at end of row 20. 45 [47: 49: 51: 53] sts.

Change to 3¼mm (US 3) needles.

Beg and ending rows as indicated, using the fairisle technique as described on the information page and repeating the 106 row patt rep throughout, cont in patt from chart for sleeve, which is worked entirely in st st beg with a K row, as follows:

Inc 1 st at each end of 3rd and every foll 4th row to 73 [77: 83: 91: 99] sts, then on every foll 6th row until there are 85 [89: 93: 97: 101] sts, taking inc sts into patt.

Cont straight until sleeve measures 44 [45: 46: 46: 46]cm, ending with RS facing for next row.

Shape top

Keeping patt correct, cast off 5 [6: 7: 8: 9] sts at beg of next 2 rows. 75 [77: 79: 81: 83] sts.

Dec 1 st at each end of next 5 rows, then on every foll alt row until 51 sts rem, then on foll 13 rows, ending with RS facing for next row. 25 sts.

Cast off 5 sts at beg of next 2 rows.

Cast off rem 15 sts.

MAKING UP

Press as described on the information page.

Join both shoulder seams using back stitch, or mattress stitch if preferred.

Neckband

With RS facing, using 2¾mm (US 2) needles and yarn A, beg and ending at front opening edges, pick up and knit 38 [38: 39: 39: 42] sts up right side of neck, 44 [44: 46: 46: 48] sts from back, then 38 [38: 39: 39: 42] sts down left side of neck. 120 [120: 124: 124: 132] sts.

Row 1 (WS): K1, P2, *K2, P2, rep from * to last st, K1.

Join in yarn B.

Row 2: Using yarn A K3, using yarn B yfrn, P2tog (to make 9th buttonhole), using yarn A K2, *using yarn B P2, using yarn A K2, rep from * to last st, using yarn A K1.

Row 3: Using yarn A K1, P2, *using yarn B K2, using yarn A P2, rep from * to last st, using yarn A K1.

Row 4: Using yarn A K3, *using yarn B P2, using yarn A K2, rep from * to last st, using yarn A K1.

Row 5: As row 3.

Break off yarn B.

Row 6: K3, *P2, K2, rep from * to last st, K1.

Cast off in rib (on WS).

Left front facing

Using 2¾mm (US 2) needles and yarn A, cast on 7 sts.

Row 1 (RS): K2, P1, K1, P1, K2.

Row 2: K1, (P1, K1) 3 times.

These 2 rows form rib.

Cont in rib until facing fits up entire left front opening edge, from cast-on edge to cast-off edge of neckband, ending with RS facing for next row.

Cast off in rib.

Right front facing

Work as given for left front facing with the addition of 9 buttonholes worked to correspond with buttonholes along right front opening edge as follows:

Buttonhole row (RS): K2, P1, yrn, P2tog (to make a buttonhole), K2.

Slip stitch facings to front opening edges, then fold facings to inside and neatly sew in place.

See information page for finishing instructions, setting in sleeves using the set-in method.

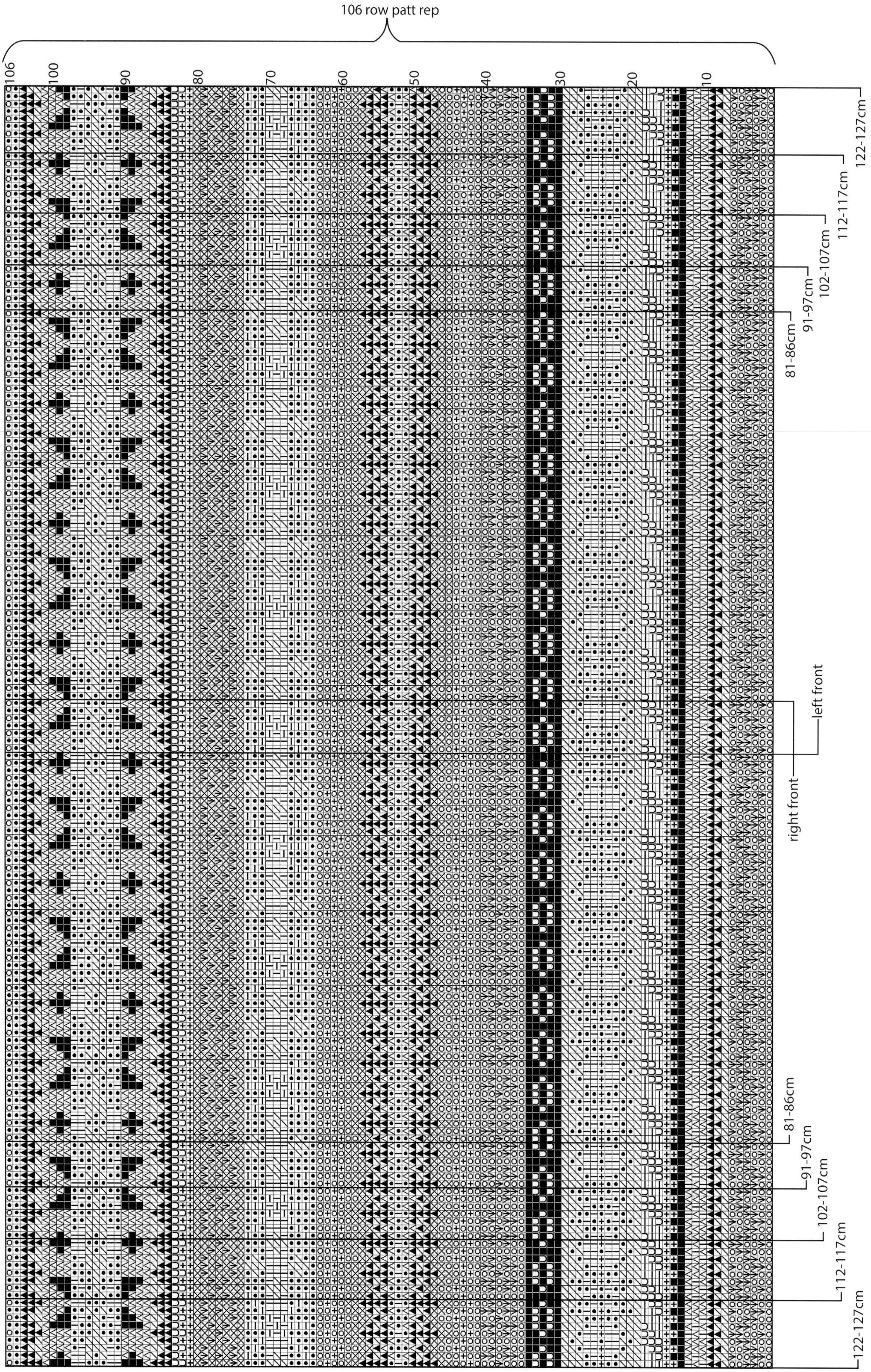

106 row patt rep

106 100 90 80 70 60 50 40 30 20 10

122-127cm
112-117cm
102-107cm
91-97cm
81-86cm

left front

right front

81-86cm
91-97cm
102-107cm
112-117cm
122-127cm

Body

200

Sleeves

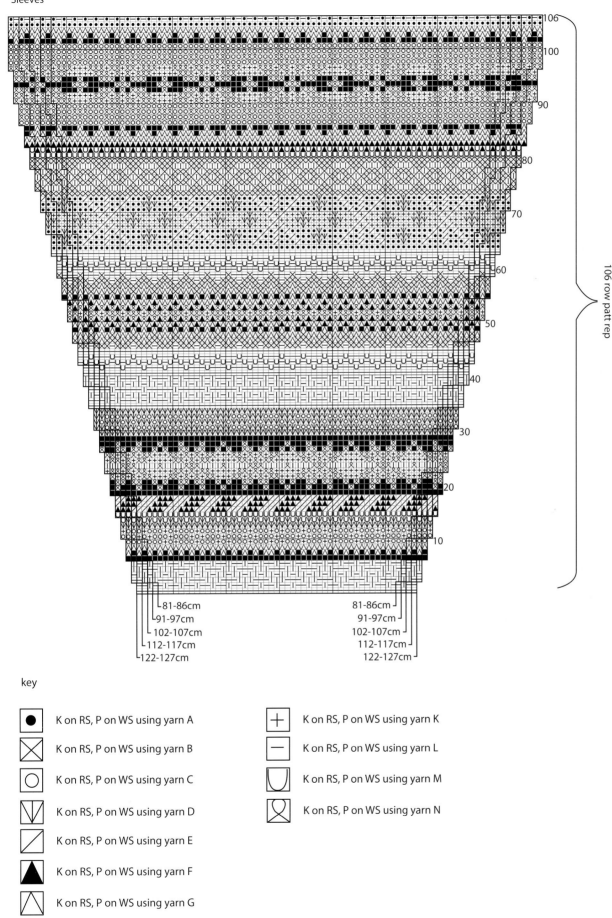

106 row patt rep

81-86cm
91-97cm
102-107cm
112-117cm
122-127cm

81-86cm
91-97cm
102-107cm
112-117cm
122-127cm

key

●	K on RS, P on WS using yarn A	
⊠	K on RS, P on WS using yarn B	
○	K on RS, P on WS using yarn C	
⋁	K on RS, P on WS using yarn D	
⟋	K on RS, P on WS using yarn E	
▲	K on RS, P on WS using yarn F	
△	K on RS, P on WS using yarn G	
│	K on RS, P on WS using yarn H	
■	K on RS, P on WS using yarn I	

+	K on RS, P on WS using yarn K
−	K on RS, P on WS using yarn L
⋃	K on RS, P on WS using yarn M
⊗	K on RS, P on WS using yarn N

PLAID COAT

Kim Hargreaves

● ● ●

SIZE

To fit bust

81	86	91	cm
32	34	36	in

Actual bust measurement of garment

138.5	144.5	150.5	cm
54½	57	59	in

YARN

Rowan Brushed Fleece

A Rock 273

15	16	16	x 50gm

Rowan Softyak DK

★B Steppe 231

2	2	2	x 50gm

★C Prairie 233

1	1	1	x 50gm

★Use Softyak DK **DOUBLE** throughout.

NEEDLES

1 pair 5½mm (no 5) (US 9) needles
1 pair 6mm (no 4) (US 10) needles

BUTTONS – 5 x 25mm single shank (leather look) from Groves and Banks. Please see information page for contact details.

TENSION

13 sts and 19 rows to 10cm (4in) measured over st st using 6mm (US 10) needles and yarn A.

BACK

Using 5½mm (US 9) needles and yarn A, cast on 80 [84: 88] sts..

Row 1 (RS): ★K1, P1, rep from ★ to end.
Row 2: ★P1, K1, rep from ★ to end.
These 2 rows form moss st.
Work in moss st for a further 4 rows, ending with RS facing for next row.
Change to 6mm (US 10) needles.
Row 7 (RS): (K1, P1) twice, K to last 5 sts, (P1, K1) twice, P1.
Row 8: (P1, K1) twice, P to last 5 sts, (K1, P1) twice, K1.
These 2 rows set the sts for the back vents – st st central panel with 5 moss sts at each side.
Cont in patt as set for a further 22 rows, ending with RS facing for next row.
Beg with a K row, cont in st st throughout as folls:
Inc 1 st at each end of next and 4 foll 12th rows. 90 [94: 98] sts.
Cont in st st for a further 13 rows, ending with RS facing for next row.

Shape armholes
Cast off 5 sts at beg of next 2 rows.
80 [84: 88] sts.

Sizes 91-97 and 102-107 only
Next row (Dec): K2, K3tog, K to last 5 sts, K3tog tbl, K2.
Next row: Purl.
Rep last 2 rows [1: 0] times. [76: 84] sts.

All sizes
Work 2 rows in st st.
Next row (Dec): K2, K3tog, K to last 5 sts, K3tog tbl, K2.
Next row: Purl.
Rep the last 4 rows, until 28 sts rem.
Work 3 rows in st st.
Next row: K2, K3tog, K2 and turn, leaving rem sts on a holder. 5 sts.
Work each side of neck separately.
Next row: Cast off 4 sts. 1 st.
Fasten off.
With RS facing, rejoin yarn to rem sts.
Next row: Cast off centre 14 sts, K1, K3tog tbl, K2. 5 sts.
Complete to match first side, reversing shapings.

POCKET LININGS (Make 2)

Using 6mm (US 10) needles and yarn A, cast on 22 sts.
Beg with a K row work 34 [34: 36] rows in st st.
Leave sts on a holder.

LEFT FRONT

Using 5½mm (US 9) needles and yarn A, cast on 40 [42: 44] sts.
Work 6 rows in moss st as given for back.
Change to 6mm (US I0) needles.
Row 7 (RS): (K1, P1) twice, K to last 5 sts, (P1, K1) twice, P1.
Row 8: (P1, K1) twice, P to last 5 sts, (K1, P1) twice, K1.
These 2 rows set the sts for the left front vent and front opening – st st central panel with 5 moss sts at each side.
Cont in patt as set for a further 22 rows, ending with RS facing for next row.
Next row (RS inc): K1, M1, K to last 5 sts, (P1, K1) twice, P1. 41 [43: 45] sts.
Next row: (P1, K1) twice, P to end.
This sets the sts for the left front – st st with 5 moss sts at front opening.
Cont in patt as set throughout as folls:
Inc 1 st at beg of foll 11th row. 42 [44: 46] sts.
Work 3 [3: 5] rows in patt, ending with RS facing for next row.
Place pocket lining
Next row: K7 [9: 9], place rem 35 [35: 37] sts on a second holder, K across 22 pocket lining sts from first holder. 29 [31: 31] sts.
Inc 1 st at beg of 8th [8th: 6th] row.
30 [32: 32] sts.
Work 2 [2: 4] rows in st st, ending with WS facing for next row.
Leave these 30 [32: 32] sts on a holder for back of pocket.
With RS facing, rejoin yarn to rem 35 [35: 37] sts from second holder.
Cont in patt of st st with moss st front opening, cast off 4 sts at beg of next and 4 foll alt rows, then cast off 2 sts at beg of foll alt row, ending with WS facing for next row. 13 [13: 15] sts.
Next row: P across 13 [13: 15] sts on needle and 30 [32: 32] sts from holder for back of pocket. 43 [45: 47] sts.

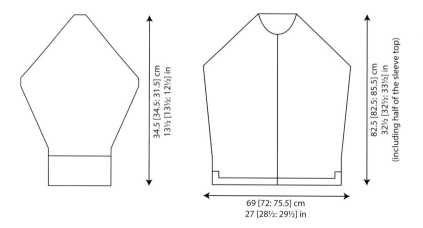

34.5 [34.5: 31.5] cm
13½ [13½: 12½] in

82.5 [82.5: 85.5] cm
32½ [32½: 33½] in
(including half of the sleeve top)

69 [72: 75.5] cm
27 [28½: 29½] in

Cont in patt as set, inc 1 st at beg of
9th [9th: 7th] row and foll 12th row.
45 [47: 49] sts.
Cont in patt for a further 13 rows, ending with
RS facing for next row.
Shape armhole
Cast off 5 sts at beg of next row. 40 [42: 44] sts.
Next row: Patt to end.
Sizes 91-97 and 102-107 only
Next row (Dec): K2, K3tog, patt to end.
Next row: Patt to end.
Rep last 2 rows [1: 0] times. [38: 42] sts.
All sizes
Work 2 rows in patt.
Next row (Dec): K2, K3tog, patt to end.
Next row: Patt to end.
Rep the last 4 rows, until 20 sts rem, ending
with a **dec** row, and WS facing for next row.
Shape front neck
Next row (WS): Cast off 4 sts, patt to end.
16 sts.
Dec 1 st at neck edge on next 3 rows, then foll
4 alt rows, and **at the same time** dec as set at
armhole edge (i.e. K2, then K3tog) on
3rd and 3 foll 4th rows. 1 st.
Fasten off.

RIGHT FRONT
Using 5½mm (US 9) needles and yarn A, cast on
40 [42: 44] sts.
Work 6 rows in moss st as given for back.
Change to 6mm (US I0) needles.
Row 7 (RS): (K1, P1) twice, K to last 5 sts,
(P1, K1) twice, P1.
Row 8: (P1, K1) twice, P to last 5 sts, (K1, P1)
twice, K1.

These 2 rows set the sts for the right front vent
and front opening - st st central panel with
5 moss sts at each side.
Cont in patt as set for a further 22 rows, ending
with RS facing for next row.
Next row (RS inc): (K1, P1) twice, K to
last st, M1, K1. 41 [43: 45] sts.
Next row: P to last 5 sts, (K1, P1) twice, K1.
This sets the sts for the right front − st st with
5 moss sts at front opening.
Cont in patt as set throughout as folls:
Inc 1 st at end of foll 11th row. 42 [44: 46] sts.
Work 3 [3: 5] rows in patt, ending with RS
facing for next row.
Place pocket lining
Next row: Break yarn, place first 35 [35: 37] sts
on a second holder, K across 22 pocket lining sts
from first holder and k7 [9: 9] rem sts on needle.
29 [31: 31] sts.
Inc 1 st at end of 8th [8th: 6th] row.
30 [32: 32] sts.
Work 2 [2: 4] rows in st st, ending with WS
facing for next row.
Leave these 30 [32: 32] sts on a holder for back
of pocket.
With WS facing, rejoin yarn to rem
35 [35: 37] sts from second holder.
Cont in patt of st st with moss st front opening,
cast off 4 sts at beg of next and 4 foll alt rows,
then cast off 2 sts at beg of foll alt row, ending
with RS facing for next row. Break yarn.
13 [13: 15] sts.
Next row (WS): P across 30 [32: 32] sts from
holder for back pocket, then P across
13 [13: 15] sts on needle. 43 [45: 47] sts.
Complete to match left front, reversing shapings.

SLEEVES
Using 6mm (US I0) needles and yarn A, cast on
40 sts.
Beg with a K row, work 66 [66: 60] rows in st st,
at the same time, inc 1 st at each end of 9th,
and every foll alt row to 72 [72: 84] sts, then for
81-86 and **91-97 sizes only,** every 4th row to
80 [80] sts, ending with RS facing for
next row.
Shape top
Cast off 5 sts at beg of next 2 rows.
70 [70: 74] sts.
Next row: K2, K3tog, K to last 5 sts, K3tog tbl,
K2.
Next row: Purl.
Rep the last 2 rows 2 [2: 1 times more.
58 [58: 66] sts.
Work 2 rows in st st.
Next row: K2, K3tog, K to last 5 sts,
K3tog tbl, K2.
Work 3 rows in st st.
Rep the last 4 rows until 10 sts rem.
Cast off.

COLLAR
Using 5½mm (US 9) needles and yarn A, cast
on 74 sts.
Beg and ending rows as indicated and using
the **intarsia** technique as described on the
information page, and using yarns B and C
doubled throughout, work 51 rows in patt from
Chart for Collar, which is worked entirely in
st st beg with a K rows as folls:

KEY
☐ A
 B used double
☒ C used double

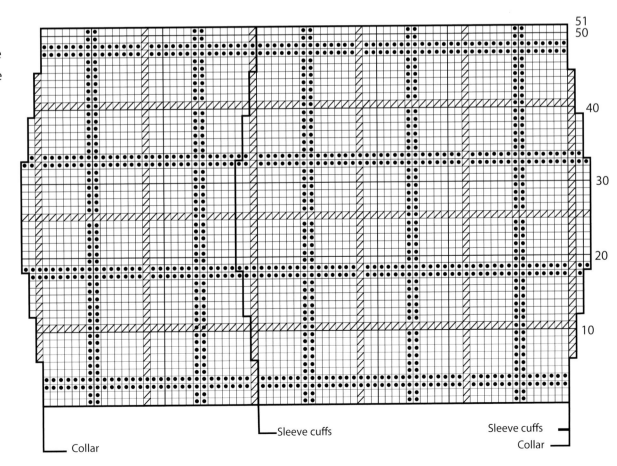

Collar

Sleeve cuffs

Sleeve cuffs
Collar

Shape sides by inc 1 st at each end of rows 7,
13 and 19, and dec 1 st at each end of rows 34,
40 and 46.
Cast off in A (on WS).

CUFFS
Using 5½mm (US 9) needles and yarn A, cast on
44 sts.
Work as given for collar but using the Chart for
the Sleeve cuffs.

MAKING UP
Press as described on the information page.
Join raglan seams, sleeve and side seams using
back stitch or mattress stitch if preferred.
Button band
Using 5½mm (US 9) needles and yarn A, cast on
6 sts.
Work in moss st as given for back until band fits
up left front when slightly stretched.
Slip st band into place.
Mark position of 5 buttons, the first to come
20cm from cast-on edge, the fifth to come 2.5cm
from top of band, the others spaced
evenly between.
Buttonhole band
Work as for button band with the addition of
5 buttonholes to correspond with markers,
making buttonholes as follows:
Buttonhole row (RS): Patt 2, cast off 2 sts,
patt 1.
Next row: Patt 2, cast on 2 sts, patt 2.
Slip st band into place.
Pocket tops (both alike)
With RS facing, using 5½mm (US 9) needles
and yarn A, pick up and knit 23 sts along
pocket edge.
Row 1 (RS): ★K1, P1, rep from ★ to last st, K1.
Last row forms moss st.
Work 5 more rows in moss st.
Cast off in moss st.
Slip st pocket tops into place on RS, and pocket
linings into place on WS.
With RS facing fold cuffs in half and stitch the
row ends together. Press seams well, on WS.
With WS together fold cuffs in half and with
seams matching slip st cast-on and cast-off edges
to bottom of sleeves.
With RS facing fold collar in half length ways
and stitch row ends together. Press seams on WS
then turn RS out. Placing edge of collar halfway
across front bands and matching centre back of
collar to centre back of neck, slip st cast-on and
cast-off edges of collar to coat neck edge.
Press seams.
Sew on buttons.

PLAIN CELLINI
Marie Wallin

● ● ● ●

SIZE

To fit bust

81-86	91-97	102-107	112-117	cm
32-34	36-38	40-42	44-46	in

Actual bust measurement of garment

93	103	114	128	cm
37	41	45	50	in

YARN

Rowan Felted Tweed

11	13	14	16	x 50gm

(photographed in Bilberry 151)

NEEDLES

1 pair 3¼mm (no 10) (US 3) needles
3¼mm (no 10) (US 3) circular needle

TENSION

26 sts and 48 rows to 10cm (4in) measured over g stitch using 3¼mm (US 3) needles.

BACK (worked sideways, beg at left side seam edge)

Using 3¼mm (US 3) needles cast on
172 [177: 182: 188] sts.
Place marker after 56th [59th: 61st: 64th] st from end of cast-on edge (beg of first row) to denote base of armhole.
Noting that first row is a WS row, now work in g st throughout as follows:
Work 7 rows, ending with RS facing for next row.
Inc 1 st at end of next and 5 [5: 5: 6] foll
6th [8th: 10th: 12th] rows.

---

178 [183: 188: 195] sts.
Work 1 [3: 7: 1] rows, ending with RS facing for next row.

Shape dart

Row 1 (RS): K101 [103: 106: 109], wrap next st (by slipping next st from left needle to right, taking yarn to opposite side of work between needles and then slipping same st back onto left needle – when working back across wrapped sts work the wrapped st and the wrapping loop together) and turn.
Row 2 and every foll alt row: knit to end.
Row 3: K95 [97: 101: 103], wrap next st and turn.
Row 5: K89 [91: 95: 97], wrap next st and turn.
Row 7: K83 [85: 89: 91], wrap next st and turn.
Row 9: K77 [79: 83: 85], wrap next st and turn.
Row 11: K71 [73: 77: 79], wrap next st and turn.
Row 13: K65 [67: 71: 73], wrap next st and turn.
Row 15: K59 [61: 65: 67], wrap next st and turn.
Row 17: K53 [55: 59: 61], wrap next st and turn.
Row 19: K47 [49: 53: 55], wrap next st and turn.
Row 21: K41 [43: 47: 49], wrap next st and turn.
Row 23: K35 [37: 41: 43], wrap next st and turn.
Row 25: K29 [31: 35: 37], wrap next st and turn.
Row 27: K23 [25: 29: 31], wrap next st and turn.
Row 29:, K17 [19: 23: 25], wrap next st and turn.
Row 31: K11 [13: 17: 19], wrap next st and turn.
Row 33: As row 29.
Row 35: As row 27.
Row 37: As row 25.
Row 39: As row 23.
Row 41: As row 21.
Row 43: As row 19.
Row 45: As row 17.
Row 47: As row 15.
Row 49: As row 13.

Row 51: As row 11.
Row 53: As row 9.
Row 55: As row 7.
Row 57: As row 5.
Row 59: As row 3.
Row 61: As row 1.
Row 63: K101 [103: 106: 109], wrap next st and turn.
Row 64: As row 2.
These 64 rows complete dart.
Work 4 [4: 2: 10] rows, ending with RS facing for next row.
Inc 1 st at end of next and 1 [1: 1: 0] foll 6th [8th: 10th: –] row. 180 [185: 190: 196] sts.
Work 12 [10: 8: 10] rows, ending with WS facing for next row.

Shape back neck

Cast off 3 sts at beg of next row, then dec 1 st at end of foll row.
Rep last 2 rows once more.
172 [177: 182: 188] sts.★★
Dec 1 st at shaped neck edge of 8th and 2 foll 8th rows. 169 [174: 179: 185] sts.
Work 21 [21: 23: 23] rows, ending with RS facing for next row.
Work the 64 dart rows once more.
Work 22 [22: 24: 24] rows, ending with RS facing for next row.
Inc 1 st at end of next and 2 foll 8th rows.
172 [177: 182: 188] sts.
Work 7 rows, ending with RS facing for next row.
★★★Inc 1 st at end of next row, then cast on 3 sts at beg of foll row.
Rep last 2 rows once more. 180 [185: 190: 196] sts.
Neck shaping is now complete.
Dec 1 st at end of 13th [11th: 9th: 11th] and 1 [1: 1: 0] foll 6th [8th: 10th: –] row.
178 [183: 188: 195] sts.
Work 3 [3: 1: 9] rows, ending with RS facing for next row.
Work the 64 dart rows once more.
Dec 1 st at end of 3rd [5th: 9th: 3rd] and 5 [5: 5: 6] foll 6th [8th: 10th: 12th] rows.
172 [177: 182: 188] sts.
Work 6 rows, ending with WS facing for next row.

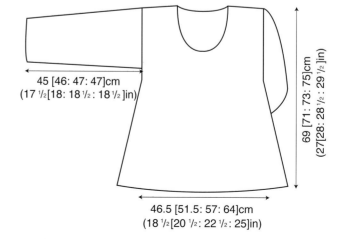

45 [46: 47: 47]cm
(17 ½[18: 18 ½: 18 ½]in)

69 [71: 73: 75]cm
(27[28: 28 ½: 29 ½]in)

46.5 [51.5: 57: 64]cm
(18 ½[20 ½: 22 ½: 25]in)

Cast off (on WS), placing marker after
56th [59th: 61st: 64th] cast-off st to denote base
of armhole.

FRONT
Work as given for back to ★★.
Cast off 2 sts at beg of next row.
170 [175: 180: 186] sts.
Dec 1 st at shaped neck edge of next 21 rows,
then on foll 3 alt rows, then on 2 foll 4th rows.
144 [149: 154: 160] sts.
Work 9 [9: 11: 11] rows, ending with RS facing
for next row.
Work the 64 dart rows once more.
Work 10 [10: 12: 12] rows, ending with RS
facing for next row.
Inc 1 st at neck edge of next and 2 foll 4th rows,
then on foll 3 alt rows, then on foll 20 rows.
170 [175: 180: 186] sts.
Cast on 2 sts at beg of next row, ending with RS
facing for next row. 172 [177: 182: 188] sts.
Complete as given for back from ★★★.

SLEEVES (both alike)
Using 3¼mm (US 3) needles cast on
80 [82: 84: 84] sts.
Noting that first row is a WS row, now work in
g st throughout as follows:
Dec 1 st at each end of 30th and 2 foll 30th
rows. 74 [76: 78: 78] sts.
Work 27 rows, ending with RS facing for
next row.
Inc 1 st at each end of next and every foll
6th [6th: 6th: 4th] row to 88 [100: 106: 90] sts,
then on every foll 8th [8th: 8th: 6th] row until
there are 98 [104: 108: 112] sts.
Cont straight until sleeve measures
45 [46: 47: 47] cm, ending with WS facing
for next row.
Cast off (on WS).

MAKING UP
Press as described on the information page.
Join right shoulder seam using back stitch, or
mattress stitch if preferred.
Neckband
With RS facing, using 3¼mm (US 3) needles,
pick up and knit 31 sts down left side of front
neck, 24 [24: 26: 26] sts from front, 31 sts up
right side of front neck, then 50 [50: 52: 52] sts
from back. 136 [136: 140: 140] sts.
Cast off knitwise (on WS).
Join left shoulder and neckband seam.
Hem edgings (both alike)
With RS facing, using 3¼mm (US 3) circular
needle, pick up and knit 208 [220: 234: 250] sts
evenly along lower row-end edge.
Cast off knitwise (on WS).
See information page for finishing
instructions, setting in sleeves using the
straight cast-off method.

POWDER PUFF

Kaffe Fassett

SIZE

To fit bust

81	86	91	97	102	cm
32	34	36	38	40	in

Finished bust measurement of garment

100	105	110	116	121	cm
39	41	43	46	48	in

YARN

Rowan Kidsilk Haze

A Romance 681					
7	7	8	8	8	x 25gm

B Candy Girl 606					
2	2	2	3	3	x 25gm

C Grace 580					
1	1	1	1	1	x 25gm

D Dewberry 600					
1	1	1	1	1	x 25gm

E Majestic 589					
1	1	1	1	1	x 25gm

F Pearl 590					
1	1	1	1	1	x 25gm

G Shadow 653					
1	2	2	2	2	x 25gm

H Trance 582					
1	1	1	1	1	x 25gm

J Jelly 597					
1	1	1	2	2	x 25gm

L Heavenly 592					
1	1	1	1	1	x 25gm

Use Kidsilk Haze **DOUBLE** throughout.

NEEDLES

1 pair 3mm (no 11) (US 2/3) needles
1 pair 3¾mm (no 9) (US 5) needles

TENSION

23 sts and 32 rows to 10cm (4in) measured over stocking stitch using 3¾mm (US 5) needles and yarn **DOUBLE**.

BACK

Using 3mm (US 2/3) needles and yarn B **DOUBLE** cast on 115 [121: 127: 133: 139] sts.
Work in g st for 8 rows, ending with RS facing for next row.
Change to 3¾mm (US 5) needles.
Using the **intarsia** technique as described on the information page and starting and ending rows as indicated, cont in patt from chart, which is worked entirely in st st beg with a K row, as folls: Cont straight until chart row 118 [122: 122: 124: 124] has been completed, ending with RS facing for next row. (Work measures approx 39 [40: 40: 41: 41] cm.)

Shape armholes

Keeping patt correct, cast off 5 sts at beg of next 2 rows. 105 [111: 117: 123:129] sts.
Dec 1 st at each end of next 7 rows. 91 [97: 103: 109: 115] sts.
Cont straight until chart row 198 [202: 206: 208: 210] has been completed, ending with RS facing for next row. (Armhole measures approx 25 [25: 26: 26: 27] cm.)

Shape shoulders and back neck

Cast off 8 [8: 9: 10: 11] sts at beg of next 2 rows. 75 [81: 85: 89: 93] sts.
Next row (RS): Cast off 8 [8: 9: 10: 11] sts, K until there are 11 [13: 14: 14: 15] sts on right needle and turn, leaving rem sts on a holder.
Work each side of neck separately.
Cast off 4 sts at beg of next row. Cast off rem 7 [9: 10: 10: 11] sts.
With RS facing, rejoin yarns to rem sts, cast off centre 37 [39: 39: 41: 41] sts, K to end.
Complete to match first side, reversing shapings.

FRONT

Work as given for back until chart row 186 [190: 194: 194: 196] has been completed, ending with RS facing for next row.

Shape neck

Next row (RS): Patt 35 [37: 40: 43: 46] sts and turn, leaving rem sts on a holder.
Work each side of neck separately.
Cast off 5 sts at beg of next row. 30 [32: 35: 38: 41] sts.
Dec 1 st at neck edge of next 5 rows, then on foll 2 [2: 2: 3: 3] alt rows. 23[25: 28: 30: 33] sts.
Work 1 row, ending after chart row 198 [202: 206: 208: 210] and with RS facing for next row.

Shape shoulder

Cast off 8 [8: 9: 10: 11] sts at beg of next and foll alt row.
Work 1 row.
Cast off rem 7 [9: 10: 10: 11] sts.
With RS facing, rejoin yarns to rem sts, cast off centre 21 [23: 23: 23: 23] sts, patt to end.
Complete to match first side, reversing shapings.

SLEEVES

Using 3mm (US 2/3) needles and yarn B **DOUBLE** cast on 69 [69: 71: 73: 73] sts.
Work in g st for 8 rows, ending with RS facing for next row.
Change to 3¾mm (US 5) needles.
Starting and ending rows as indicated, cont in patt from chart, shaping sides by inc 1 st at each end of 7th and every foll 6th row to 103 [103: 105: 111: 103] sts, then on every foll 4th row until there are 117 [117: 121: 121: 125] sts.
Cont straight until chart row 144 [144: 148: 148: 148] has been completed, ending with RS facing for next row. (Sleeve measures approx 47 [47: 48: 48: 48] cm.)

Shape top

Keeping patt correct, cast off 5 sts at beg of next 2 rows. 107 [107: 111: 111: 115] sts.
Dec 1 st at each end of next and foll 6 alt rows. 93 [93: 97: 97: 101] sts.
Work 1 row, ending with RS facing for next row.
Cast off.

MAKING UP

Press as described on the information page.
Join right shoulder seam using back stitch, or mattress st if preferred.

Neckband

With RS facing, using 3mm (US 2/3) needles and yarn B **DOUBLE**, pick up and knit 20 [20: 20: 22: 22] sts down left side of neck, 21 [23: 23: 23: 23] sts from front, 20 [20: 20: 22: 22] sts up right side of neck, then 45 [47: 47: 49: 49] sts from back. 106 [110: 110: 116: 116] sts.
Work in g st for 4 rows, ending with RS facing for next row.
Cast off knitwise (on WS).
See information page for finishing instructions, setting in sleeves using the shallow set-in method.

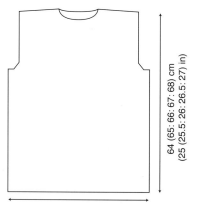

50 (52.5: 55: 58: 60.5) cm
(19.5 (20.5: 21.5: 23: 24) in)

64 (65: 66: 67: 68) cm
(25 (25.5: 26: 26.5: 27) in)

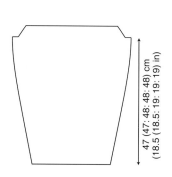

47 (47: 48: 48: 48) cm
(18.5 (18.5: 19: 19: 19) in)

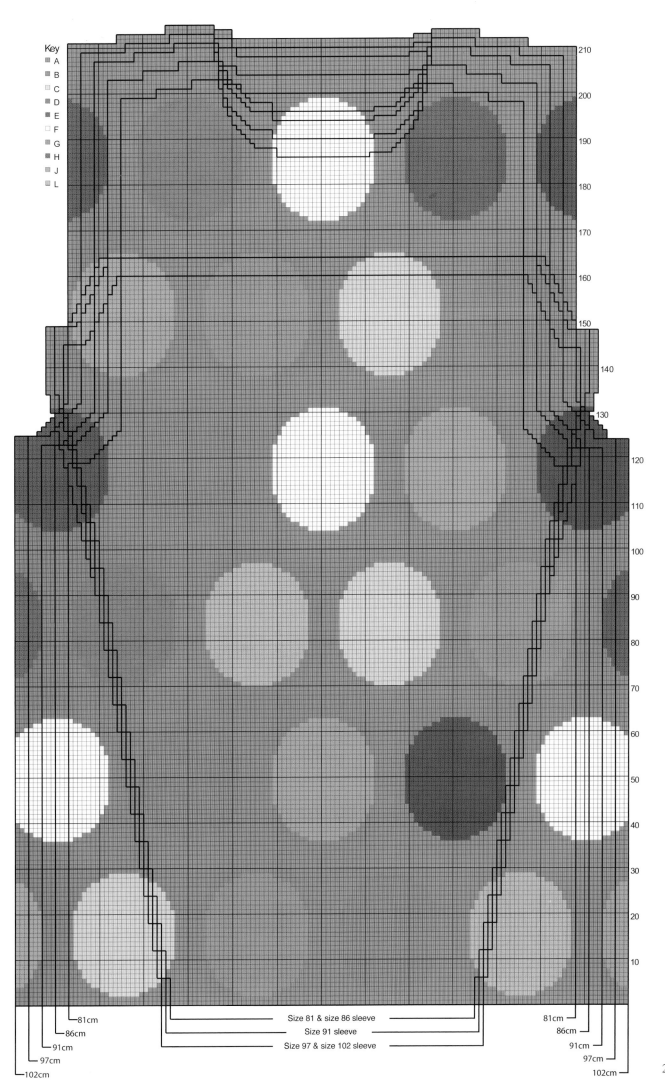

Key
A
B
C
D
E
F
G
H
J
L

210

200

190

180

170

160

150

140

130

120

110

100

90

80

70

60

50

40

30

20

10

81cm

86cm

91cm

97cm

102cm

Size 81 & size 86 sleeve

Size 91 sleeve

Size 97 & size 102 sleeve

81cm

86cm

91cm

97cm

102cm

209

ROBINIA
Marie Wallin

● ● ●

SIZE
To fit bust

81–97	102–117	122–127	cm
32–38	40–46	48–50	in

Actual bust measurement of garment

128	153	166	cm
50	60	65	in

YARN
Rowan Felted Tweed

A Duck Egg 173

8	10	11	x 50gm

B Carbon 159

3	4	4	x 50gm

C Seafarer 170

2	2	2	x 50gm

NEEDLES
1 pair 3¼mm (no 10) (US 3) needles
3¼mm (no 10) (US 3) circular needle, at least 120cm long

BUTTONS
3 x BN1368B from Bedecked. Please see information page for contact details.

TENSION
24 sts and 32 rows to 10cm (4in) measured over st st, 25 sts and 29 rows to 10cm (4in) measured over patterned st st, both using 3¼mm (US 3) needles.

BACK
Using 3¼mm (US 3) needles and yarn B, cast on 139 [169: 185] sts.
Row 1 (RS): K1, *P1, K1, rep from * to end.
Row 2: As row 1.
These 2 rows form moss st.
Work in moss st for a further 12 rows, ending with RS facing for next row.
Break off yarn B and join in yarn A.
Beg with a K row, work in st st until back measures 11 [13: 14]cm, ending with RS facing for next row.
Inc 1 st at each end of next and 4 foll 16th rows. 149 [179: 195] sts.
Work 2 rows, ending with WS facing for next row.
Next row (WS): P16 [31: 39], M1, (P29, M1) 4 times, P17 [32: 40]. 154 [184: 200] sts.
Place chart
Using the intarsia technique as described on the information page, now place chart for body, which is worked entirely in st st beg with a K row, as follows:
Next row (RS): K3 [18: 26], work next 148 sts as row 1 of chart for body, K3 [18: 26].
Next row: P3 [18: 26], work next 148 sts as row 2 of chart for body, P3 [18: 260].
These 2 rows set the sts – central 148 sts in patt from chart with edge sts in st st using yarn A.
Cont as set, inc 1 st at each end of 11th and foll 16th row. 158 [188: 204] sts.
Cont straight until all 73 rows of chart have been completed, ending with WS facing for next row.
Break off yarn B and cont using yarn A only.
Next row (WS): P18 [33: 41], P2tog, (P28, P2tog) 4 times, P18 [33: 41]. 153 [183: 199] sts.
Beg with a K row, cont in st st until back measures 70 [74: 76]cm, ending with RS facing for next row.
Shape shoulders
Cast off 4 [5: 6] sts at beg of next 8 [10: 26] rows, then 5 [6: 7] sts at beg of foll 24 [22: 6] rows, ending with RS facing for next row.
Fasten off rem 1 st.

LEFT FRONT
Using 3¼mm (US 3) needles and yarn B, cast on 69 [83: 91] sts.

Work in moss st as given for back for 14 rows, inc 0 [1: 1] st at end of last row and ending with RS facing for next row. 69 [84: 92] sts.
Break off yarn B and join in yarn A.
Beg with a K row, work in st st until left front measures 11 [13: 14]cm, ending with RS facing for next row.
Inc 1 st at beg of next and 4 foll 16th rows. 74 [89: 97] sts.
Work 2 rows, ending with WS facing for next row.
Next row (WS): P12, M1, (P24, M1) twice, P14 [29: 37]. 77 [92: 100] sts.
Place chart
Beg and ending rows as indicated, now place chart for body as follows:
Next row (RS): K3 [18: 26], work last 74 sts as row 1 of chart for body.
Next row: Work first 74 sts as row 2 of chart for body, P3 [18: 26].
These 2 rows set the sts – front opening edge 74 sts in patt from chart with edge sts in st st using yarn A.
Cont as set, inc 1 st at beg of 11th and foll 16th row. 79 [94: 102] sts.
Cont straight until all 73 rows of chart have been completed, ending with WS facing for next row.
Break off yarn B and cont using yarn A only.
Next row (WS): P11, P2tog, (P23, P2tog) twice, P16 [31: 39]. 76 [91: 99] sts.
Beg with a K row, cont in st st until left front matches back to beg of shoulder shaping, ending with RS facing for next row.
Shape shoulder
Cast off 4 [5: 6] sts at beg of next and foll 3 [4: 12] alt rows, then 5 [6: 7] sts at beg of foll 11 [10: 2] alt rows.
Work 1 row, ending with RS facing for next row.
Cast off rem 5 [6: 7] sts.

RIGHT FRONT
Using 3¼mm (US 3) needles and yarn B, cast on 69 [83: 91] sts.
Work in moss st as given for back for 14 rows, inc 0 [1: 1] st at beg of last row and ending with RS facing for next row. 69 [84: 92] sts.
Break off yarn B and join in yarn A.

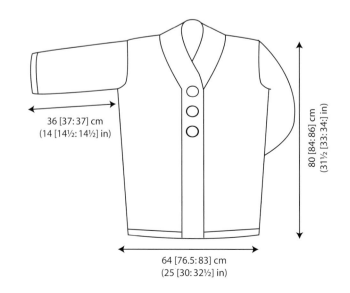

36 [37: 37] cm
(14 [14½: 14½] in)

80 [84: 86] cm
(31½ [33: 34¼] in)

64 [76.5: 83] cm
(25 [30: 32½] in)

Beg with a K row, work in st st until right front measures 11 [13: 14]cm, ending with RS facing for next row.

Inc 1 st at end of next and 4 foll 16th rows. 74 [89: 97] sts.

Work 2 rows, ending with WS facing for next row.

Next row (WS): P14 [29: 37], M1, (P24, M1) twice, P12. 77 [92: 100] sts.

Place chart

Beg and ending rows as indicated, now place chart for body as follows:

Next row (RS): Work first 74 sts as row 1 of chart for body, K3 [18: 26].

Next row: P3 [18: 26], work last 74 sts as row 2 of chart for body.

These 2 rows set the sts - front opening edge 74 sts in patt from chart with edge sts in st st using yarn A.

Cont as set, inc 1 st at end of 11th and foll 16th row. 79 [94: 102] sts.

Cont straight until all 73 rows of chart have been completed, ending with WS facing for next row.

Break off yarn B and cont using yarn A only.

Next row (WS): P16 [31: 39], P2tog, (P23, P2tog) twice, P11. 76 [91: 99] sts.

Beg with a K row, cont in st st until right front matches back to beg of shoulder shaping, ending with WS facing for next row.

Shape shoulder

Cast off 4 [5: 6] sts at beg of next and foll 3 [4: 12] alt rows, then 5 [6: 7] sts at beg of foll 11 [10: 2] alt rows.

Work 1 row, ending with WS facing for next row.

Cast off rem 5 [6: 7] sts.

SLEEVES (both alike)

Using 3¼mm (US 3) needles and yarn B, cast on 63 [65: 67] sts.

Work in moss st as given for back for 14 rows, ending with RS facing for next row.

Break off yarn B and join in yarn A.

Beg with a K row, work in st st, shaping sides by inc 1 st at each end of 3rd and 2 [4: 4] foll 6th [4th: 4th] rows. 69 [75: 77] sts.

Work 3 [1: 1] rows, inc 1 st at centre of last row and ending with RS facing for next row. 70 [76: 78] sts.

Place chart

Beg and ending rows as indicated, now place chart for appropriate sleeve as follows:

Next row (RS): K6 [9: 10], work next 58 sts as row 1 of appropriate sleeve chart, K6 [9: 10].

Next row: P6 [9: 10], work next 58 sts as row 2 of appropriate sleeve chart, P6 [9: 10].

These 2 rows set the sts - centre 58 sts in patt from chart with edge sts in st st using yarn A.

Cont as set, inc 1 st at each end of next and 6 [1: 4] foll 6th [4th: 4th] rows, then on 3 [10: 8] foll 8th [6th: 6th] rows. 90 [100: 104] sts.

Work 6 [2: 2] rows, completing all 69 rows of chart and ending with WS facing for next row.

Break off yarn B and cont using yarn A only.

Next row (WS): P44 [49: 51], P2tog, P44 [49: 51]. 89 [99: 103] sts.

Beg with a K row, work in st st for 8 [10: 10] rows, inc 1 st at each end of next [3rd: 3rd] row and ending with RS facing for next row. 91 [101: 105] sts. Sleeve should measure 36 [37.5: 37.5]cm.

Shape top

Cast off 4 sts at beg of next 16 rows, ending with RS facing for next row.

Cast off rem 27 [37: 41] sts.

MAKING UP

Press as described on the information page. Join both shoulder seams using back stitch, or mattress stitch if preferred. **(Note: There is no back neck edge as front shoulder edges meet at centre back neck fasten-off point.)**

Front band

With RS facing, using 3¼mm (US 3) circular needle and yarn C, beg and ending at cast-on edges, pick up and knit 212 [222: 228] sts up right front opening edge to back neck fasten-off point, then 212 [222: 228] sts down left front opening edge. 424 [444: 456] sts.

Row 1 (WS): K1, P2, ★K2, P2, rep from ★ to last st, K1.

Row 2: K3, ★P2, K2, rep from ★ to last st, K1. These 2 rows form rib.

Work in rib for a further 9 rows, ending with RS facing for next row.

Row 12 (RS): Rib 100 [104: 104], ★cast off 3 sts (to make a buttonhole - cast on 3 sts over these cast-off sts on next row), rib until there are 14 [16: 17] sts on right needle after cast-off, rep from ★ once more, cast off 3 sts (to make 3rd buttonhole - cast on 3 sts over these cast-off sts on next row), rib to end.

Work in rib for a further 13 rows, ending with RS facing for next row.

Cast off in rib.

Mark points along side seam edges 20 [22: 23]cm either side of shoulder seams and sew shaped cast-off edges of sleeves to body between these points.

See information page for finishing instructions.

left sleeve

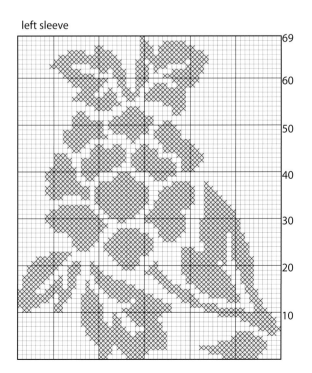

right sleeve

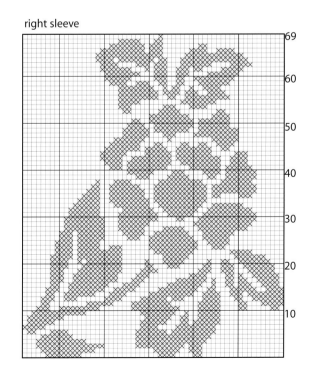

key

□ A

☒ B

Body Chart

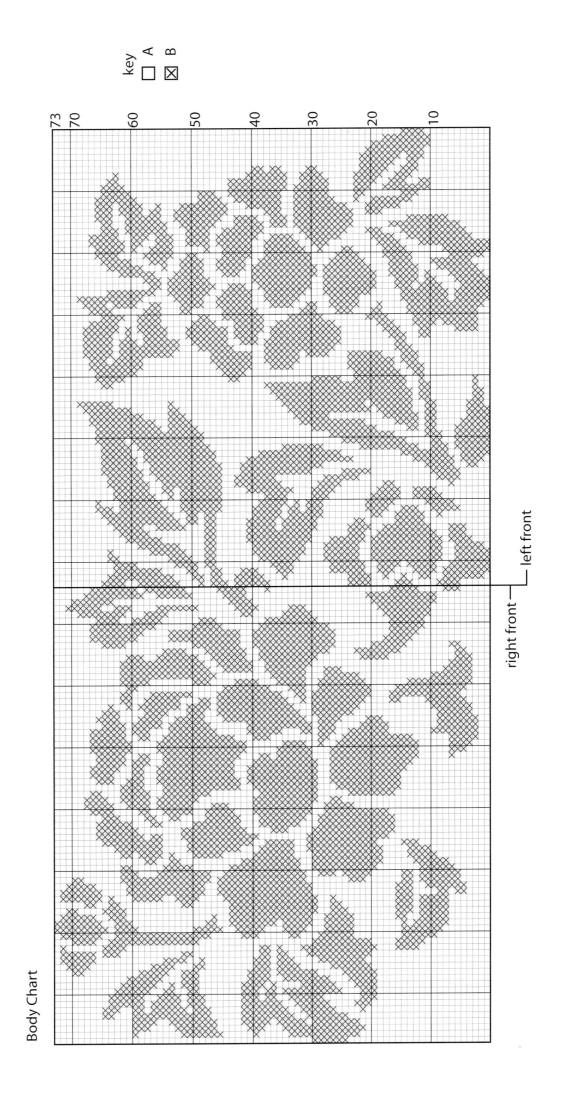

key
□ A
☒ B

73
70
60
50
40
30
20
10

right front
left front

213

SOUMAK WRAP

Lisa Richardson

• •

FNISHED SIZE

Completed wrap is 45 cm (17½ in) wide and approx 181cm (71½ in) long.

YARN

Rowan Felted Tweed

A Seasalter 178	2	x 50gm
B Watery 152	1	x 50gm
C Amethyst 192	2	x 50gm
D Rage 150	1	x 50gm
E Barn Red 196	2	x 50gm
F Mineral 181	2	x 50gm
G Seafarer 170	2	x 50gm
H Peony 183	1	x 50gm
I Ginger 154	2	x 50gm
K Pine 158	1	x 50gm

NEEDLES

1 pair 3¼mm (no 10) (US 3) needles

TENSION

32 sts and 50 rows to 10cm (4in) measured over patt using 3¼mm (US 3) needles.

Pattern note: All slipped sts should be worked with yarn held at WS of work – this is back of work on RS rows and front of work on WS rows.

WRAP

Using 3¼mm (US 3) needles and yarn A, cast on 144 sts.
Row 1 (RS): Knit.
Row 2: K3, P2, ★K6, P2, rep from ★ to last 3 sts, K3.
Joining and breaking off colours as required, now work in patt as follows:
Row 3 (RS): Using yarn B, K3, ★sl 2 (see pattern note), K6, rep from ★ to last 5 sts, sl 2, K3.
Row 4: Using yarn B, K3, ★sl 2 (see pattern note), K2, P2, K2, rep from ★ to last 5 sts, sl 2, K3.
Row 5: Using yarn A, K7, ★sl 2, K6, rep from ★ to last st, K1.
Row 6: Using yarn A, K3, P2, K2, ★sl 2, K2, P2, K2, rep from ★ to last st, K1.
Rows 3 to 6 form patt.
Keeping patt correct, cont in stripes as follows:
Rows 7 and 8: Using yarn B.
Rows 9 and 10: Using yarn C.
Rows 11 and 12: Using yarn B.
Rep last 4 rows once more.
Rows 17 and 18: Using yarn C.
Rows 19 and 20: Using yarn D.
Rep last 4 rows once more.
Rows 25 and 26: Using yarn E.
Rows 27 and 28: Using yarn D.
Rep last 4 rows once more.
Rows 33 and 34: Using yarn E.
Rows 35 and 36: Using yarn F.
Rep last 4 rows once more.
Rows 41 and 42: Using yarn A.
Rows 43 and 44: Using yarn F.
Rep last 4 rows once more.
Rows 49 and 50: Using yarn A.
Rows 51 and 52: Using yarn G.
Rep last 4 rows once more.
Rows 57 and 58: Using yarn H.
Rows 59 and 60: Using yarn G.
Rep last 4 rows once more.
Rows 65 and 66: Using yarn H.
Rows 67 and 68: Using yarn I.
Rep last 4 rows once more.
Rows 73 and 74: Using yarn K.
Rows 75 and 76: Using yarn I.
Rep last 4 rows once more.
Rows 81 and 82: Using yarn K.
Rows 83 and 84: Using yarn F.
Rep last 4 rows once more.
Rows 89 and 90: Using yarn C.
Rows 91 and 92: Using yarn F.
Rep last 4 rows once more.
Rows 97 and 98: Using yarn C.
Rows 99 and 100: Using yarn E.
Rep last 4 rows once more.
Rows 105 and 106: Using yarn G.
Rows 107 and 108: Using yarn E.
Rep last 4 rows once more.
Rows 113 and 114: Using yarn G.
Rows 115 and 116: Using yarn I.
Rep last 4 rows once more.
Rows 121 and 122: Using yarn A.
Rows 123 and 124: Using yarn I.
Rep last 4 rows once more.
Rows 129 and 130: Using yarn A.
Rows 3 to 130 form stripe sequence.

Rep rows 3 to 130 6 times more, and then rows 3 and 4 again, ending after 2 rows using yarn B and with RS facing for next row.
Next row (RS): Using yarn A, Knit.
Next row: Using yarn A, K3, P2, ★K6, P2, rep from ★ to last 3 sts, K3.
Using yarn A, cast off.

MAKING UP

Press as described on the information page.

WAYFARER

Lisa Richardson

●●

SIZE

To fit bust

81-97	102-117	cm
32-38	40-46	in

YARN

Rowan Cocoon

9	10	x 100gm

(photographed in Breeze 850)

NEEDLES

1 pair 7mm (no 2) (US 10½) needles
6mm (no 4) (US 10) circular needle
Cable needle

TENSION

14 sts and 16 rows to 10cm (4in) measured over st st using 7mm (US 10½) needles.

SPECIAL ABBREVIATIONS

C6B = slip next 3 sts onto cable needle and leave at back of work, K3, then K3 from cable needle; **C6F** = slip next 3 sts onto cable needle and leave at front of work, K3, then K3 from cable needle; **C12B** = slip next 6 sts onto cable needle and leave at back of work, K6, then K6 from cable needle; **C12F** = slip next 6 sts onto cable needle and leave at front of work, K6, then K6 from cable needle.

FIRST LOOP

Using 7mm (US 10½) needles and waste yarn cast on 63 sts.
Row 1 (WS): Purl.
Break off waste yarn and join in main yarn.
Now work in patt as folls:
Row 1 (RS): P3, (K5, P1, K6, P3, K6, P1, K5, P3) twice.
Row 2: K3, (P5, K1, P6, K3, P6, K1, P5, K3) twice.
Row 3: P3, (K5, P1, C6B, P3, C6F, P1, K5, P3) twice.
Row 4: As row 2.
Rows 5 to 8: As rows 1 to 4.
Rows 9 and 10: As rows 1 and 2.
Row 11: P3, (C12F, P3, C12B, P3) twice.
Row 12: K3, (P6, K1, P5, K3, P5, K1, P6, K3) twice.
Row 13: P3, (K6, P1, K5, P3, K5, P1, K6, P3) twice.
Row 14: As row 12.
Row 15: P3, (C6F, P1, K5, P3, K5, P1, C6B, P3) twice.
Row 16: As row 12.
Rows 17 to 28: As rows 13 to 16, 3 times.
Rows 29 and 30: As rows 13 and 14.
Row 31: P3, (C12B, P3, C12F, P3) twice.
Row 32: As row 2.
Rows 33 to 40: As rows 1 to 4, twice. These 40 rows form patt.
Rep last 40 rows 4 [5] times more, ending with RS facing for next row. (Strip should meas approx 125 [150] cm.)
Unravel waste yarn and slip the 63 sts of the first row in main yarn onto a spare needle.

Holding both sets of 63 sts tog with RS facing (and ensuring strip is not twisted) now cast off both sets of sts tog, taking one st from front needle tog with corresponding st from back needle.

SECOND LOOP

Using 7mm (US 10½) needles and waste yarn cast on 60 sts.
Row 1 (WS): Purl.
Break off waste yarn and join in main yarn.
Now work in patt as folls:
Row 1 (RS): P3, (K6, P2) 7 times, P1.
Row 2: K3, (P6, K2) 7 times, K1.
Row 3: P3, (C6B, P2, C6F, P2) 3 times, C6B, P3.
Row 4: As row 2. These 4 rows form patt.
Cont in patt until second loop meas same as first loop, ending after patt row 4 and with RS facing for next row.
Unravel waste yarn and slip the 60 sts of the first row in main yarn onto a spare needle.
Slip one end of this loop through centre of first loop (so resulting joined loops will be interlocked tog) and, holding both sets of 60 sts tog with RS facing (and ensuring this strip is not twisted) now cast off both sets of sts tog, taking one st from front needle tog with corresponding st from back needle.

MAKING UP

Do NOT press.
Lay joined loops flat to form an X shape. Mark the 2 adjacent row-end edges of the 2 loops at the top of the X – these are the upper edges.

Upper borders (both alike)
With RS facing and 6mm (US 10) circular needle, beg and ending at "seam" joining ends of strip, pick up and knit 120 [144] sts evenly along entire marked row-end edge of one loop.
Round 1 (RS): *K2, P2, rep from * to end.
This round forms rib.
Work in rib for a further 9 rounds. Cast off in rib.

Lower borders (both alike)
With RS facing and 6mm (US 10) circular needle, beg and ending at "seam" joining ends of strip, pick up and knit 180 [216] sts evenly along entire free row-end edge of one loop.
Work in rib as given for upper border for 10 rounds. Cast off in rib.
See information page for finishing instructions.

INFORMATION

TENSION

Obtaining the correct tension is perhaps the single factor which can make the difference between a successful garment and a disastrous one. It controls both the shape and size of an article, so any variation, however slight, can distort the finished garment. Different designers feature in our books and it is **their** tension, given at the **start** of each pattern, which you must match. We recommend that you knit a square in pattern and/or stocking stitch (depending on the pattern instructions) of perhaps 5 - 10 more stitches and 5 - 10 more rows than those given in the tension note. Mark out the central 10cm square with pins. If you have too many stitches to 10cm try again using thicker needles, if you have too few stitches to 10cm try again using finer needles. Once you have achieved the correct tension your garment will be knitted to the measurements indicated in the size diagram shown at the end of the pattern.

CHART NOTE

Many of the patterns in the book are worked from charts. Each square on a chart represents a stitch and each line of squares a row of knitting. Each colour used is given a different letter and these are shown in the **materials** section, or in the **key** alongside the chart of each pattern. When working from the charts, read odd rows (K) from right to left and even rows (P) from left to right, unless otherwise stated. When working lace from a chart it is important to note that all but the largest size may have to alter the first and last few stitches in order not to lose or gain stitches over the row.

WORKING A LACE PATTERN

When working a lace pattern it is important to remember that if you are unable to work both the increase and corresponding decrease and vica versa, the stitches should be worked in stocking stitch.

KNITTING WITH COLOUR

There are two main methods of working colour into a knitted fabric: **Intarsia** and **Fairisle** techniques. The first method produces a single thickness of fabric and is usually used where a colour is only required in a particular area of a row and does not form a repeating pattern across the row, as in the fairisle technique.

Fairisle type knitting: When two or three colours are worked repeatedly across a row, strand the yarn **not** in use loosely behind the stitches being worked. If you are working with more than two colours, treat the "floating" yarns as if they were one yarn and always spread the stitches to their correct width to keep them elastic. It is advisable not to carry the stranded or "floating" yarns over more than three stitches at a time, but to weave them under and over the colour you are working. The "floating" yarns are therefore caught at the back of the work.

Intarsia: The simplest way to do this is to cut short lengths of yarn for each motif or block of colour used in a row. Then joining in the various colours at the appropriate point on the row, link one colour to the next by twisting them around each other where they meet on the wrong side to avoid gaps. All ends can then either be darned along the colour join lines, as each motif is completed or then can be "knitted-in" to the fabric of the knitting as each colour is worked into the pattern. This is done in much the same way as "weaving- in" yarns when working the Fairisle technique and does save time darning-in ends. It is essential that the tension is noted for intarsia as this may vary from the stocking stitch if both are used in the same pattern.

FINISHING INSTRUCTIONS

After working for hours knitting a garment, it seems a great pity that many garments are spoiled because such little care is taken in the pressing and finishing process. Follow the text below for a truly professional-looking garment.

PRESSING

Block out each piece of knitting and following the instructions on the ball band press the garment pieces, omitting the ribs. Tip: Take special care to press the edges, as this will make sewing up both easier and neater. If the ball band indicates that the fabric is not to be pressed, then covering the blocked out fabric with a damp white cotton cloth and leaving it to stand will have the desired effect. Darn in all ends neatly along the selvage edge or a colour join, as appropriate.

STITCHING

When stitching the pieces together, remember to match areas of colour and texture very carefully where they meet. Use a seam stitch such as back stitch or mattress stitch for all main knitting seams and join all ribs and neckband with mattress stitch, unless otherwise stated.

CONSTRUCTION

Having completed the pattern instructions, join left shoulder and neckband seams as detailed above. Sew the top of the sleeve to the body of the garment using the method detailed in the pattern, referring to the appropriate guide:
Straight cast-off sleeves: Place centre of cast-off edge of sleeve to shoulder seam. Sew top of sleeve to body, using markers as guidelines where applicable.
Square set-in sleeves: Place centre of cast-off edge of sleeve to shoulder seam. Set sleeve head into armhole, the straight sides at top of sleeve to form a neat right-angle to cast-off sts at armhole on back and front.
Shallow set-in sleeves: Place centre of cast off edge of sleeve to shoulder seam. Match decreases at beg of armhole shaping to decreases at top of sleeve. Sew sleeve head into armhole, easing in shapings.
Set-in sleeves: Place centre of cast-off edge of sleeve to shoulder seam. Set in sleeve, easing sleeve head into armhole.
Join side and sleeve seams.
Slip stitch pocket edgings and linings into place.
Sew on buttons to correspond with buttonholes.
Ribbed welts and neckbands and any areas of garter stitch should not be pressed.

PATTERN QUERIES

For all pattern queries, please contact:
mail@knitrowan.com

ABBREVIATIONS

K	knit
P	purl
st(s)	stitch(es)
inc	increas(e)(ing)
dec	decreas(e)(ing)
st st	stocking stitch (1 row K , 1 row P)
g st	garter stitch (K every row)
beg	begin(ning)
foll	following
rem	remain(ing)
rev st st	reverse stocking stitch (1 row K , 1 row P)
rep	repeat
alt	alternate
cont	continue
patt	pattern
tog	together
mm	millimetres
cm	centimetres
in(s)	inch(es)
RS	right side
WS	wrong side
sl 1	slip one stitch
psso	pass slipped stitch over
p2sso	pass 2 slipped stitches over
tbl	through back of loop
M1	make one stitch by picking up horizontal loop before next stitch and knitting into back of it
M1P	make one stitch by picking up horizontal loop before next stitch and purling into back of it
yfwd	yarn forward
yrn	yarn round needle
meas	measures
0	no stitches, times or rows
–	no stitches, times or rows for that size
yon	yarn over needle
yfrn	yarn forward round needle
wyib	with yarn at back

CROCHET TERMS

UK crochet terms and abbreviations have been used throughout. The list below gives the US equivalent where they vary.

ABBREV.	UK	US
dc (sc)	double crochet	(single crochet)
htr (hdc)	half treble	(half double crochet)
tr (dc)	treble	(double crochet)
dtr (tr)	double treble	(treble)

EXPERIENCE RATING - for guidance only

⬤ Beginner Techniques
For the beginner knitter, basic garment shaping and straight forward stitch technique.

⬤ ⬤ Simple Techniques
Simple straight forward knitting, introducing various, shaping techniques and garments.

⬤ ⬤ ⬤ Experienced Techniques
For the more experienced knitter, using more advanced shaping techniques at the same time as colourwork or more advanced stitch techniques.

⬤ ⬤ ⬤ ⬤ Advanced Techniques
Advanced techniques used, using advanced stitches and garment shaping along with more challenging techniques

BUTTONS, BEADS AND RIBBONS USED IN THIS BOOK ARE SOURCED FROM:

Bedecked Haberdashery
Barningham Park Coach House
Barningham, Nr Richmond
North Yorkshire
DL11 7DW
United Kingdom
Tel: +44 (0)1833 621 451
Email: thegirls@bedecked.co.uk

Groves and Banks
Eastern Bypass
Thame, Oxfordshire
OX9 3FU
Web: www.grovesltd.co.uk
Email: groves@stockistenquiries.co.uk

Debbie Abrahams Beads
26 Church Drive
Nottingham
NG5 2BA
Tel: 0115 960 7991
Email: beads@debbieabrahams.com
Web: www.debbieabrahamsbeads.co.uk

WASH CARE INFORMATION

To help you to care for your knitting and crochet more easily below are the symbols you are likely to on our ball bands and shade cards and a brief explanation of each.

MACHINE WASH SYMBOLS

Machine Wash, Cold | Machine Wash, Cold, Gentle | Machine Wash, Warm | Machine Wash, Warm, Gentle

HAND WASH SYMBOLS

Do Not Wash | Hand Wash, Normal | Hand Wash, Cold | Hand Wash, Warm

DRY CLEAN SYMBOLS

Do Not Dry Clean | Dry Clean | Dry Clean, in Certain Solvents, Consult Cleaner | Dry Clean, Any Solvent

IRONING SYMBOLS

Do Not Iron | Iron Low Heat | Iron Medium Heat

DO NOT BLEACH SYMBOL

Do Not Bleach

DRYING SYMBOLS

Do Not Tumble Dry | Tumble Dry, Gentle, Low Heat | Dry Flat in Shade | Do Not Wring

SIZING GUIDE

When you knit and wear a Rowan design we want you to look and feel fabulous. This all starts with the size and fit of the design you choose. To help you to achieve a great knitting experience we have looked at the sizing of our womens and menswear patterns.

Dimensions in the charts below are body measurements, not garment dimensions, therefore please refer to the measuring guide to help you to determine which is the best size for you to knit. We also now give full garment measurements around chest/bust at the beginning of each pattern so that you can see how much ease there will be for your size.

STANDARD WOMENS SIZING GUIDE

The sizing within this chart is also based on the larger size within the range.

To fit bust	32 – 34	36 – 38	40 – 42	44 – 46	48 – 50	inches
	81 – 86	91 – 97	102 – 107	112 – 117	122 – 127	cm
To fit waist	24 – 26	28 – 30	32 – 34	36 – 38	40 – 42	inches
	61 – 66	71 – 76	81 – 86	91 – 97	102 – 107	cm
To fit hips	34 – 36	38 – 40	42 – 44	46 – 48	50 – 52	inches
	86 – 91	97 – 102	107 – 112	117 – 122	127 – 132	cm

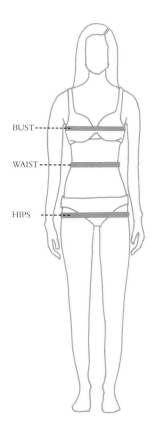

SIZING & SIZE DIAGRAM NOTE

The instructions are given for the smallest size. Where they vary, work the figures in brackets for the larger sizes. **One set of figures refers to all sizes.** Included with most patterns in this magazine is a '**size diagram**' - see image on the right, of the finished garment and its dimensions. The measurement shown at the bottom of each '**size diagram**' shows the garment width 2.5cm below the armhole shaping. To help you choose the size of garment to knit please refer to the sizing guide. Generally in the majority of designs the welt width (at the cast on edge of the garment) is the same width as the chest. However, some designs are 'A-Line' in shape or have a flared edge and in these cases the welt width will be wider than the chest width.

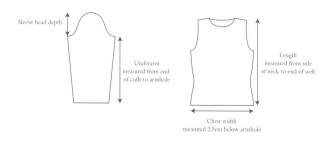

MEASURING GUIDE

For maximum comfort and to ensure the correct fit when choosing a size to knit, please follow the tips below when checking your size.

Measure yourself close to your body, over your underwear and don't pull the tape measure too tight!

Bust/chest – measure around the fullest part of the bust/chest and across the shoulder blades.

Waist – measure around the natural waistline.

Hips – measure around the fullest part of the bottom.

To be extra sure, measure your favourite jumper and then compare these measurements with the Rowan size diagram given at the end of the individual instructions.

Finally, once you have decided which size is best for you, please ensure that you achieve the tension required for the design you wish to knit.

Remember if your tension is too loose, your garment will be bigger than the pattern size. If your tension is too tight, your garment could be smaller than the pattern size both of which will alter the amount of yarn used to that stated in the pattern.

Furthermore if your tension is incorrect, the handle of your fabric will be too stiff or floppy and will not fit properly. It really does make sense to check your tension before starting every project.

YARNS

ROWAN

From time to time some of our yarns may become discontinued. We have provided a table below, which outlines the yarns featured in this book, and the standard stocking stitch tension for those yarns.
This will enable you to try to find a substitute yarn for your design.

All of the 20 designs that have been re-photographed and restyled are made using current yarns, and we have adjusted the patterns to work with the chosen yarns.
More information on our yarns can be found at www.knitrowan.com

YARN	YARN WEIGHT SYMBOL	STANDARD ST ST TENSION
Rowan Alpaca Cotton	4 MEDIUM	16 sts and 23 rows
Rowan Kidsilk Haze	0 LACE to 4 MEDIUM	18-25 sts and 23-34 rows
Rowan Yorkshire Tweed 4ply	1 SUPER FINE to 2 FINE	26-28 sts and 38-40 rows
Rowan 4ply Soft	1 SUPER FINE	28 sts and 36 rows
Rowan Handknit Cotton	4 MEDIUM	19-20 sts and 28 rows
Rowan 4ply Cotton	1 SUPER FINE	27-29 sts and 37-39 rows
Rowan Cotton Glace	4 MEDIUM	23 sts and 30 rows
Rowan Fox Tweed	3 LIGHT	22-24 sts and 30-32 rows
Rowan Kid Silk	3 LIGHT	22-24 sts and 28-30 rows
Rowan D.D.K	3 LIGHT	22-24 sts and 30-32 rows
Rowan Silk/Wool	3 LIGHT	22 sts and 30 rows
Rowan Felted tweed	3 LIGHT	22-24 sts and 30-32 rows
Rowan Cocoon	5 BULKY	14 sts and 16 rows
Rowan Wool Cotton	3 LIGHT	22 sts and 30 rows
Rowan Pure Wool DK	3 LIGHT	22 sts and 30 rows

YARN	YARN WEIGHT SYMBOL	STANDARD ST ST TENSION
Rowan Kid Classic	4 MEDIUM	18-19 sts and 23-25 rows
Lurex Shimmer	1 SUPER FINE	29 sts and 41 rows
Rowan Purelife Organic Cotton DK	3 LIGHT	22 sts and 30 rows
Rowan Rowanspun DK	3 LIGHT to 4 MEDIUM	20-21 sts and 29-30 rows
Rowan Rowanspun 4ply	1 SUPER FINE to 2 FINE	26-28 sts and 29-30 rows
Rowan Fine Cotton Chenille	2 FINE to 4 MEDIUM	20-25 sts and 36-44 rows
Rowan DK Soft	3 LIGHT	22-24 sts and 31-33 rows
Rowan Felted Tweed Aran	4 MEDIUM	16 sts and 28 rows
Rowan Alpaca Classic	2 FINE	23 sts and 31 rows
Rowan Brushed Fleece	5 BULKY	13 sts and 19 rows
Rowan Softyak Dk	3 LIGHT	22 sts and 30 rows

PLEASE NOTE

We would always suggest that you use the yarn specified in the pattern, where this isn't possible in the case of discontinued yarns choose a replacement with exactly the same stocking stitch tension to ensure the garment works out correctly.

Check your tension before knitting your garment to ensure you achieve the pattern tension, changing needle size if needed.

ACKNOWLEDGEMENTS

....

R O W A N

Rowan's success is due to the team behind the brand which consists of many people; designers, knitters, retailers, graphics team, marketing and sales teams to name just a few. They work hard to create the well–loved brand, so a big thank you must go to all of the Rowan team both today and from the past forty years.

It is the talent, love and enthusiasm for the brand that everyone has brought with them and continues to give, that makes the brand as strong as it is today and ready for the next forty years.

We would like to thank everybody that has helped produce this fantastic overview of our 40 years, with a special thanks to Darren Brant from Quail Publishing for getting us to focus in busy times and make this possible and to Trisha Malcolm from Soho Publishing for supporting the book on its global journey.

We hope that you enjoy it as much as we have putting it together!

SHARON BRANT
ROWAN BRAND DIRECTOR

DAVID MACLEOD
ROWAN BRAND MANAGER